The Latin Masks of
Ezra Pound

Studies in Modern Literature, No. 4

A. Walton Litz, General Series Editor

Professor of English
Princeton University

George Bornstein

Consulting Editor for Titles on Ezra Pound
Professor of English
University of Michigan

Other Titles in This Series

No. 6   *The Last Courtly Lover: Yeats and the Idea of Woman*   Gloria C. Kline

No. 8   *The Presence of the Past: T.S. Eliot's Victorian Inheritance*   David Ned Tobin

No. 13   *Hamlet and the New Poetic: James Joyce and T.S. Eliot*   William H. Quillian

No. 14   *Faulkner's Changing Vision: From Outrage to Affirmation*   Doreen Fowler

No. 15   *The Sources and Structures of James Joyce's "Oxen"*   Robert Janusko

No. 16   *Yeats's Daimonic Renewal*   Herbert J. Levine

No. 17   *A Reading of Eliot's* Four Quartets   Julia Maniates Reibetanz

No. 18   *D.H. Lawrence and the Literature of Travel*   Billy T. Tracy, Jr.

No. 19   *Circe's Craft: Ezra Pound's* Hugh Selwyn Mauberley   Jo Brantley Berryman

No. 20   *Faulkner's Un-Christlike Christians: Biblical Allusions in the Novels*   Jessie McGuire Coffee

No. 22   *William Carlos Williams's* A Dream of Love   Steven Ross Loevy

No. 23   *James Joyce and the Beginnings of* Ulysses   Rodney Wilson Owen

The Latin Masks of
Ezra Pound

by
Ron Thomas

UMI RESEARCH PRESS

Ann Arbor, Michigan

Grateful acknowledgment for permission to reprint is made to New Directions Publishing Corporation for the following:

Ezra Pound, *The Cantos of Ezra Pound.* Copyright © 1934, 1937, 1940, 1948, 1956, 1959, 1962, 1963, 1966, 1968 by Ezra Pound. Copyright © 1972 by the Estate of Ezra Pound.

Ezra Pound, *The Literary Essays of Ezra Pound.* Copyright © 1935 by Ezra Pound.

Ezra Pound, *Personae.* Copyright © 1967 by Ezra Pound.

Ezra Pound, *A Lume Spento.* Copyright © 1967 by Ezra Pound. All Rights Reserved.

Ezra Pound, *Confucius to Cummings.* Copyright © 1964 by New Directions Publishing Corporation.

Portions of chapter 1 were published in *Paideuma*; portions of chapter 5 were published in *Helix* (Melbourne, Australia). Both appear here in revised form by permission of the editors.

Produced and distributed by
UMI Research Press
an imprint of
University Microfilms International
Ann Arbor, Michigan 48106

Library of Congress Cataloging in Publication Data

Thomas, Ronald Edward.
  The Latin masks of Ezra Pound.

    (Studies in modern literature ; no. 4)
    Revision of thesis (Ph.D.)–University of Michigan,
1977.
    Bibliography: p.
    Includes index.
    1. Pound, Ezra, 1885-1972–Knowledge–Literature.
2. Pound, Ezra, 1885-1972–Sources. 3. Latin poetry–
History and criticism. 4. Latin poetry–Translations
into English–History and criticism. I. Title. II. Series.

    PS3531.O82Z864 1983   811'.52   83-5734
    ISBN 0-8357-1407-1

M'amour, m'amour

       what do I love and

         where are you?

That I lost my center

         fighting the world.

The dreams clash

         and are shattered —

and that I tried to make a paradiso

            terrestre.

for Mary

Maiden Gathering Flowers
Fresco, Stabiae, first century A.D.
(National Museum of Naples, NM 89)
Photo: Alinari

Errata

page	line	
27	last	for "grave" read "grove"
37	4	for "deed" read "dead"
58	3	for "pendants" read "pedants"
64	15	for "to" read "of"
67	20 from end	for "Demotes" read "Demeter"
79	16	for "fame" read "fane"
	22	for "enrolling" read "unrolling"
85	5 from end	for "lost" read "last"
92	3 from end	for "The" read "This"
98	9	for "statute" read "statue"
	14	for "shall" read "shell"
149	19 from end	Sentence reads: The Sibyl even warns Aeneas' uninitiated comrades ("profani") away from the grove that hides the portal to hell (*Aen.* VI. 258-59); we recall that Pound, too, would accent the "profanum," not the "vulgus." He himself, after all, was of that vast American "vulgus" ...

Contents

Abbreviations   *xi*

Preface   *xiii*

Introduction   *1*

1   Virgil as Antimask   *9*

2   Catullus as Lyric Mask   *21*

3   Propertius as Dramatic Mask   *39*

4   Ovid as Epic Mask   *59*

5   Horace as Demimask   *117*

Conclusion   *141*

Notes   *151*

Appendix   *165*

Bibliography   *167*

Index   *175*

Abbreviations

The following abbreviations of Ezra Pound's writings are used throughout this work:

ABC   *ABC of Reading* (New Directions, 1951).

ALS   *A Lume Spento* (New Directions, 1965).

Ca   *Canzoni* (London, 1911).

CtC   *Confucius to Cummings* (New Directions, 1964).

GB   *Gaudier-Brzeska: A Memoir* (London, 1960).

GtK   *Guide to Kulchur* (London, 1952).

"H"   "Horace," *The Criterion* (Jan. 1930).

In   *Instigations* (New York, 1920).

L   *Selected Letters,* ed. by Donald Paige (New Directions, 1960).

LE   *Literary Essays,* ed. with intro. by T. S. Eliot (New Directions, 1968).

Lu   *Lustra* (New York, 1917).

"OCiG"   "On Criticism in General," *The Criterion* (Jan. 1923).

PD   *Pavannes and Divisions* (New York, 1918).

PE   *Polite Essays* (Freeport, New York, 1967).

Per   *Personae* (New Directions), 1971).

P/J   *Pound/Joyce: Letters,* ed. with com. by Forrest Read (New Directions, 1967).

SP   *Selected Prose,* ed. with intro. by William Cookson (London, 1973).

SPs   *Selected Poems,* ed. with intro. by T. S. Eliot (London, 1928).

SR   *The Spirit of Romance* (New Directions, 1968).

Preface

Halfway through this book I mention Mark Twain for his romantic use of masks in *Huckleberry Finn,* and might well have referred to that book's famous non-ending in closing my own. Here I will say that had I known how hard it was going to be to write this particular book, perhaps I would have chosen someone less controversial than "Hailey's Comet." Pound's self-consciousness sensitizes us to our own intellectual honesty; his search for self reveals our own painful preoccupations with integrity. Too often even the most prominent Poundians offer little real relief, themselves busied with making the admittedly impressive aesthetic case for Pound — who frankly encourages cultural pedantry — without rendering much of an objective judgment on his political machinations. Such devotion, by scholars, presses, and journals, can become too inbred. How refreshing it is, therefore, and often how revealing about our subject, to peruse material seemingly unrelated to Pound — for instance, M. H. Abrams' *Natural Supernaturalism: Tradition and Revolution in Romantic Literature.* Yet from this perspective, too, we note how some of the most distinguished critics of romanticism in our time seem intent on burying Pound by ignoring him, as if extolling a high romantic tradition that omits his work could seal his ignominious fate. Cant about Pound and his own anti-romanticism (itself part of the cant), then, are the Scylla and Charybdis between which I have sailed to bring this book, my odyssey, home to its own imperfect and provisional completion. As perhaps few others besides Pound himself would understand, working so *in quadriviis et angiportis* has provided its own rewards.

The Latin Masks of Ezra Pound is not simply another influence study about Pound and [pick a language], because Latin for Pound was *not* just another language. Nor is translation, for Pound, a neoclassical pastime. Instead, it is a process of transformation or metamorphosis or renewal of personality, and less finally the predecessor's (merely the fertilizer) than one's own (the plant itself). Such translation involves an evolution of self in relation to the selves of the past, and becomes an almost assumptive, biological, or scientific process. Dead and decaying matter, then, promotes new growth. So much for Pound's surface and well known anti-romanticism, which were it all this book was about would qualify it as a disappointing contribution to knowledge indeed.

By contrast, I would root Pound's anti-romanticism in a classical Latin past as it has not been grounded before. This animus of Pound's we might generally and conveniently label Hellenism, by which I mean the Greco-Roman cultural heritage and all those individuals down through the ages who have or who would venerate it, including Pound in his poetry. Conversely, I employ the term Hebraism, which defined might include not only Protestant and Judeo-Christian tradition generally but also romantic aesthetics, to describe Pound's anti-romantic bias. Hebraism's continuing vitality in the West, as opposed to Hellenism's two-thousand year decline as a moral force, posed the supreme obstacle for a post-protestant American poet working aginst his time. Interestingly enough, Hellenism underwent something of a modern resurgence or renaissance in this century prior to World War II, no doubt as a result of World War I's undermining of traditional Judeo-Christian values concerning love, brotherhood, and the meaning of life. Sadly, Pound's own anti-Semitic outbursts during the thirties and forties seem part of this widespread reactionary revival, and unfortunately our reaction to the fascist excesses of World War II still clouds our appraisals not only of Pound but also of the Hellenism he represents. As a young modern poet Pound left the fold in search of a new morality, while as a mature modern the master found himself in the unfortunate, improbable, and nonplussing position of having to defend his Hellenic belief against the ironic charge of immorality. Despite the validity of this indictment, and two major American wars later, some interested critics still cannot discuss either the man or his achievement dispassionately. The fact remains that Pound began his career, although quite prodigally, in a moral quest for self or psychic and social integrity. And this insight illuminates a more important aspect of Pound's anti-romanticism. For while he remained consistently loyal to the classical past, Pound nevertheless was always contemplating his own poetic and therefore society's political end, a notably romantic obsession to say the least.

Simply put, the book deals with another permutation, an often complex one at that, of the typical early modern reaction to romanticism (or rather to aestheticism, its debased, *fin de siècle* offspring), which served Pound well enough as mother's milk but which, longing to become himself, he tried to escape from more radically than most. In his case, however, he never quite had time to effect a satisfactory reconciliation. In terms of the book's principal metaphor concerning Latin poetry, Virgil was Pound's poetic father whom the son could not love freely and fully without first disobeying (chapter 1). This he did by running successively with the wrong crowd: Catullus, Propertius, and Ovid (chapters two, three, and four). But when the time came to return to his father's fields, in something like the humility of genuine poetic achievement, Pound was confronted by a hostile audience and felt ostracized for his wandering just when he most wished to come home. At any rate, events compel Pound to seek partial reconciliation with uncle Horace rather than with father Virgil (chapter 5), and thus my conclusion represents a consideration of the reunion that never occurred.

But since Pound's interest in Latin poetry really represents an interest in himself, Virgil is less the poet to outperform than Whitman who "broke the new wood": Whitman, that great, pre-modern, American poet, so mindful himself of the benefits and the burdens of the past, yet also gifted enough to envision an eminently moral future for himself *and* for his country. Poets will be our new priests, he boldly proclaimed, not unaware of the inroads that science was even then making upon religion. Thus, the appropriate context for reading Pound, still more than appreciating his inherent romanticism, involves understanding his preoccupation with the perennial, romantic, but especially modern problem of the poet's role in an imperfect and often violent society. Is religious emotion too great a burden for poetry to bear? Is science the new god? And what about poets who would like, besides selfishly renewing themselves with their mystic rites, to redeem as well the world? As for Pound, the chief editor of Eliot's *Waste Land,* let us call him a Tiresias whose long anticipated apocalypse simply failed to happen, at least not in the way he had originally intended.

This book has entailed numerous debts. I am more obliged than mere footnotes can tell to the many fine scholars working in the field and hope that those with whom I explicitly disagree will regard my remarks as testimony to the continuing importance of their work rather than as poor reward for their admirable labors. I would like to thank Hugh Kenner for "being the first," Carroll Terrell for "continuing the work" in both *Paideuma* and his *Companion to The Cantos,* and Donald Gallup for helping me to locate some of the more isolated material incorporated in my text. More personally, it is my pleasure to acknowledge the members of my original dissertation committee: Professors Stuart McDougal and Herbert Barrows in the English Department, and Professor David Ross in the Classics Department, all of the University of Michigan. In particular I would like to express my deep appreciation and gratitude to Professor George Bornstein, the Chairman of my committee, who apart from his major work on Shelley, Yeats, Eliot, and Stevens has written an acute little book on Pound

(*The Postromantic Consciousness of Ezra Pound,* ELS, 1977), and who thereby has taught and continues to teach me a great deal about the difficult art of writing well. This book as perhaps some of my colleagues at Baylor University are well aware has had a rather long gestation, during which I have benefitted from several anonymous reviews of the manuscript. I am grateful, too, to my department chairman, Professor James Barcus, for arranging my teaching schedule so as to allow me to work most efficiently during this last often hectic year, and to my former student and graduate assistant, Francisco Gonzalez, for helping me with some of the early proofing. Finally, my wife has endured the trials of writing this book as well as I, and has supported me greatly, especially when I needed it most, with her customary encouragement and generosity.

This project was begun under a fellowship from the Horace B. Rackham School of Graduate Studies, University of Michigan, continued under a grant from the American Council of Learned Societies, and completed under a fellowship from the Faculty Development Program at Baylor University in conjunction with the Andrew W. Mellon Foundation.

> Sunt bona, sunt quaedam mediocria, sunt mala plura
> quae legis hic. aliter non fit, Avite, liber.
> Martial, *Epigrams,* 1.16

Introduction

"I have seen what I have
seen" (2/9).

Sooner or later most youthful but enthusiastic admirers of Ezra Pound must confront the reality of his racism. Resulting less from naivete than from a desire to give the poet his day in court, this dilemma is difficult because no one likes to think he or she has misspent time and effort once the rumors prove true. I would hope that my hard-won solution to the problem of Pound involves neither sympathy fostered by self-justification nor antipathy fanned by self-dismay. Nor does this study constitute another of the more recent redemptions of the poet's mythical from his historical (i.e., politico-economic) interests. Since the ugliness in Pound's life derives insidiously from the beauty of his art, my own recourse has been to contemplate his unfolding tragedy the better to be lessoned thereby.

Toward education, one might begin by considering Pound's career as an heroically modern struggle to discover meaning in an apparently meaningless age. Somewhat surprisingly, this traditionally romantic and therefore Hebraic (Judeo-Christian) quest for identity compelled Pound to seek himself through translation; that is, he came to see his poetic future in the recorded past. He chose to carry this past into the present in order to carry himself into a sense of psychic integrity or wholeness. Thus, what remains a classroom exercise for most of us became a rite of self-renewal for Pound, or as in his famous statement in *Gaudier-Brzeska: A Memoir* (1916):

In the "search for oneself," in the search for "sincere self-expression," one gropes, one finds some seeming verity. One says "I am" this, that, or the other, and with the words scarcely uttered one ceases to be that thing.... I began this search for the real in a book called *Personae,* casting off, as it were, complete masks of the self in each poem. I continued in a long series of translations, which were but more elaborate masks. (*GB,* 85)

And so we proceed paradoxically: the anti-Semite was really Hebraic at heart, seeking his redemption through time; yet time means without time (*achronos*) for the poet who finds, and also hides, himself in masks from the past.

Why was Pound, in particular, so determined and often desperate to root himself through translation? The reasons are many and complex. In childhood there was his sense of genteel poverty; in adolescence, his growing alienation as an aesthete in a practical, anti-intellectual land. No wonder he turned to romance languages in college, to esoteric Latin especially as an anodyne to common English. There is the matter of Pound's Protestant upbringing: his general frustration with a seemingly bankrupt moral tradition, and more specifically the fateful day his academic career was aborted with his dismissal from fundamentally Baptist and midwestern Wabash College for befriending a needy chorus girl. From America, the path to Europe and poetry appeared clear; from London, after years of poverty, increasing notoriety, and hellish war, through a purgatory of socio-economic turmoil, the poetry pointed only to paradise.

The real paradox of Pound's escape, however, lies not in his romantic race after masks, but in his pursuit of personae from the classical past. Here the subliminal importance of the Christian paradigm to Pound's poetic program should be emphasized. Without a strong sense of identity, there is no self-confidence, without which there can be no love, without which no meaningful sense of community or polity or paradise. Thus in seeking selfhood, although earnestly longing to love, Pound instead reacts Hellenically to what he sees as a decadently Hebraic Western culture. In short, anxious for Christian *agape,* he spitefully elopes with pagan *eros.* Aside from the tragic implications of his refusal or inability to accept the meaningful potential of historical process, Pound's reactionary endeavors truly mark him as a translator in the most profound sense of the word: one who transfers the work of predecessors by transforming or transfiguring it into his own. Pound's poetics prescribe, therefore, not apocalypse for the future but metamorphosis from the past. His technique, by choice, entails not imaginative vision but associative memory. Moreover, the present for such a poet is more apt to tyranize over him than to set him free, because "home" implies nostalgia for something lost, whether Lesbia, the *Monobiblos,* or the Heroic Age.

If one were to consider the essential components of Pound's Hellenic (Graeco-Roman) animus, in increasing order of importance to his poetry, Eleusis should probably come first, Homer's *nekuia* next, and then the *Metamorphoses* of Ovid. Interestingly enough, Ovid appears earliest in Pound's work (ca. 1908), followed by Homer (ca. 1917), and then the mysteries (ca. 1930). Ovid thus listed signifies Pound's transformations of the classical past in general. So far so good, but how can the term "Hellenic" possibly include such topics in Pound's canon as Provence, Renaissance Italy, or modern Europe, much less China and eighteenth-century America? In an obvious sense it cannot, nor does this book pretend to treat in any detailed way, for example, the Chinese or the Adams Cantos. Yet the term "Hellenic" as I would inclusively use it does imply a way of integrating our discussion of Pound's Latin poetry with his other poetic interests. The integration has been imagistic rather than metaphorical.

The Latin Masks of Ezra Pound can legitimately relate Rome to Cathay, by synechdoche as it were, for three principal reasons. First, Pound's repeated claim that Ovid (i.e., primarily Latin poetry, as we shall see) has been one of his two most important poetic influences can be documented by examining his college transcripts: While accumulating 24 hours in Latin, Pound accumulated 12 hours in Italian, only 3 in Provençal and none in either Greek or Chinese. Second, Pound's work with Latin suffices as the "adequate symbol" since Confucius, his other most important influence, himself assumes a strongly Hellenic role particularly in the *Cantos*. Pound's Kung is a secular humanist who practices an historiography that itself honors a static (i.e., un-Hebraic) view of history. This is why Pound's treatment of Western history in the *Cantos* resembles an Alexandrian catalog of exempla without any real sense of historical process. And third, Pound's Latin masks readily represent his other work because myth in the *Cantos* remains primarily Western, and history an ideogrammic presentation of private views disguised as public fact, wherein Pound's Hellenic heroes typically war with his Hebraic villains.

In other words, Pound's Hellenism, fundamentally deriving from his work with classical Latin poetry, not only characterizes his aesthetics, but eventually determines his economics and his politics. Instead of redeeming beauty from ugliness, myth from history, or art from life, we must conclude that the poet metamorphoses into the anti-Semitic fascist. One can, however, be instructed by Pound's finally unrepentant lessening. For in recognizing his personal anxiety and subsequent tragedy as symptomatic of our time, we may yet, even though he lost his way, find ourselves.

In searching for sincere self-expression, Pound wrote one poetic mask after another. Because the resultant poetry invariably reflects less the predecessor's personality than Pound's own, studying these masks over time reveals his maturation. *The Latin Masks of Ezra Pound* explores this evolution in poetic distortion with respect to the successive influence that Virgil, Catullus, Propertius, Ovid, and Horace had on Pound's career. Therefore, the term "mask" extends figuratively from specific performances to periods of greatest influence, wherein a particular Latin poet dominates among

Pound's Latin masks, and speaks synecdochically for all of Pound's poetry within that period. Blending analysis (with reference to the original Latin) and biography, the book utilizes the whole of Pound's poetry and criticism in measuring the significance of these masks. Within this context, and encouraged by Pound's own candor about personae, I have approached his criticism and his proficiency in Latin with some skepticism. As moderns endeavoring to refashion poetry for their time, both Pound and Eliot had vested interests in creating a criticism that essentially justified their own work. Consequently, what Pound says about other poets often glosses best his own current progress. As for Pound's notorious "ignorance" of Latin, it emerges as a nonissue. Given his adequate reading knowledge of the language (see appendix), his recurrent mistranslation epitomizes the distortion inherent in his method.

Various models deriving from either romantic or classical tradition could well describe the nature of Pound's search for identity. One could, for example, characterize his career as a secular theodicy wherein redemption lies in progressive self-education. Pound's life as a prodigal poet also fulfills the Christian metaphor of the exile's pilgrimage toward home and bride. Occultism's myth of sexual division, opposition, and reconjunction might serve as well. Or perhaps one could employ the procession and epistrophe of neoplatonism. Pound himself, particularly in the *Cantos,* preferred the allegorical analogue of Homer's Odysseus. This careful choice registers his lifelong resistance within a pervasively Christian tradition to our "obsession by monotheism and monotheistical backwash." Although appreciating the importance of Pound's gods to his epic designs, we are inclined to be more tolerant of our Hebraic heritage. Because it seems less culture-bound, I have chosen a much simplified variant of Harold Bloom's psychological metaphor concerning the family. Dedicated to being a great poet, Pound rejected Virgil as the obvious father figure. He spent a lifetime in opposition, first as Catullus, then as Propertius, and last as Ovid. Finally, having experienced "fatherhood" himself, Pound returned somewhat reconciled, playing Virgil by outboasting Horace. Never knowing what he wanted until he had achieved it, Pound struggled self-consciously to become worthy of himself, to be at home with himself in his otherness.

In the prologue of his career, quite simply, Pound loathed Virgil. Of the Latin poets important to his maturation, he failed to achieve rapport only with Virgil. Virgil functions like a Yeatsian antimask or "dominus" whom, in order to make space for himself, the adolescent son subconsciously represses. Rarely afforded an opportunity to speak, Virgil merely baits Pound's contempt as the Latin poet alluded to most in his criticism and least in his poetry. Pound's Virgil wrote the *Aeneid,* and Pound was anxious about Virgil's great achievement. Thus, in seeking to revitalize modern poetry, Pound spurned Virgil and what he saw as the Virgilian (i.e., the Miltonic) in English poetry. Pound's sense of Virgil (and Milton) as the Puritan establishment rival testifies to his own early poetic ambition to write an Hellenic epic. Instead of rhetoric, Pound valued intensity; instead of Latinized syntax, speech ionized with irony; and instead of monotheism, paganism. Pound's quest led him through his lyric, dramatic, and epic periods, underscoring respectively the personal, the social, and the historical themes of his own work. Indeed, with the help of Catullus, Propertius, and Ovid, Pound would resolutely write his own impressive but non-Virgilian epic.

Catullus in the lyric mode, Propertius in the dramatic, and Ovid in the epic constitute Pound's great triumvirate of classical Latin masks. The *Carmina,* the *Elegiae,* and the *Metamorphoses* aptly define the generic development of Pound's work from the early poetry through the *Homage* and *Mauberley* to the *Cantos.* Moreover, Pound appreciated Catullus' intensity, which generates lyric and satiric verse that together produce a poignant sense of loss. In Catullus' work Pound discovered Lesbia as an image of what developed into a central tension of his own poetry: the contrast between an ideal Hellenic past and the real Hebraic present. Through Propertius as his dramatic mask, Pound expanded this contrast into a parallel between his perception of Propertius' anti-imperialism and his own anti-imperialism toward *fin de siècle* Britain. Propertius suits Pound so well because just as the Umbrian after the great success of his *Monobiblos* began hesitantly to move toward a more Callimachian style of verse, so Pound in 1917 was most anxiously contemplating how he might package his increasingly reactionary belief in an epic form suitable for a potentially hostile public. Then, by melding Ovidian assocation with the Chinese ideogram, Pound matured his Hellenic-Hebraic contrast into an evaluation of mainly Western history by means of classical myth. Besides offering a static historiography, Confucius helps here by suggesting to Pound how he need not attain the tribe's approval, after all, of his Hellenic belief, so long as he both masks it with the ideogrammic method and gains the favor of at least the Prince of State (il Duce). At any rate, Ovid's moments of physical metamorphosis are transformed into Pound's "magic moments" wherein the gods appear to the speaker both as private ritual and as public condemnation. More important, in the crucible of the *Pisan Cantos* Pound poignantly literalizes what most often had been the gods' psychological or poetic presence in order to proclaim that his idealized past could be incorporated into the real present. Due at last to the personal suffering experienced near Pisa, Ovidian metamorphosis temporarily triumphs over Catullan loss. Most significant, however, the momentary trinity of ritual (canto LXXIX), visionary chant (canto LXXXI), and cognitive calm (canto LXXXIII) sadly for Pound but fortunately for the West fails to verify his ambitious anti-Virgilian, epic, and, above all, Hellenic success. Ever reactionary, the older Ovidian poet can only privately confirm his youthful Catullan claim that Sirmione would someday lead to paradise on earth, even as he validates his more mature Propertian malaise about being able to "write paradise" in the *Cantos*. Hence the late liaisons with Martinelli and Spann, followed by the final admissions of failure in *Drafts and Fragments*.

In the epilogue of his career, Pound partially returned to the fold. Like Virgil in epic, Horace was an establishment poet in lyric, and Pound never could accept Horace's Augustanism. As he associated Virgil's Augustan Puritanism with Milton, so he associated Horace's Hebraic didacticism with English neoclassicism. But from the distance of old age, and mindful of his own mixed success as Virgil's rival in celebrating a resurgent Rome (*fasces: fascisti*), Pound eagerly identified with Horace's lesser achievement in lyric poetry. In fact, from his early poetry through the *Cantos* to his late translations, Pound had been preoccupied with Horace's famous boast about his greatness in *Odes* 3.30. Such absorption signifies both Pound's abiding ambition to claim at least as much for himself and his final inability to do so honestly except by settling for second best. Horace becomes a demimask, therefore, because when Pound eventually does translate *Odes* 3.30 to judge his own work, his boast rings hollow as an estimation of epic endeavor, although true enough as testament to the lyric traces therein. Forever the Hellene "in half-mask's space," Pound lacked the confidence to let love lead to polity.

As a translator, Pound practiced the poetic paradox of deducing himself from the past. The pertinent Latin infinitive is "deducere," which means to "lead down" as in time, or figuratively to "spin out" as in song. Horace used this verb in Pound's favorite ode (*Odes,* 3.30.13–14) to assert his originality in composing Aeolic song into Italian verse, itself an echo of Virgil's own use in his statement of Alexandrian poetics (*Ec.* 6.3–5). Virgil's Aeneas later marvels that his Trojan comrades would follow wherever he might *lead* across the sea (*Aeneid,* II.800). Surely Virgil had in mind here raising his own "Rome" from the remains of Homeric "Troy." So perhaps Pound, after a career of Odyssean wanderings, should dearly have preferred to have followed in Aeneas' more fateful footsteps with his own great *deductum carmen,* the *Cantos.* For while cunning Odysseus left Troy for Penelope, pious Aeneas left Dido for Rome. Like Janus *bifrons,* then, the premier poet of *personae* died pondering both the anxiety that had brought him far and the repose that had always eluded him. Such is the joy, and the sorrow, of Latin masks used to seek oneself from the past and to hide oneself from the present. They are like an unbalanced door that is easy to open but hard to close, or like a "theatre of war": "'theatre' is good. There are those who did not want / it to come to an end" (78/447). Pound surely wanted his lifelong search for self to end successfully; he just did not know how to end it: "to close the Temple of Janus bifronte / the two-faced bastard" (78/477). And so it was closed for him.

1

Virgil as Antimask

"Not Virgil, especially not the
Aeneid, where he has no story
worth telling, no sense of
personality" (*LE,* 215).

Gauging Pound's Virgilian criticism is a bit like guessing the size of an iceberg by walking on its surface. But on consideration, three important insights emerge: Pound rejected Virgil for his epic success in the *Aeneid*, he identified with Gavin Douglas as an unacknowledged translator who was "a great poet," and he maligned Milton as the English Virgil. Consequently, in depreciating the chief romantic spokesman for Puritanism in English, Pound valued the emotion, irony, and polytheism that he found in classical Latin poetry excluding Virgil. Indeed, animated by a strong filial respect, the son would soon depart in self-exile to seek his own poetic identity.

In demeaning Virgil himself, and in comparison to Homer and Dante, Pound betrays his anxiety about the *Aeneid*.[1] Though while a sophomore in college he studied Virgil, his early reticence toward him, compared to, say, Catullus, conveys his distaste. In 1923 Pound conceived his first list of "the tradition," ranking Virgil with Petrarch as not "affecting the main form of the story."[2] In "How to Read" (1928), he discarded Virgil "without the slightest compunction" from his list of authors "who actually invented something" (*LE,* 27–28). And in his essay on Cavalcanti (1934), Pound proffered that "prudery is not a particularly Christian excrescence. There is plenty of prudery in Virgil" (*LE,* 151). Through such reactionary criticism Pound would distance himself from Virgil.

When comparing Virgil to Homer, Pound shows more clearly why he found the Roman a "second-rater" (*L,* 87). In 1915 he praised the Renaissance for its revival of realism: "the substitution of Homer for Virgil; the attitude of Odysseus for that of the snivelling Aeneas (who was probably not so bad as Virgil makes out)."[3] Pound's preference for the mythically circular (Hellenic) *Odyssey* over the historically linear (Hebraic) *Aeneid* suits well his own youthful identity. To insist Virgil had no sense of personality suggests that Rome's founding antagonized Pound in his own uncertain pursuit of polity more than Odysseus' wandering. Pound's remark about realism also previews his appreciation of Douglas, whose precision enhances Virgil's accuracy. Pound later explained that Virgil derived his *nekuia* from Homer (*ABC,*123), which clarifies why he chose Divus' version of Homer's descent into hell (rather than Douglas' of Virgil's) for canto I. In his *Cantos* Pound would return to the source: "The *Nekuia* shouts aloud that it is older than the rest, all that island, Cretan, etc., hinter-time, that is *not* Praxiteles, *not* Athens of Pericles, but Odysseus" (*L,* 274). In sailing after self-knowledge, Pound had little choice but to deny Virgil's psychic validity.

Pound's Virgil suffered also in comparison to Dante, though more subtly because of Dante's own evident respect. Dante's Virgil embodied the pagan ideals of honesty and stoicism acceptable to Pound. He quoted Dante after having inveighed against the simonists (*Inferno,* XIX): "I believe, indeed, that this pleased my guide" (*SR,* 134). For Pound, Dante here is invoking the honesty of Virgil's "pagan enlightenment to rebuke the corruption of the Church in a way that will not stir up the rabble" (*SR,* 134). Again, according to Pound, Dante's weeping for the sorcerers and diviners (*Inferno,* XX) prompts Virgil's "classic stoicism: 'Art thou, too, like the other fools? Here liveth pity when it were well dead. Who is more impious than he who sorrows at divine judgment?'" (*SR,* 134–35). Making Virgil palatable to Pound, "Dante was right to respect him, for Dante had no Greek, and the *Aeneid* would have stood out nobly against such literature as was available in the year 1300" (*LE,* 215). "No Greek" excludes Homer, whose medical and geographical precision (*ABC,* 43–44) prefigures Dante's own imagistic intensity. Undaunted by Virgil's derivative chthonic influence on Dante, Pound would praise his own anti-Virgilian model for the *Cantos:* "Dante makes all his acknowledgements to Virgil (having appreciated the best of him), but the direct and indirect effect of Ovid on Dante's writing is possibly greater than Virgil's" (*ABC,* 45).

In addition, Gavin Douglas as an unsung translator-poet reminded Pound of himself. In the same essay where he evinced initial interest in Ovid, Pound admired the sixteenth-century Scottish poet's translation of the "XIII Bukes of Eneados" (*LE,* 245). Deciding that Douglas (as did Dante) improved on Virgil,[4] Pound offered selected passages that explain his belief. Having discussed Douglas' work in "Notes on Elizabethan Classicists" (1917) and again in *The ABC of Reading* (1934), Pound shifted his focus from Aeneas' encounter with his mother in book one to his descent into hell in book six. Briefly, Douglas' precision especially enhanced for Pound Virgil's descriptions of Venus, the sea, and the golden bough.

Significantly, the first half of the *Aeneid* deals with Aeneas' Odyssean wanderings toward Italy; Pound did not consider the Italian half of the poem at all. In 1917 he dwelt on Aeneas' first meeting with Venus along the strand, thereby foreshadowing her importance in the *Cantos*. Aeneas, like Pound, has set out to explore:

> [To whom his mother appeared in the middle of the forest
> bearing the face and dress of a girl and the arms of
> a Spartan maid, or like Thracian Harpalyce who tires
> out horses and outstrips the swift Hebrus with her flight.
> For the huntress had hung by habit a light bow from her
> shoulders and let her hair stream in the wind,
> her knee was bare, and her flowing robe gathered in a knot.
> And she spoke first....]
>   *(Aeneid,* I.314–21)[5]

> Amyd the wod hys moder met thame tway
> Semand a maid in vissage and aray
> With wapynnys like the virgynys of Spartha
> Or the stowt wench of Trace, Harpalica,
> Hastand the hors hir fadir to reskew,
> Spedyar than Hebrum, the swyft flude, dyd persew;
> For Venus eftyr the gys and maner thar
> Ane active bow apon hir schuldir bar
> As sche had bene a wild hunteres,
> With wynd waving hir haris lowsit of tres,
> Hir skyrt kiltit til hir bair kne,
> And first of other, onto thame thus spak sche....
>   (Douglas, I.vi.17–28)[6]

Concisely accurate, Douglas did well with his pentameter couplets to stay within four lines of Virgil's hexameters. He did fall behind when glossing (as indicated from his note) Virgil's own indirect allusion to "Harpalyca"'s rescue of her father, "Ligurgus," from the "pepil of Getya," and again when glossing Hebrus as a "swyft flude." But he also enlivened his diction with the literal "virgyns of Spartha," the expansion of Virgil's "Threissa" as "the stowt wench of Trace," and the thoroughly Scottish "skyrt kiltit til hir bair kne." Such phrasing demonstrates how Douglas could idiomatically preserve his subject. His inversions seem conventional enough; he was using couplet rhyme.

Omitting Venus' humorously coy question—"Have you seen my sister wandering around here?"—Pound selected Douglas on Aeneas' marveling at the girl's appearance. Explaining that he and the Trojans are lost,

Aeneas continues his questions. The goddess replies with a lengthy explanation of Carthage's founding, and then asks Aeneas to identify himself.
He, no doubt much to Pound's chagrin, replies, "sum pius Aeneas." Venus
encourages her son by allaying his fears, directing him to Dido's court,
and assuring him through a simile about swans once scattered but now
regrouped that he and his men have come to a safe port. Only when Aeneas
recognizes his mother (*Aeneid,* I.402–06) does Pound again quote Douglas
(Douglas, I.vi.162–68). Though we can readily appreciate such excerpts
with reference to the original, reading Douglas alone would soon interest
only the translator intrigued by his Scottish dialect. But, of course, Pound
himself had more than just a translator's interest in mind. As he remarked
after Aeneas' recognition of Venus, "Gavin Douglas was a great poet" (*LE,*
248). Moreover, by excluding everything that distracts our attention from
his muse, Pound suggests another reason why he liked Douglas' Virgil: his
own *Cantos* would consist of recurrent lyrical glimpses without the less
intense connecting links of conventional epic.

Pound had said in 1917 that Douglas improved on Virgil whenever the
text treated the sea (*SP,* 356), and again in 1928 that the *Eneados* was
"better than the original, as Douglas had heard the sea" (*LE,* 35). But not
until returning to Douglas in *The ABC of Reading* (1934) did he buttress
his assertion with a view of Juno, determined to swamp the Trojans in a
squall.

> [As he uttered such words a gale, roaring with the North wind,
> struck the sail in front, and lifted the waves to the stars.
> The oars were crushed, then the prow yawed and turned
> sideways to the sea, a mountain of water towering....]
>   (*Aeneid,* I.102–05)

> And al invane thus quhil Eneas carpit,
> A blastrand bub out from the north brayng
> Gan our the forschip in the baksaill dyng,
> And to the starnys up the flude gan cast.
> The aris, hechis and the takillis brast,
> The schippis stevin frawart hir went gan wryth,
> And turnyt hir braid syde to the wallis swyth,
> Heich as a hill the iaw of watir brak....
>   (Douglas, I.iii.14–21)

In footnoting an earlier passage, Douglas himself had quoted the line, "a
blastrand bub out from the north brayng," to exemplify Virgil's use of the
north wind. Hence Douglas has suggested Pound's selection, which reveals
Douglas' rendering of the winds, the ship, and the sea. Douglas' translation
is packed with technical terms referring to the ship. Where Virgil, the
writer of bucolic and georgic poetry, had used the relatively flat diction of

"velum" and "remi" and "prora," Douglas was more precise: "forschip" and "baksaill" and "aris" and "hechis" and "takillis" and "stevin." Such specificity intrigued Pound; when glossing "wryth" in the line, "the ship's prow away from her path did twist," he pondered Douglas' dialect: "? also technical nautical *ware* 'faire virer,' cause to turn. Possibly a textual error, I don't make out whether the ship's stem, main keel timber twists forward, i.e. wyrd or wrything loose from the ribs, or whether it is merely a twisted forward lurch of the ship" (*ABC,* 118). Pound, too, in exile knew the sea.

Also in 1934, Pound examined Douglas' version of Aeneas' descent into hell in book six, which reflects his own choice (after 1917) of making the *nekuia* a major theme of the *Cantos*.[7] Even so, Pound respected book six of the *Aeneid* less for its *nekuia* predating Homer, than for its treatment reflecting Virgil's interest in Italian folklore. As he admonished, "the lover of Virgil who wishes to bring a libel action against me would be well advised to begin his attack by separating the part of the *Aeneid* in which Virgil was directly interested (one might almost say, the folk-lore element) from the parts he wrote chiefly because he was trying to write an epic poem" (*ABC,* 45). Pound's distinction denotes his preference for Aeneas' preparations—especially discovering the golden bough—over his tour through hell itself. Interestingly, the psychically itinerant Pound thereby avoided Anchises' prophecy about Rome's founding, which forms the last two-thirds of the book. That he considered Virgil's golden bough folklore can be supported by his earlier reference to Chaucer's open-mindedness, "let us say to folklore, to the problems [Sir James] Frazer broaches" (*ABC,* 102–3). Just as Frazer had employed Virgil's bough to suggest his collection of the religio-cultural myths of the past, so Pound used it to represent his own intense interests in ancient culture. The runaway slave longed to become, as his Pisan references to Nemi sadly confirm, the *rex nemorensis,* and Aeneas' passkey becomes the symbolic token for Pound's own rites of passage toward polity. Pound's hell is the quest for meaning of the *Cantos:* "sa gret desyre and luf [he] has / Twys [i.e., once now, alive, and again once dead] til oursayll [oversail] of Stix the dedly layk, / And twys behald blak hellis pyt of wraik [wrath, danger]," for "sa huge laubour delytis" him.[8] Pound's "descent" into the past that should allow his "ascent" into self-knowledge, love, and paradise requires the ritual key, the golden bough of cultural knowledge, of folklore.

Aeneas' prayers are answered, the birds fulfill their office, and his mother is indeed "favorable to his way." Behold, Pound seems to say through Douglas, the bough itself:

> [As mistletoe, which its own tree does not produce, in the wood
> in winter's cold is wont to grow green with new foliage,
> and to surround the smooth trunk with its yellow fruit,

so on the dark oak was a sight of leafy gold,
so its metal leaf tinkled in the gentle breeze.
Aeneas seized it directly....]
    (*Aeneid*, VI.205-10)

Lyke as ful oft, in chil wyntiris tyde,
The gum or glew, amyd the woddis wide,
Is wont to seym zallow on the grane new,
Quhilk nevir of that treis substance grew,
With saffron hewit frute doyng furth sprowt,
Circulis and wymplis rownd bewis about—
Siklyke was of this gold the figur brycht,
That burgionyt fayr on the rank akis hycht.
Evir as the branch for pypand wynd reboundit,
The golden schakeris ratlis and resoundit.
Eneas smertly hynt the grayn at schone,
And but delay hes rent it doun anone....
    (Douglas, VI.iii.93-104)

Douglas' heightened description of the bough's "golden" nature determines Pound's use of it to symbolize his own interest in ancient culture. Douglas dropped Virgil's "solet...virere" ("is wont to grow green") for his own "is wont to seym zallow [yellow]." Where Virgil first had compared the bough to mistletoe, with its "croceo fetu," Douglas matched him with "saffron hewit frute." Even as Douglas lessened Virgil's contrast between the green plant and its yellow fruit, he also lessened the contrast between the golden bough and the dark oak, "species auri...opaca / ilice," with his own "gold...brycht, / That burgionyt fayr on the...akis." And where Virgil had used only "brattea" ("metal leaf"), Douglas highlighted the bough yet again with "golden schakeris [thin metal plates]," conceiving his trisyllabic rhyme ("reboundit" / "resoundit") for a "tinkling" effect. Thus, where Virgil had used only "saffron" and "gold" in his simile to describe the bough, Douglas used "yellow," "saffron," "gold," "fair," and "golden" to embellish his (and Pound's) vision.[9]

After examining Douglas in *The ABC of Reading*, Pound had little more to say about him. In 1937 he implied that Douglas' being out of print reflected a decline in the study of Latin authors themselves (*PE*, 143)—a measure of how much Douglas *was* Virgil for Pound. In 1938 he claimed that Douglas created "something glorious and different" from the original (*L*, 311). That same year, Pound professed: "Of the books that a man would read. The books that I shall, I hope, reread, with more diligence, and a deeper comprehension...Gavin Douglas' with reference to the Latin original" (*GtK*, 150). He summed up Douglas' work thus: "Gavin Douglas recreated us Virgil, or rather we forget Virgil in reading Gavin's *Eneados* and know only the tempest, *Acheron*, and the eternal elements that Virgil for most men glazes over" (*GtK,* 249). By 1942 Pound ranked among the most beautiful books of poetry in the English language, "Douglas' *Eneados,* done...in a Scots dialect that no one can read today without a glossary" (*SP,* 249). The comparison with the *Cantos* is clear.

Besides sympathizing with his obscure fate as a translator-poet, Pound admired Gavin Douglas for his precision. This chief Poundian virtue enhanced Douglas' descriptions of Venus, the sea, and the golden bough, all of which held great aesthetic significance for Pound. Though in time he progressed from goddess to bough, Pound kept returning to the beginning of Douglas' *Eneados.* After quoting from it in 1917 and in 1934, he did so again in 1948 (*Cantos,* 78/478-79) and in 1964 (*CtC,* 34). One couplet, in particular, stands out:

> Gret pane in batail sufferit he alsso
> Or [ere] he his goddis brocht in Latio....
> (Douglas, I.i.7–8)

In maligning Milton as the English Virgil, and thus rejecting English romantic tradition for a classical Latin one excluding Virgil, Pound first explained that Milton did not invent "Miltonism." Before discussing Douglas in "Elizabethan Classicists," he had quoted briefly from Tottle's edition (1557) of Surrey's "Certain Bokes of Virgiles Aenaeis" (*LE,* 244). Important less as a translation of Virgil, or even as a foil to Douglas, Pound's selection clarifies what he meant by Miltonic poetry. After excerpting from the opening of book two, where Aeneas begins to tell of Troy's fall,[10] Pound exclaims that "The quality of translations declined in measure as the translators ceased to be absorbed in the subject matter of their original. They ended in the 'Miltonian cliche'; in the stock and stilted phraseology of the usual English verse as it has come down to us" (*LE,* 247). In short, Surrey's blank verse is "'so Miltonic'" (*LE,* 244) because, for example, its syntactic inversion to metronomize meter and its highly periodic clause structure imitate Latin but suffocate English.[11]

Despite the development of blank verse from Surrey to Milton, Pound's association of Surrey's translation with Milton's poetry testifies to his belief not only that translation is poetry, but also that Milton is the English Virgil. Pound made the critical juxtaposition between Virgil and Milton as early as 1914: "Virgil is a man on a perch. All these writers of pseudo *épopée* are people on perches....Milton and Virgil are concerned with decorations and trappings and they muck about with a moral" (*LE,* 217). C. S. Lewis, of course, has argued famously that poets such as Virgil and Milton wrote literary or secondary epic, while poets such as Homer and the author of *Beowulf* wrote primary epic.[12] In Lewis' (and Pound's) sense, then, Milton is an English Virgil, which means that Pound saw him as a

ironic overtones of Pound's speech develop primarily from his satiric struggle to contemporize such aspects as the diction, rhythm, and voices of his verse. Stated differently, Pound's *Homage* finally represents less his preservation of Propertius than another more dramatic—i.e., watershed— effort to discover his own poetic identity through translation.

Third, besides censuring his rhetoric and his latinism, Pound would preempt Milton's Puritanism with polytheism. In fact, Pound's contempt for Virgil as a prude and Aeneas as a priest modulated into his "disgust with what [Milton] has to say, his asinine bigotry, his beastly hebraism, the coarseness of his mentality" (*LE*, 238). Not only did he dislike Milton's theology, but he blamed "monism and monotheistical backwash" (*LE*, 397) for many of the ills of our time: "most of the tyrannies of modern life, or at least a lot of stupidities, are based on Xtn taboos, and can't really be got rid of radically until Xtianity is taken lightly and skeptically" (*L,* 141). Pound related the modern world's stupidities to the rise of usury in a Christian tradition wherein the classical tradition had declined: "Anything that profanes the mysteries or tends to obscure discrimination...goes hand in hand with drives toward money profit.... The whole of Protestant morals, intertwined with usury-tolerance, has for centuries tended to obscure perception of degrees, to debase the word moral to a single groove, to degrade all moral perceptions outside the relation of the sexes, and to vulgarize the sex relation itself" (*GtK,* 281–82). This dissociation of Eleusis with usury graphically displays the conviction underlying Pound's use of Hellenic myth to evaluate Hebraic history in the *Cantos.* Rejecting Milton's Hebraic influence on English poetry, Pound honored instead the gods of Hellenic tradition in heralding his renaissance for poetry and society at large.

Proscribing Hebraism, Pound revered polytheism. In "Terra Italica" (1931–32), explaining the fusion of Eleusis and the late Roman worship of Mithras, a Persian sun-god, he suggested that Christianity had adopted many of the worst traits of Mithraism while suppressing the Eleusinian impulse. Following Frazer (if not Farnell and Foucart) and making his own sexual associations with Sappho, the Roman elegists, medieval love poetry, and Remy de Gourmont, Pound himself preferred to associate the ancient rites of Eleusis, which venerated Demeter and Persephone as agricultural goddesses, with Aphrodite, the goddess of love. Christianity had "produced nothing to match the grace of the well-curb of Terracina" (*SP,* 58), where Pound would erect a statue of the *alma mater* to symbolize Hellenism. This spurious association of Eleusis with Aphrodite underscores Pound's conventional view that she represented a lost but moral tradition, based upon celebrating the erotic as an embodiment of nature's mysterious and divine life-force.[15] Ironically, however, the quaint analogy between agriculture and sex ("ploughing," etc.) probably derives less from Eleusis than from the polemical church fathers via the vivid imagination of a Scottish *fin de siècle* anthropologist. Nevertheless, though insisting that Italy had "lived more fully than other nations because she has kept up the habit of placing statues in gardens" (*SP,* 332), Pound pleaded repeatedly in the *Pisan Cantos* that "the grove calls for the column: *Nemus aram vult*" (*SP,* 332). Since "to replace the marble goddess on her pedestal at Terracina is worth more than any metaphysical argument" (*SP,* 290), Ovid with his compendium of myths about the gods became crucial to Pound's poetic if not political restoration of Cytherean Hellenism.[16]

Pound's reaction to Milton strongly distorted his estimation of English poetry in general, and especially of high romantic tradition. Notwithstanding a few notable exceptions along the way, Pound's misrepresentation of romanticism in search of his own Hellenic identity is remarkable. Spenser seems to have escaped his critical eye altogether. Milton, of course, was "a thorough-going decadent" and "the worst possible food for a growing poet" (*LE,* 216-17). Blake was "dippy" (*LE,* 72), and Wordsworth "a silly old sheep" who "buried" his talent for natural description "in a desert of bleatings" (*LE,* 277). Even Pound's admiration for Coleridge's "magical definition of beauty—KALON quasi KALOUN" (*SR,* 149)—while informing his own precociously Plotinan pursuit of "the Fatherland," had masked Milton's sympathetic defense of beauty in the dialogue of "The Principles of Genial Criticism." As George Bornstein shows, Pound sympathized more with Keats, Shelley, and Byron because of their own self-exile and contemporary ignominity.[17] Still, *Endymion* was "not very well-written verse,"[18] and "The Sensitive Plant" was "one of the rottenest poems ever written" (*LE,* 51). Pound's antiromantic appreciation of Byron's social satire was more complex: just as he and Eliot often assailed a public who wished they were Keats and Shelley, so Byron often satirized the vatic stance of his romantic contemporaries. Pound nixed the nineties for their "muzziness" and "softness" (*LE,* 363), and the common verse of Britain from 1890 to 1910 for being "a doughy mess of third-hand Keats, Wordsworth, heaven knows what, fourth-hand Elizabethan sonority blunted, half-melted, lumpy" (*LE,* 205). And in 1920, the "idyllic and romantic," he sneered, "were W.B.Y.'s particular line" (*L,* 155). Obviously, Pound preferred Hellenism to Hebraism.

Besides forecasting the sadness of his anti-Semitic flirtation with fascism, Pound's antiromantic rivalry with Virgil and Milton precipitated more immediate and profound aesthetic consequences. As an early modern (i.e., prodigal) poet, he was struggling to create a new sort of poetic art that was really an old sort (*LE,* 55); for him tradition did not begin "in A.D. 1870, nor in...1632, nor...even with Chaucer" (*LE,* 91). Initially gainless in Greek but returning beyond Provence and Tuscany, Pound loved the Latin past because the Roman poets had approximately "the same problems as we have. The metropolis, the imperial posts to all corners of the known world. The enlightenments" (*L,* 90). And though "Homer is better than Virgil" (*LE,* 240), Catullus, Propertius, and Ovid have preserved a great deal not in Greek (*SP,* 225). Certainly, they promoted Pound's own poetic powers of precision, satire, and metamorphosis in his consciously classical but subconsciously romantic quest for self, love, and paradise. Sallying forth, then, to reclaim the Golden Age, the ephebe first found himself in Sirmio.

2

Catullus as Lyric Mask

"Catullus offers neatness,
hardness" ("OCiG," 154).

Valuing his lyric and satiric intensity, Pound claimed Catullus as his first
love among the Roman poets. His Catullan translations isolate Lesbia as
an image either of divine love or of base desire; in this dual role she represents Pound's personal ambivalence about his own poetic program to
resuscitate the past. His allusions to Catullus' work more derivatively treat
this seminal contrast between an ideal past and the real present by previewing the social form it takes in his work with Propertius. Pound's tan-
gentially Catullan enshrining of Sirmio provides the *locus amoenus* from
which he set out under Ovid's influence to write paradise by synthesizing
myth and history in the *Cantos*. Indeed, while Pound tragically failed to
reconcile his Roman head with his Christian heart, his late return to Sirmio
both confirms the locale of his poetic beginning and conveys his own consciously Catullan sense of loss.

Pound's early translations of Catullus did not occur in a critical vac-
uum. He had studied Catullus as a sophomore and as an M.A. student in
college, which would predate the influence of Ford and French literature,
of imagisme, and of Fenellosa and the ideogram. As Pound himself said in
1942, "I consider the hours spent... copying a prose translation of Catullus
by W. McDaniel [a distinguished Latin professor at the University of
Pennsylvania] more important than any contemporary influences" (*SP*,
289); and again in 1963, "I did have *some* things in my head when I got to
London, and I *had* heard of Catullus before I heard about modern French
poetry."[1] Just as Pound saw Homer behind Virgil, so he saw Sappho
behind Catullus, though to Sappho's disadvantage (*LE*, 240). Among his
Roman peers, Catullus mattered most to Pound for his intensity (*SP*, 87);
he even outranked Horace as "the most skillful metrist" and as "the greatest
lyricist in Latin" ("H," 217, 225). Although echoing Landor here,[2] Pound
in 1914 legitimized his own youthful lead in pursuing poetic identity:

"poets like Villon, Sappho, and Catullus differ from poets like Milton, Tasso, and Camoens, and...size is no more a criterion of writing than it is of painting" (*LE,* 215).

Pound's initial and unusually literal translations of Catullus begin to characterize the lyric-satiric nature of his influence. The first translation, "To Formianus' Young Lady Friend, after Valerius Catullus" (*Poetry and Drama,* II.i. [Mar. 1914], 20–21), is of Catullus 43.[3]

> All Hail! young lady with a nose
>   by no means too small,
> With a foot unbeautiful,
>   and with eyes that are not black,
> With fingers that are not long, and with a mouth undry,
> And with a tongue by no means too elegant,
> You are the friend of Formianus, the vendor of cosmetics,
> And they call you beautiful in the province,
> And you are even compared to Lesbia.
>
> O most unfortunate age!
>   (*Lu,* 56)

Though John Espey senses its pedantry,[4] this translation cleverly transforms Catullus' mockery of Mamura into Pound's own depreciation of false beauty. Catullus' allusion to "the bankrupt of Formiae" would be unclear without knowing Catullus 29, where Mamura was scorned for squandering his ancestral estates and the gifts of his patrons.[5] Recasting the reference, Pound derives "Formianus" from Formiae and "vendor of cosmetics" presumably from associating "decoctoris" with decoction and then concocter. As in the original, Pound's young lady is considered pretty in the province, but now she tawdrily pursues a cosmetic beauty. Whereas Catullus wondered whether Lesbia was compared with Mamura's "amica," Pound asserts that Formianus' friend is "even compared to Lesbia," thereby presenting her as a prior ideal. Such provinciality only piques Pound's panache: "O most unfortunate age!" His translation, in effect, clarifies Catullus' own distinction between false and true beauty.

Pound's next two translations develop Catullus 43's motif of true versus false beauty by confirming the contrast between an ideal past and the real present. Pound conceived this contrast only gradually, for several allusions to the originals surround the translations themselves. Examining Pound's work with each poem—his preceding allusions, translation, and succeeding allusions—explains his juxtaposition of them into a diptych of past ideality versus present reality. The first translation (found in ur-canto II, *Poetry,* 10.4 [July 1917], 181–82) is of Catullus 51, and complements Catullus 43's implication that Lesbia manifests true beauty. Pound not surprisingly considered Catullus' poem (itself a translation of Sappho 2) a prototype of medieval European love poetry. As early as 1910 he associated it with Piere Vidal's "'Good Lady, I think I see God when I gaze on your delicate body'" (*SR,* 96), and with Dante's "'Whence is he blest who first looketh on her'" (*SR,* 122), and later with Daniel's "En Breu Brisaral Temps Braus" (*SP,* 41). Pound's appreciation of Catullus 51's archetypal value explains why he initially selected it for Canto II.

Catullus 51 measures the effects of Lesbia's beauty on the speaker himself, constituting Catullus' (and Sappho's) clinical definition of love as madness:

> Ille mi par esse deo videtur,
> ille, si fas est, superare divos
> qui sedens adversus identidem te
>   spectat et audit
>
> dulce ridentem, misero quod omnis
> eripit sensus mihi: nam simul te,
> Lesbia, adspexi, nihil est super mi
>
> ....
>
> lingua sed torpet, tenuis sub artus
> flamma demanat, sonitu suopte
> tintinant aures, gemina teguntur
>   lumnia nocte. (51)
>
> "God's peer that man is in my sight—
> Yea, and the very gods are under him,
> Who sits opposite thee, facing thee, near thee,
> Gazing his fill and hearing thee,
> And thou smilest. Woe to me, with
> Quenched senses, for when I look upon thee, Lesbia,
> There is nothing above me
> And my tongue is heavy, and along my veins
> Runs the slow fire, and resonant
> Thunders surge in behind my ears,
> And the night is thrust down upon me."
>   (*Poetry,* 10.4, 181–82)

Pound appreciated Catullus 51's lyric intensity. The poem, by cataloging Lesbia's direct effects on the speaker, more strongly idealizes beauty than did Catullus 43. As analysis of his translation shows, Pound would even heighten Catullus' emotion in English (e.g., "resonant thunders surge" for "ringing"). But surely he also foretells of Cavalcanti's ecstatic epiphany and of Aphrodite's Plotinan hypostasis in the *Cantos.* Like Lesbia herself, Pound's illuminating recollection of love is fragile, and fleeting, and once lost gone forever, unless invocable again through poetry.

Catullus' eventual disappearance from canto II suggests Pound's own realization after 1919 of the inappropriateness of beginning his epic poem with the work of a lyric poet. He merely summarized Catullus 51 in the second version of canto II (*Lu,* 190). But for a time Catullus 51 retained its strong appeal. Within a year after his translation's initial appearance, Pound referred to the poem as the age-old "bogie of 'Sapphics,'" which Catullus alone had imitated with success (*LE,* 230). About the same time, he offered that it "is possibly better than the Aeolic original; harder in outline,"[6] thereby emphasizing how Catullus used parts of the body to portray love as madness. Catullus had become the quintessential *imagiste* using objects to evoke emotion. Pound last alluded to Catullus 51, through Landor, at Horace's expense. Landor had said, "Catullus was, what Horace claims for himself, the first who imported into Latin poetry any vast variety of meters" (*Works,* vol. II, p. 203). Pound repeated with slightly more vehemence: "Horace is a liar of no mean pomposity when he claims to have been the first to bring in the 'Aeolic modes,' for Catullus preceded him, and Catullus wrote better Sapphics. Catullus frankly translated one poem and frequently improves on Greek style" ("H," 217).

Classicists themselves have entertained the idea that, of the two Sapphics Catullus wrote, lyric Catullus 51 was the first poem he wrote to Lesbia, and invective Catullus 11 was the last. For the satiric poem of his own diptych in ur-canto II, Pound chose Catullus 58, an even more effective statement of what Catullus' relationship had degenerated into than Catullus 11. As with his translation of Catullus 51, a substantial body of allusions both precede and follow Pound's translation of Catullus 58. He first alluded to the poem, itself rather typical of Catullus' own risque "acridity," in "Lesbia Illa,"one of a series (originally "Le Donne," and then changed to "Ladies") of caustic poems about women that originally appeared in *Poetry,* 4.5 (Aug. 1914), 169–177:

> Memnon, Memnon, that lady
> Who used to walk about amongst us
> With such gracious uncertainty,
> Is now wedded
> To a British householder.
> *Lugete, Veneres! Lugete, Cupidinesque!*
> (*Lu,* 42)

Alluding to Catullus 58, Pound presumably intended parallels between the Lesbia Catullus once loved and the lady of once "gracious uncertainty," and between Lesbia now fornicating among the crowd and the lady having married a "British householder." The Latin tag of the last line — Weep Venuses! And weep Cupids! — which echoes Catullus' mock heroic lament over the death of Lesbia's sparrow, has a noticeably caustic tone in its new context as a comment on the lady's deed. The pejorative expression, "British householder,"as a sign of economic decadence presages the economic and political direction of Pound's later career. Wanting to delete "Lesbia Illa" because of its bad taste, Harriet Monroe elicited his "Now who could blush at 'Lesbia Illa'????????? Who???.... Can one [not] presuppose a public which has read at least some of the classics?" (*L,* 37). Referring once more to Catullus 58 prior to his translation's appearance in ur-canto II, Pound used Catullus' line explaining where the sluttish Lesbia plied her trade—"in the crossroads and alleyways"—to gloss where the artist in 1916 must live.[7] He felt that while modern society compelled artists to work under impoverished conditions, their task was to revive the live tradition.

Against the past ideal of Catullus 51, then, in ur-canto II Pound juxtaposed Catullus 58 as the present reality of Catullus' relationship with Lesbia:

> [Caelius, my Lesbia, that Lesbia,
> that Lesbia, whom alone Catullus
> loved more than himself and all his friends
> now in the crossroads and alleyways
> screws the descendents of greatminded Remus.] (58)

> "*Caelius, Lesbia illa*—
> That Lesbia, Caelius, our Lesbia, that Lesbia
> Whom Catullus once loved more
> Than his own soul and all his friends,
> Is now the drab of every lousy Roman."
> (*Poetry,* 10.4, 182)

"Every lousy Roman," or earlier, by implication, "British householder," cancels Catullus' irony in "descendants of great-minded Remus," one of the legendary founders of Rome. Supporting his earlier and later use of Catullus' line four (and explaining why he omitted it here), Pound relinquished the irony of Catullus' phrase partly because he saw himself, at least, as trying to recapture that magnanimity. He liked Catullus 58 for its analogous condemnation of British reality, but would distance himself from that reality.

As not with Catullus 51, Pound retained his translation of Catullus 58 for the *Lustra* (1917) version of Canto II, with only minor variation in the first few lines (*Lu,* 190); but as with Catullus 51, he then dropped the poem from the early *Cantos* altogether. Pound referred to it one last time in 1948:

> "wd." said the guard "*take* everyone of them g.d.m.f. generals
> c.s. all of 'em fascists"

> Oedipus, nepotes Remi magnanimi
> so Mr Bullington lay on his back like an ape
> singing: O sweet and lovely
> o Lady be good"
>   in harum ac ego ivi
> Criminals have no intellectual interests?
>   (74/439)

Like Oedipus, Pound sits entrapped in the DTC by his own poetic program to revive the Hellenic past. In roundly chastising all generals as "fascists," the guard appears incognizant of Pound's own political sympathies, thus qualifying with the rest of his captors as "nepotes Remi magnanimi." Bullington, too, seems a modern caricature, singing his pop tune like Catullus to Lesbia: "Lady be good." Thus, despite his youthful dream to redeem Lesbia as Aphrodite, the poet regretfully has lost her amid Circe's pigsty, where only his comic dramatic irony can save him. For who says criminals have no intellectual interests! Catullus 58 lingered with Pound longer than Catullus 51, which Peter Whigham confirms with his anecdote about Santayana quoting "glubit magnanimi Remi nepotes" in reference to what transpired beyond the confines of Santo Stefano during World War II. Having written to Pound of Santayana's story, Whigham received a reply confirming that Santayana's experience was possible: "Old Jarge must have been leanin' over the fence an' usin' a pair of opry glasses."[8]

Pound juxtaposed Catullus 51 and 58 in ur-canto II to illuminate Catullus' theme of betrayal in love that Lesbia so signified. Itself an adequate symbol, Catullus 58 shows how Catullus often used his stormy relationship with Lesbia to generalize about Roman society.[9] The poem typifies Catullus' exploration of the tension between past and present, love and hate, ideal and real in that relationship. Pound's diptych, therefore, reinforces the risk of loss in love by representing Catullus,[10] who is but one of the European writers mentioned whose works emphasize the theme of loss. Indeed, the theme of the canto as Pound originally intended it concerned "the tears of things" in human affairs. The entire canto, with its modulation from simple private to complex public relationships, demonstrates that Pound (unlike Frederic Vance) intended not to betray his aesthetic calling, as his final injunction, "Take my Sordello," makes clear.

After 1917 Pound did not translate Catullus for two decades; instead he repeatedly referred to the difficulty of translating him.[11] This predicament resulted not only from Pound's respect for Catullus' lyric ability, but also from his own preoccupation with the *Cantos*. Then, in 1940 he continued the pattern of betrayal, but with an interest less in "Lesbia" than in "society at large." With "The Draughty House" (*Furioso,* 1.2 [1940], 5), Pound translated Catullus 26, wherein the poet derides Furius' poverty by punning on "opposita est" as "to mortgage." While foregoing Catullus' likely gibe at the low cost of Furius' villa, Pound does retain the pun (though on "ventus"). Although "Furius" becomes "Furus" (and "Favonius," "Favonus"), Pound's three different sums humorously echo his own five different winds. Moreover, his choice of "this house" for "your little villa" suggests, given his politico-economic views and the poem's date, that "draft" signifies the "blast" of war as well. Thus, the "draughty house" modulates from speaker to villa to Europe on the eve of World War II, and the "ventus" blowing through it will be "horribilis atque pestilens" indeed.[12]

While Pound's youthful allusions to Catullus' work more derivatively modulate his influence (wherein the satiric equals the lyric betrayed), they often forecast either the form or the content of his Propertian ravings as well. These allusions are critical and poetic, and half of them refer to Catullus 61, the first of Catullus' marriage hymns. Since Pound referred most often and latest to this poem, his other allusions (the majority occurring before 1918) deserve initial consideration. Within this miscellaneous group he referred earliest to Catullus 34, a festival hymn to Diana, which except for Catullus 61 is the only Catullan poem to resurface in the *Cantos*.

Pound appreciated Catullus 34's solemnity: the children's singing; their recognition of Diana as the threefold goddess; their association of her with the seasons and the harvest; and, finally, their prayer beseeching her blessing. In 1910 he had praised "the beautiful flowing of garments which Catullus had presumably in mind when he wrote 'Dianae sumus in fide / Puellae et pueri integri'" (*SR*, 40).[13] This interest in Dianan dancing reappears in the *Homage* where, once she has escaped death, Cynthia is ordered "back to Great Dian's dances bearing suitable gifts" (*Per*, 224). Of course, Cynthia is named for the Cynthian goddess, born with her brother near mount Cynthus on Delos. Later, in canto XXXIX (1934), Pound invoked part of Catullus 34's opening stanza—"sumus in fide...puellaeque canamus"—to begin his own grain rite, as it were, "beaten from flesh into light" (39/196). Pound's harvesting of aesthetic from sexual energy—"Not I but the handmaid kindled / Cantat sic nupta / I have eaten the flame" (39/196)—prompts us to recall the Eleusinian implications of an earlier Propertian remark: "My genius is no more than a girl" (*Per*, 217). In between these two allusions to Catullus 34, then, Propertius' Cynthian achievement, which he would take as his "not unworthy gift...to Persephone" (*Per*, 219), promotes Pound's own Eleusinian interests. One might add, recalling Diana's appearance as a huntress in canto XXX (1930), that only through resisting the status quo could the *rex* achieve his priesthood of the grave.

Pound next alluded to Catullus 4 with his more obviously Propertian parody, "'Phasellus Ille'" (*Ripostes,* 1912), which ridicules the British *fin de siècle* publishing establishment. While Catullus honored the yacht that brought him safely home from Bithynia to Sirmio, Pound distinctly dishonors his own "papier-mâché editor."[14] His first two lines follow Catullus' opening,

> [That boat, which you see, friends,
> was the fastest of ships....]
>   (4.1–2)

> This *papier-mâché,* which you see, my friends,
> Saith 'twas the worthiest of editors....
>   (*Lu,* 159)

Catullus' statement of his ship's origin and subsequent tasks loosely implies Pound's own for his editor, and Catullus' description of his boat's seaworthiness (4.19–21) becomes parodically in Pound: "Nay, should the deathless voice of all the world / Speak once again for its sole stimulation / 'Twould not move it one jot from left to right" (*Lu,* 160). Catullus' conclusion suggests Pound's own, with St. Anthony, the founder of monachism, replacing Castor and Pollux, the patron stars of sailors:

> [...now reconditioned
> it grows old in quiet and dedicates itself to you,
> twin Castor and twin of Castor.]
>   (4.25–27)

> Come Beauty barefoot from the Cyclades,
> She'd find a model for St. Anthony
> In this thing's sure *decorum* and behaviour.
>   (*Lu,* 160)

Predictably enough Pound has split Catullus' image of the "phaselus" into its lyric and satiric components. On the one hand, he venerates not the boat, but "Beauty barefoot" (rather a syncretism of Ameana's, Hymen's, Aurunculeia's, and Lesbia's famous feet), who has Hellenically sustained him from the Cyclades of the past. On the other hand, for such pre-Odyssean adventures, he must contend with an Hebraically Victorian editor's "sure *decorum* and behavior." Aside from sniffing something of Pound's attitude toward Horace in the *Homage* (II) and *Mauberley* (I.iv), one recalls Pound's praise of Swinburne as a poet "who kept alive some spirit of paganism and of revolt in a papier-mâché era" (*LE,* 293). Thus, Pound's "'Phasellus Ille'" anticipates not only the *Homage*'s parodic highjinks but also as a central concern of that poem the consequences of satirizing one's audience.

In "To A Friend Writing on the Cabaret Dancers" (*Cathay*, 1915), Pound borrowed a term from Catullus 86 to contrast the "Quintia" 's of "these dark northern climates" with his example of a "Lesbia" from Venice. Catullus had asserted that Quintia was less beautiful than Lesbia because she lacked the necessary "grain of salt." After his realistic portraits of "Pepita" and "Euhenia,"[15] Pound's poet-speaker generalizes about the local London dancers: "We can't preserve the elusive '*mica salis*'" (*Per*, 163). The decline from Nell Gwynn to Edward's mistresses to the prudent whore reveals the speaker's own ennui by suggesting that beauty has not "lasted well" in northern climates. By contrast, he says of his new-found southern "Lesbia":

> Now in Venice, 'Storante al Giardino, I went early,
> Saw the performers come: him, her, the baby,
> A quiet and respectable-tawdry trio;
> An hour later: a show of calves and spangles,
> "*Un e duo fanno tre,*"
> Night after night,
> No change, no change of program, "*Che*!
> "*La donna è mobile.*"
> (*Per*, 163)

Pound's riposte to "Hedgethorn," including his "innocent and innocuous" (*L*, 82) Venetian trio, confirms his own iconoclastic determination to escape the norms of ornamental beauty, despite outlawing himself as a result with indecorous poets like Catullus, or "Propertius of Cynthia, taking his stand / among these" (*Per*, 230).[16]

Appreciating Catullus 34's solemnity, Pound admired Catullus 61's celebration of marital love. Commemorating the wedding of Manlius Torquatus and Vinia Aurunculeia, Catullus 61 is less an epithalamium than a series of lyric reminiscences about a Roman marriage.[17] Indeed, Pound employed the poem to sanction his own increasingly illicit union with the Hellenic past, especially as celebrated in the early *Cantos*. Showing an early critical interest in Catullus 61, he qualified his dissociation of its physicality from the spirituality of "trobar clus" by suggesting that "Catullus, recording his own emotion, could say: 'More as a father than a lover.'"[18] Here Pound associates Aurunculeia with Lesbia as Catullus lyrically viewed her before their relationship began to sour. Catullus himself seems to have made a similar association in Catullus 68, where after trying to console Manlius for Aurunculeia's untimely death, he describes Lesbia as if she were Aurunculeia by comparing her to the loving bride Laodamia. (Intriguingly, Laodamia lost her husband Protesilaus at Troy, where Catullus more recently lost his brother, whose death alone in Catullus' work rivals the loss of Lesbia's love.) But the Alexandrian conceit crumbles when Catullus recalls his first *mira nox* of love: Lesbia came to him (not he to her) in adultery (not matrimony) by stepping on (not over) the threshold with a sandal that *creeked!* Not unlike Catullus, then, Pound would soon use Aurunculeia to redeem his lyric view of Lesbia as expressed in ur-canto II, which in turn implies his rededication to the poetic program of resuscitating the past in the *Cantos* to come.

Two years later while discussing the troubadours and Cavalcanti, Pound used a word perhaps derived from Pater in reference to Catullus 61: "It is the artist's business to find his own *virtù*. This *virtù* may be what you will.... It may be something which draws Catullus to write of scarlet poppies, of orange-yellow slippers, of the shaking, glorious hair of the torches..." (*SP,* 29). The references to Hymen's slippers (61.9–10), the torches as the bride appears (61.76–78), and her poppy-colored mouth (61.193–195) signify not only Pound's respect for Catullus 61, but also his own Catullan search for a poetic *virtù* that entails marital virtue. And so he substitutes Aurunculeia for Lesbia in the early *Cantos,* not because he loved the Hellenic past any less during his final years in London, but because in gaining notoriety as a poet seeking to impose that past on an unwilling public, he needed to reconsecrate his love in order to begin his epic in earnest.

Realizing that lyricism would not suffice to open his epic poem, Pound deleted Catullus from the final version of the first two cantos. But his allusions to Catullus 61 in cantos III, IV, and V do strike an ambivalently celebrative note, as if comparing Lesbia to Aurunculeia were finally wishful thinking. Though the complement to Catullus 61's promise would toll much later with elegiac regularity, Pound began in canto III with the little girl "reading the writ *voce tinnula*" (3/11) to Ruy Diaz. Hymen himself had come with "tinkling voice," harmonizing nuptial songs (61.12–13). Anticipating Pound's allusions to the poem in canto IV, the phrase also implies success for Diaz (Pound)[19] as a man of action. Catullus 61 next sounds its lyric note at the beginning of canto IV:

> Palace in smoky light,
> Troy but a heap of smouldering boundary stones,
> ANAXIFORMINGES. Aurunculeia!
> Hear me.
>   (4/13)

The plaintive apostrophe—"Hear me"—to both Pindar's "Lords of the lyre" and Catullus' bride plumbs Pound's ambivalence about setting out for paradise in a world where the sexual energy of poetic creation can readily metamorphose into the destructive wiles of a Helen, a Lesbia, or an Eleanor. Very tentatively Aurunculeia betokens hope in the poetic pursuit of beauty:

> Torches melt in the glare
>> set flame of the corner cook-stall,
> Blue agate casing the sky (as at Gourdon that time)
>> the sputter of resin,
> Saffron sandal so petals the narrow foot: Hymenaeus Io!
>> Hymen, Io Hymenaee! Aurunculeia!
> One scarlet flower is cast on the blanch-white stone.
>> 4/15)

Pound probably intended, with his reference to Gourdon, to link Catullus'
bride with his own wife Dorothy,[20] but Aurunculeia as his lyric mask for
Lesbia seems the poppy cast upon the tragically white stone of time. For
Pound in canto V, she symbolizes his Catullan vision of beauty in life,
however fleeting, however

> ...flitting
> And fading at will. Weaving with points of gold,
> Gold-yellow, saffron...The roman shoe, Aurunculeia's
> And come shuffling feet, and cries "Da nuces!
> "Nuces!" praise, and Hymenaeus "brings the girl to her man."
>> (5/17)

Yet when reviewing Pound's Hellenic career in retrospect, we do not see
Aurunculeia's "aureolos pedes" (61.167), but rather hear Lesbia's "arguta
solea" (68.72). The cry of "Give nuts," which were tossed out ceremonially
during Roman weddings, is uttered in Catullus 61 by the slaveboy who
must bid farewell to his carefree life.

Pound wanted the Catullan "tinkling of sound" about him, always
(5/17). Having liked the rhythm of Catullus 34, whose meter is similar to
Catullus 61's, he characteristically had said in 1916: "There is the Poikilo-
thron [Sappho 1] and then Catullus, 'Collis O Heliconii,' and some Propertius, that one could do worse than know by heart for the sake of knowing
what rhythm really is" (*L*, 91). Pound appreciated Catullus 61 as music
because lyric poetry has traditionally exhibited the rhythm of song. As
Hugh Kenner has admirably shown, he made the point with Catullus 61 at
the beginning of canto XX (1927),[21] and did so again in association with
Marcabrun, the troubadour who employed the "pastorela," in canto
XXVIII (1930). But the "tinkling" from Catullus 61 grew so faint that
Pound alluded little more to the poem.[22] Though he returned to Catullus in
the *Cantos,* counterpointing Catullus 61's note of promise and beauty with
a note of loss, he would be dealing with the setting around Lake Garda
sacred to Catullus and himself.

Just as Pound valued Catullus 51 and 61 most among his Catullan translations and allusions, so he prized Catullus 31 most when creating a Catullan

landscape in his poetry. Catullus' haunts included Garda (the lake), Sirmio (the peninsular village that held his villa), and Verona (the town nearby where he was born). Pound employed this setting chiefly in his early poetry (pre-1918), in order to create a *locus amoenus* from which he set forth under Ovid's influence to synthesize myth and history in the *Cantos*. Then he re-employed it intermittently in the later *Cantos* (post-1948), when elegiacally evoking his own lyrical youth. Significantly, Pound's initial infatuation with Sirmio most clearly demonstrates how he began his quest to proclaim a pagan paradise with Catullus. And so his sad return in poetry and life to the locale of his beginning reveals his shortfall.

Although Pound notably depicted his Catullan setting in such early work as "'Blandula, Tenella, Vagula'" and the initial versions of canto I, he began the process of enshrining Sirmio even earlier. In 1908 he had translated M. A. Flaminius' *Lusus* I, a Renaissance Latin poem that invokes the Muse of Catullus from Sirmio.[23] A year later Pound referred to his idyllic landscape in "Guillaume de Lorris Belated: A Vision of Italy," an early poem describing cities as women, where the speaker encounters

> ...svelte Verona [whom] first I met at eve;
> And in the dark we kissed and the way
> Bore us somewhile apart.
> And yet my heart keeps tryst with her,
> So every year our thoughts are interwove
> As fingers were, such times as eyes see much, and tell.
> (*Per,* [1909], 43)

In 1910, having published *The Spirit of Romance* (containing part of *Lusus* I [SR, 230]), Pound actually visited Sirmio in late March—staying at the Hotel Eden—where he spent his time sunbathing, and wrote to his mother that except for the electric light it was "the same old Sirmio that Catullus raved over a few years back, or M. A. Flaminius more recently."[24] He was alluding both to Flaminius' poem and to Catullus 31, written on Catullus' return from Bithynia.[25]

Pound's references to the haunts of Catullus intensified in 1911, for he published in *Canzoni* both "The Flame" (originally "Und Drang, VIII" in *Personae* [1909]), and "'Blandula, Tenella, Vagula.'" In "The Flame" he addresses Garda ("Lacus Benacus" in Flaminius' poem):

> Sapphire Benacus, in thy mists and thee
> Nature herself's turned metaphysical,
> Who can look on that blue and not believe?
> (*Per,* 50)

Pound, as Catullus and Flaminius before him, found Garda and her environs a source of poetic inspiration. "'Blandula, Tenella, Vagula'" became his most important statement of that inspiration (except for the initial versions of canto I):

> What has thou, O my soul, with paradise?
> Will we not rather, when our freedom's won,
> Get us to some clear place wherein the sun
> Lets drift in on us through the olive leaves
> A liquid glory? If at Sirmio,
> My soul, I meet thee, when this life's outrun,
> Will we not find some headland consecrated
> By aery apostles of terrene delight,
> Will not our cult be founded on the waves,
> Clear sapphire, cobalt, cyanine,
> On triune azures, the impalpable
> Mirrors unstill of the eternal change?
>
> Soul, if She meet us there, will any rumour
> Of havens more high and courts desirable
> Lure us beyond the cloudy peak of Riva?
> (*Per,* 39)

Representing Pound's complex response to Hadrian's deathbed address to his soul,[26] "'Blandula, Tenella, Vagula'" offers the haunts of Catullus as a metaphor for paradise. Pound's rhetorical presentation of Sirmio, the peninsula, and Lake Garda reveals his own youthful speculation about his place in a lyric tradition dating back through Flaminius to Catullus himself. As "apostles of terrene delight" all three poets have "consecrated" the "headland" and absorbed "cultic" inspiration from the "triune azures" of the lake itself. Presumably, Catullus and Flaminius would be "aery" apostles because their spirits yet linger about the place; as for Pound, this preview of his epic program to replace all "rumour" of heaven-havens with an earthly garden of the gods earns him the right to return. Meeting his Muse at Sirmio, Pound in 1912 made one last remark, notable for its use of "azure" in reference to the lake: "I would much rather lie on what is left of Catullus' parlour floor and speculate the azure beneath it and the hills off to Salo and Riva with their forgotten gods moving unhindered amongst them, than discuss any processes and theories of art whatsoever" (*LE,* 9). The statement neatly summarizes the situation of "'Blandula, Tenella, Vagula,'" and articulates the process—to "speculate the azure...and the hills...with their forgotten gods"—that would provide much of the underlying inspiration for the initial versions of canto I.

Through Browning, Pound began the process of invoking his Catullan landscape in the *Cantos.* Casting about for his own beginning, Pound recalled Browning's "Appear Verona!" and seized upon Sirmio, his "chosen and peninsular village" (*Poetry,* 10.3 [June 1917], 115), as the base note for his song:

As well begin here. Began our Catullus:
"Home to sweet rest, and to the waves' deep laughter,"
The laugh they wake amid the border rushes.
This is our home, the trees are full of laughter,
And the storms laugh loud, breaking the riven waves
On "north-most rocks"; and here the sunlight
Glints on the shaken waters, and the rain
Comes forth with delicate tread, walking from Isola Garda —
                Lo soleils plovil,
As Arnaut had it in th' inextricable song.
The very sun rains and a spatter of fire
Darts from the "Lydian" ripples; "*locus undae,*" as Catullus, "*Lydiae,*"
And the place is full of spirits.
             (*Poetry,* 10.3, 115–16)

As Bush (p. 115) mentions, vestiges of Catullus 31 occur in "'Home to sweet rest'" and "'*locus undae*'...'*Lydiae,*'" although the change from "lacus" to "locus" is telling. Pound even manifests his own lyric sensibility by glossing the "laughter" of Catullus' waves: "The laugh they wake amid the border rushes." Here he also exhibits his familiar interest in the sunlight "glinting" on the lake's waves and the shore's two-toned olive leaves. But now Pound describes the rain coming across the lake "with delicate tread" and acknowledges the gods with "the place is full of spirits." The line from Daniel, "the rain falls from the sun," recurs in his "coda" to Daniel's "Lancan son passat" (*LE,* 121). Just as Pound associates "*Lo soleils plovil*" with Sirmio and Lake Garda in this canto, so the diction of his coda in 1920, "no pleasure's won like this freedom," echoes "where our freedom's won" in "'Blandula, Tenella, Vagula.'" Moreover, the comment in ur-canto II on Catullus' relationship with Lesbia — "So much for him who puts his trust in woman" (*Poetry,* 10.4, 182) — suggests that Pound identified Daniel's wariness toward women with Catullus' and his own anxiety about harnessing sexual energy for poetic creation. Hence he considered his setting a place of inspiration based less on loving a woman than on loving poetry, which only Lesbia as a *Candida diva* can give.

Pound's extended dialogue with Browning in canto I signals his own search for a way to begin, as the young poet's question in 1917 reveals: "What's left for me to do?" (*Poetry,* 10.3, 117). Though he eventually answered his question in the same canto, he answered it more concisely a few months later in *Lustra:*

    Gods float in the azure air,
    Bright gods and Tuscan, back before dew was shed...
    'Tis the first light — not half-light — Paniks
    And oak-girls and the Maelids have all the wood;
        Our olive Sirmio

Lies in its burnished mirror, and the Mounts Balde and Riva
Are alive with song, and all the leaves are full of voices.
"Non è fuggi."
"It is not gone." Metastasio
Is right, we have that world about us.
And the clouds bowe above the lake, and there are folk upon them
Going their windy ways, moving by Riva,
By the western shore, far as Lonato,
And the water is full of silvery almond-white swimmers,
The silvery water glazes the upturned nipple.
      (Lu, 185)

For his own classical beginning, the self-exile returned to "our olive Sirmio," to the gods in the woods, air, and water of Garda itself. But "return" is not quite right, for that world to Pound "is not gone."

Pound's Catullan landscape from the initial versions of canto I made its final appearance in canto III of the *Cantos* (1925). The canto contrasts Pound, the impoverished young poet, "sitting on the Dogana's steps" in 1908, with Ruy Diaz, El Cid, seeking to overcome his poverty. But in between these two vignettes Pound described the paradise that he, Cid-like, would write in epic:

Gods float in the azure air,
Bright gods and Tuscan, back before dew was shed.
Light: and the first light, before ever dew was fallen.
Panisks, and from the oak, dryas,
And from the apple, maelid,
Through all the wood, and the leaves are full of voices,
A-whisper, and the clouds bowe over the lake,
And there are gods upon them,
And in the water, the almond-white swimmers,
The silvery water glazes the upturned nipple,
    As Poggio has remarked.
      (3/11)

In canto III's first two versions, the girl read Diaz the writ, "a-whisper" (*Poetry,* 10.4, 185; *Lu,* 192), but now "the leaves are full of voices, a-whisper," with their own "writ" inspiring Pound to poetic action. He once intended that his Cid ride up "to Burgos in the Spring" (*Poetry,* 10.4, 185; *Lu,* 192), but eight years later his vision of the way to build a soul for man has assumed an almost private meaning. Though Catullus 64.18 may lie behind Poggio's remark about the swimmers (see Kenner, *Era,* p. 143), Pound has subordinated Catullus to Homer and Ovid as the primary spokesmen for the *Cantos.*

As Pound said in canto VV, "Topaz I manage, and three sorts of blue; / but on the barb of time" (5/17). His Catullan landscape, with its olive trees and sunlit lake of "triune azures," was perdurable but vulnerable because subject to a world of flux. Though Aurunculeia appeared for a time, Pound's symbolic setting vanished surprisingly given its tremendous importance to him as a young poet. In outgrowing Catullus, Pound forsook his vision of Sirmio as he became ensnared in economic and political affairs. Caught upon the "barb of time," he inevitably tempered his lyric sense of loss with dramatic, social, and Propertian concerns, and then with epic, historical, and Ovidian ones. Pound's Catullan contrast between an ideal past and the real present steadily burgeoned into the bittersweet triumph of the gods' return in the *Pisan Cantos*. But the high cost of such epic success can be measured by Pound's Catullan homecoming from a "Bithynian" wasteland of the spirit to the place of his poetic beginning. Wistfully, a lifetime later and after sailing from St. Elizabeths to Sirmio, he would again recall Metastasio: "The gods have not returned. 'They have never left us.' / They have not returned" (113/787).[27]

In time Pound's Catullan ambivalence toward the Lesbia of his poetic program would metamorphose under Ovid's influence into a lyric treatment of myth (Aphrodite) and a satiric treatment of history (Circe). Yet in the short term, as Aurunculeia's emergence suggests, Pound grew anxious about appearing to whore after such a publicly unworthy goal as resuscitating the pagan past through his poetry. In fact, he developed an identity crisis of severe aesthetic (not moral) proportions, soon becoming preoccupied with the problem of how to begin his Hellenic quest for polity. Indeed, rhythmically alone his dilemma was momentous: "To break the pentameter, that was the first heave." But, of course, as a young poet maturing toward epic selfhood, Pound was inclined to portray his diffidence in Catullan terms. This can be seen clearly by comparing "The Study in Aesthetics" (1914) with the opening lines of ur-canto I (*Poetry*, 10.3, 113). "Study" offers an early metaphor of Pound's malaise by implying a deterioration in the recognition of beauty, symbolized first by the woman whose beauty both speaker and children appreciate, and then by the sardines that only the child admires. Moreover, as merely one of many young Dantes and Catulli in Sirmione, he elicits the vain command of his elders to "*sta fermo!*" (*Per*, 97). Nor had Pound's self-confidence improved much three years later when he began ur-canto I by chiding Browning for having already written the "one *Sordello*": "Say I take your whole bag of tricks" and "say the thing's an art form" and "that the modern world / Needs such a rag-bag to stuff all its thought in; / Say that I dump my catch, shiny and silvery / As fresh sardines flapping and slipping on the marginal cobbles?" Pound was "mildly abashed" in "Study" because the little boy's infatuation for the sardines befits his own insecure characterization of beauty as expressed in canto I, only so many dead fish for one's elders to frown at. At least three more years would pass before Pound developed enough confidence to answer the seemingly innocuous question of canto I by transforming the day's catch into an archetypal encounter with the illustrious deed. Since in between he wrote the *Homage* and its alter ego *Mauberley,* to Propertius as Pound's dramatic mask we now turn not only to analyze his anxiety more precisely, but also to show how once again he used translation to steel himself for the epic adventures ahead.

3

Propertius as Dramatic Mask

"...sometime after his first
'book,' S. P. ceased to be the
dupe of magniloquence and began
to touch words somewhat as
Laforgue did" (*L,* 178).

Unique among Pound's triumvirate of Latin poets, Propertius with the
Elegiae evokes his only bona fide dramatic mask, *The Homage to Sextus
Propertius* (1919). Propertius himself was a semidramatic elegist who often
addressed indirectly and sometimes directly various figures in his work,
and although we miss Browning's sophistication in either the original or its
recreation, Pound's poem does presage his preoccupation with voice in
Mauberley and in the early *Cantos.* But as perhaps Pound's single most
vivacious monologue, the *Homage* is dramatic for another more important
reason: It mirrors less Propertius' than Pound's own personality during the
critical years of transition between his lyric and his epic selves. Representing the ironic results of his search for a new poetic diction, the *Homage*
demonstrates that Pound's attitude toward Propertius is really an attitude
toward himself in three principal ways. First, the poem reflects Pound's
antiromantic rejection of his own earlier aesthetic treatment of Propertius
in *Canzoni.* Also, it represents Pound's satiric reaction to contemporary
pressures from pedants, poets, publishers, and, of course, the war itself.
Third, the *Homage* silhouettes an underlying crisis of aesthetic anxiety as
Pound's secret inspiration for digging up Propertius.

Through its satire, the *Homage* exhibits Pound's newfound social consciousness by superimposing Propertius living in Augustan Rome with
himself in Georgian London. But the poem also incorporates Pound's
earlier, personal interest in Propertius. He had studied him as a sophomore
at the University of Pennsylvania (spring 1903), had evaluated him critically in *The Spirit of Romance,* and employed him poetically in *Canzoni.*
Conspicuously, these pre-*Homage* references reflect a youthfully romantic

view of the elegist that Pound gradually outgrew.[1] For example, his first allusion to a favorite line reveals less, finally, about Propertius than about the later nineteenth century's attitude toward him, and hence Pound's own nascent view. Following his remarks about the relative physicality of Catullus 61, Pound noted by contrast that "Propertius writes: 'Ingenium nobis ipsa puella f[a]cit'" (*SR,* 96). Chosen to suggest the mystical side of Propertius' love, the line underscores the prevalent *fin de siècle* feeling, which Pound had rejected by the time he wrote the *Homage,* that the center of Propertius' poetry lay in his relationship with Cynthia. Nevertheless, through this quotation Pound did begin his association of Propertius with the love poets of Provence,[2] and as his allusions to Catullus 34 have shown with his Eleusinian use of coition as a rite for poetic creation.

Pound's early flirtation with Propertius in *Canzoni* (1911) registers how much he was writing in the late-romantic style, even while beginning to break out of that mold. For his epigraph to *Canzoni,* Pound chose the pentameter—"Quos ego Persephonae maxima dona feram" (2.13.26)[3]—to one of Propertius' couplets. Imagining his own death and modest funeral procession, Propertius was saying "My procession will be dear enough, if there be three little books, / which I shall bear as my greatest gift to Persephone." Pound was interested here less in death or Persephone than in dedicating his own modest literary achievement—his greatest gift—"to Olivia and Dorothy Shakespear" (v). After returning to the same poem in the *Homage,* he used the line again in 1926 when dedicating *Personae* to W. C. Williams. Pound's own achievement was now more substantial, his college friend had recently published *Kore in Hell,* and Eleusis hovered just over the horizon. *Personae* includes the material from *Canzoni*—"Prayer for his Lady's Life," "Rome," and "Satiemus"—as well as the *Homage* itself.

Perhaps previewing his use of Homer's *nekuia* in ur-canto III, Pound's Propertian "prayer" in *Canzoni* invokes the queen of hell:

> [May this your clemency, Persephone, remain, nor
>   may you, husband of Persephone, wish to be more cruel.
> There are among the dead so many thousand beautiful women:
>   let one pretty girl live on earth!
> With you is Iope, with you fair Tyro,
>   with you Europe and unworthy Pasiphae,
> and all the beautiful women ancient Troy and all Achaia has born,
>   the destroyed kingdoms both of Thebes and of old Priam:
> and whatever Roman girl was in their number,
>   has died: the greedy flame holds them all.
> Neither is beauty forever nor fortune eternal for anyone:
>   close by or far one's own death awaits everyone.
> Since you, my light, have been spared from great danger,
>   pay Diana dances as your owed offering,

also keep guard for her now a goddess, but before a heifer;
   alas for me, pay her ten votive nights!]
     (2.28C)

Here let thy clemency, Persephone, hold firm,
Do thou, Pluto, bring here no greater harshness.
So many thousand beauties are gone down to Avernus,
Ye might let one remain above with us.

With you is Iope, with you the white-gleaming Tyro,
With you is Europa and the shameless Pasiphae,
And all the fair from Troy and all from Achaia,
From the sundered realms, of Thebes and of aged Priamus;
And all the maidens of Rome, as many as they were,
They died and the greed of your flame consumes them.

Here let thy clemency, Persephone, hold firm,
Do thou, Pluto, bring here no greater harshness.
So many thousand fair are gone down to Avernus,
Ye might let one remain above with us.
    (*Ca,* 22)

So Cynthia is sick, and the poet beseeches the corn maiden to let her live: Propertius after the *Monobiblos* has begun to doubt whether becoming a *Romanus Callimachus* is worth his reputation as a love elegist. By contrast, Pound himself in only the Catullan stage of his career proves uninterested in any talk of recovery altogether, as his emphatic repetition and therefore exclusion of Propertius' final lines makes clear. In effect, he simply refuses to let the lyric voice of his own poetry die. This can easily be confirmed by noticing the late-romantic style of Pound's poem, its diction of "thy" and "thou" and "ye," even its rendering of "beauties" for "formosarum" and "maiden" for "puella." Yet another index of Pound's poetic innocence can be recovered from his later remarks about his own translation: "There is a perfectly literal and, by the same token, perfectly lying and 'spiritually' mendacious translation of 'Vobiscum est Iope,' etc., in my earlier volume, *Canzoni,* for whosoever wants the humorless version, which vein, in this particular poem, makes it utterly impossible to translate the 'votivas noctes et mihi' at its termination" (*The New Age,* 26.5 [Dec. 4, 1919], 83). In dramatically retrospective justification, then, the poet of the *Homage* could not translate the "votivas noctes" because, following Mueller, he had read "et mihi" (3.26.16) instead of Barber's "ei mihi" (2.28c.62), and thought that Propertius was telling Cynthia to pay *him* 10 votive nights as well. This would be the perfect example of Propertian irony except that Cynthia was to pay *her,* i.e., the goddess (who is understood), 10 nights, "alas for me." Even so, despite the satiric signs of maturation, Cynthia momentarily recovers and Pound's lyric gift never quite dies. Is not the *nekuia* itself of Canto I a marvelous epic excuse to redeem all the fair dead from Pound's Hellenic past?

That Pound translated the entire poem in the *Homage* (IX.2, 3) measures how much he had tempered his antecedent aestheticism:

> (2)
> Persephone and Dis, Dis, have mercy upon her,
> There are enough women in hell,
>   quite enough beautiful women,
> Iope, and Tyro, and Pasiphae, and the formal girls of Achaia,
> And out of Troad, and from the Campania,
> Death has his tooth in the lot,
>   Avernus lusts for the lot of them,
> Beauty is not eternal, no man has perennial fortune,
> Slow foot, or swift foot, death delays but for a season.
> (3)
> My light, light of my eyes,
>   you are escaped from great peril,
> Go back to Great Dian's dances bearing suitable gifts,
> Pay up your vow of night watches
>   to Dian goddess of virgins,
> And unto me also pay debt:
> The ten nights of your company you have promised me.
>   (*Per*, 223–24)

The passage indicates Pound's newfound, and ultimately ironic, sense of style. In comparison with his earlier effort, this version is more concise, notwithstanding repetitions like "enough women. . .quite enough beautiful women" or "my light, light of my eyes," which help liberate its rhythm. Also, Pound has freshened his diction: "beauties" have become "beautiful women" and "maidens," "girls."

But the high seriousness that Pound could have achieved through concision, repetition, and new diction required ironic counterpointing as well. Pound frequently let the Latin suggest his English, which often does not retain the same meaning as in the original. For example, whereas "eternal" serves for "aeternum," "perennial" for "perennius," and "peril" for "periclo," "formal" does not mean "formas" ("beautiful women"). Pound's phrasing often intentionally undercuts the very seriousness that has come before, as with "Death has his tooth in the lot, / Avernus lusts for the lot." And with "munera Dianae debita redde choros" Pound indifferently mistranslates, taking "reddo" ("pay") for "redeo" ("return") and construing "Go back to Great Dian's dances bearing suitable gifts." Moreover, for unity's sake and to insure the comic and ironic reading he saw in the original, Pound dropped the reference to Io altogether and added the ironic "Dian goddess of virgins," which of course would ill suit Cynthia. In short, once outgrowing his own aestheticism, Pound trained his satiric cannons on a British establishment that had not by debunking their nineties view of

Propertius. Since poetic anxiety animates his Propertian pursuits, the
Homage's regrettable reception only determined Pound to defend the
Hellenic *lux* of his eyes against modern muzziness more fiercely in
Mauberley and then more grandly in the *Cantos*.

In *Canzoni* Propertius next emerged from the epigraph to "Rome,
from the French of Joachim du Bellay" (*Ca,* 27), from the Renaissance
Latin of Vitali. Here his appearance anticipates both the *Homage* as a
dramatic mask and, more ominously, the *Cantos* as a fascist epic. The
epigraph reads simply, "Troia Roma resurges. – Propertius." It comes
from Propertius' hexameter "I will sing: 'Troy, you will fall, and Trojan
Rome you will rise anew'" (4.1.87) and, in Mueller's edition, at the end
of a passage extolling Rome's Trojan ancestry. In effect, Propertius was
announcing his desire to sing of Roman themes, which he subsequently did
in his last book. In fact, Propertius' line forecasts his fourth book just as it
does Pound's own singing on Roman themes in this poem, in the *Homage,*
and in the *Cantos* to come. According to Pound's poem, "Rome's name
alone" remains "Rome's one sole monument" that "hast conquered Rome
the town." As Vitali, du Bellay, and Pound aptly demonstrate, Rome in
literature has outlasted the place itself. With the *Homage,* too, Pound
would honor his Propertian epigraph predicting a Roman resurgence.
Propertius thought of Rome as Troy reborn, and so Pound with his
Homage conceived a cultural parallel between the Augustan and the British
empires. But the torch can be passed further, for Pound's Roman interests
did not end with his Propertian poetry. In speaking of the *Homage,* Pound
said he should have "wished to render a composite character, including
something of Ovid, and making the portrayed figure not only Propertius
but inclusive of the spirit of the young man of the Augustan Age, hating
rhetoric and undeceived by imperial hogwash" (*L,* 150). One man's hogwash is another's ambrosia, however, for with his Ovidian mask in the
Cantos Pound becomes that composite character, laboring like Hercules
to instigate his own Hellenic (i.e., fearfully fascist) happening. Thus,
an acorn about Propertius' Trojan tribute grew into the oak of Pound's
Roman reformation.

Alluding to one of Propertius' most erotic poems (2.15), "Satiemus"
(*Ca,* 43) provides the perfect envoi to his appearances in *Canzoni*. Though
Pound would deal directly with Propertius' poem in the *Homage* (VII),
here he seems concerned less with the poem itself than with Ernest Dowson's treatment of it. Dowson had used the hexameter suggesting Pound's
title – "Dum nos fata sinunt, oculos satiemus amore" (2.15.23) – for the
title of his own nineties response to Propertius' *nox candida* of love. In
presenting its *carpe diem* theme ("while the fates permit us, let us sate our
eyes with love"), Dowson's poem epitomizes the *fin de siècle* conception of

Propertius as a romantic lover, and in 1911 Pound was not unaware of Dowson's decadence.[4] "Satiemus" is the second of three poems grouped under the heading, "Victorian Eclogues." Pound's title, if not ironic, is at least ambivalent, and implies that in sating ourselves with love we should not cloy ourselves with Dowson. Manifesting its title's ambivalence, the poem itself heralds the *Homage*'s own satire (though not in section VII) of Propertius as a love poet. Dowson was much closer to Propertius (if not his unknowing caricature) in that his speaker abandons himself to senti- mentality. But Pound, whose speaker questions his mistress and recalls another "who bent her...head...as thou dost," as well as "the fair dead" mindful of their own "bright glad days,"[5] better redeems himself from tradition than Dowson does. So "Satiemus" signals Pound's postscript to Dowson, even as the *Homage* honoring Propertius' retrospective lead in 2.15 celebrates the passing of his Catullan self. In neither case should the farewell flourish be construed as more of the same.[6]

Besides debunking his own youthful aestheticism with the *Homage,* Pound also sought with his poem to rebuke the pedantic decadence of classicists in his day. Moreover, sandwiched between the achievements of a more mature W. B. Yeats — *Responsibilities* (1914) — and an ironic T. S. Eliot — *Pruefrock and Other Observations* (1917) — Pound seems to have felt the need in writing his poem to contemporize his own quaint personae. As *Mauberley*'s "Mr. Nixon" (I.ix) and its war poems (I.iv and v) more expli- citly show, Pound with the *Homage* was resisting crass publishers and, of course, the war itself. Unfortunately, several of the poem's earliest critics failed to recognize most of Pound's motivations, and when confronted with his intense if unfocused irony simply condemned the performance as a poor translation. This reception, in turn, prompted Pound near the end of the war to justify the *Homage*'s ironic distortion by asserting that he had sought not to translate a text but to superimpose a shared anti-imperialism, which defense most subsequently enlightened critics have come to accept at face value.

In criticizing the grammatical and philological bias of Latin teachers generally (*LE,* 239-40), Pound specifically chided the classicist J. W. Mackail for his late-romantic view of Propertius (*Latin Literature,* 124- 29), thereby disdaining his own aestheticism in *Canzoni.* Pound gibed that "given the 'Ride to Lanuvium,' even Professor Mackail might have sus- pected that there was something in Propertius apart from the smaragdites and chrysolites, and that this poet of later Rome was not steeped to the brim in Rossetti, Pater & Co., and that, whatever heavy sentimentality there was in Propertius' juvenilia, it is not quite the sentiment of thirteenth- century Florence decanted in the tone of the unadulterated Victorian period" (*The New Age*, 26.5 [Dec. 4, 1919], 82). Steeped in the poetic sentiments of his time, Mackail had asserted that Propertius' opening book was "the first appearance in literature of a neurotic young man, who reappeared last century in Rousseau's *Confessions* and Goethe's *Werther*" (*Latin Literature*, 125), which remark measures the professor's aestheticism. Nevertheless, Pound's own late-romantic interests in medieval Europe had earlier compelled him to associate Propertius with the troubadours and Cavalcanti; and the decadent reference to Propertius' mention of emeralds and chrysolite was Pound's, not Mackail's.[7]

After again betraying his own early view by scoffing that Mackail thought Propertius, as a student of Rossetti and Pater, was filled with reminiscences of the *Vita Nuova*, Pound quoted from the "Ride to Lanuvium," wondering whether the Propertius of that poem was always "sentimental...in the manner so dear to the contemporaries of...Mr. Gosse" (*The Observer*, Jan. 25, 1920, p. 5). Propertius' poem deals in part with the rites of Juno at Lanuvium, where virgins had to undergo the test of giving food to the serpent of the shrine. Pound quoted as ironic these lines:

> [He seizes for himself the food offered by the virgin:
>   The baskets themselves tremble in the virgin's hands.
> If they have been chaste, they return into their parents' embrace,
>   and farmers shout, "The year will be fertile."
> Hither my Cynthia was drawn by her close-clipped ponies.]
>   (4.8.11–15)

Yet he omitted the pentameter revealing Propertius' irony: "Juno was her excuse, but really her reason was Venus" (4.8.16). Echoing his use of Catullus 58's "Lesbia nostra, Lesbia illa" in canto II (1917), Pound repeated the last hexameter: "'Huc mea Cynthia'—my Cynthia, with her *cause célèbre* past... —are we to suppose that he was never ironical, that he was always talking for Tennyson's tea-table, that he was as dull and humorless as the stock contributors to Mr. Marsh's series of anthologies?" (*The Observer*, Jan. 25, 1920, p. 5). Answering his own question with another more cynical, Pound demonstrated his current view of Propertius' irony: "Or is the vaunted and recommended 'tenderness' [that Robert Nichols had missed in the *Homage*] supposed to be that quality of feeling which would prevent us from receiving our own Cynthias upon *their* returns from Lanuvium?" (*The Observer*, Jan. 25, 1920, p. 5). As late as 1937, Pound could recall, "after all Homer, Villon, and Propertius speak of the world as I know it, whereas Tennyson and Dr. Bridges did not" (*PE*, 137).

In fairness to Mackail, if his conventional, maudlin view distorted by sentimentalizing Propertius, then Pound's view, 20 years and much bitter personal experience later, distorted by satirizing him.[8] Pound himself unintentionally made this point when in 1923 he criticized Mackail's view of Propertius as "ludicrous" ("OCiG," 144). Having let his sentimental view of book one color his estimation of Propertius' work as a whole, Mackail had deplored how in time Propertius' passion yielded to his desire for literary reputation: "In the introductory poem to [book three] there is a new and almost aggressive tone with regard to his own position among the Roman poets" (*Latin Literature,* 127). That Pound himself chose the same poem to begin the *Homage* not only underscores his satiric stance toward Mackail, but suggests another reason for his antipathy. Mackail, in lamenting Propertius' desire for fame, quite incidentally had touched on the controlling motive for Pound's interest in Propertius: his concern in 1917 for the direction of his own career. Mackail also had chided Propertius for "the want of self-control" in his poetry (*Latin Literature,* 127–28).

In addition to rejecting Mackail's late romanticism, Pound wished as a poet of esoteric and minor personae to write poetry of a more contemporary nature. In *The New Poetic* (London: Hutchison Univ. Lib., 1964), C. K. Stead discusses Yeats' adoption of the mask in his later poetry as a means of becoming more relevant and hence public. Forecasting the direction his own poetry soon would take, Pound himself praised this new turn in Yeats' work when reviewing *Responsibilities* (1914): "In the poems on the Irish gallery we find this author certainly at *prise* with things as they are and no longer romantically Celtic, so that a lot of his admirers will be rather displeased with the book. That is always a gain for a poet, for his admirers nearly always want him to stay put, and they resent any signs of stirring, of new curiosity or of intellectual uneasiness" (*LE,* 380–81). Pound's phrasing, "things as they are" and "no longer romantically Celtic," suggests a growing uneasiness with his own early work neither contemporary nor unromantic in nature. He was beginning to feel the need to modernize his own masks by creating portraits not just of past personalities but of personalities that spoke to the present as well.

Three years later Pound praised T. S. Eliot's poetry for its complete "depiction of our contemporary condition" (*LE,* 419). For the first time in his criticism, he raised the name of Laforgue: "It is quite safe to compare Mr. Eliot's work with anything written in French, English or American since the death of Jules Laforgue" (*LE,* 418). Pound admired Eliot's metaphor that was a "wholly unrealizable, always apt, half-ironic suggestion," his "method of conveying a whole situation and half a character by three words of a quoted phrase," and his "constant aliveness" and "mingling of a very subtle observation with the unexpectedness of a backhanded cliche" (*LE,* 419). His remarks describe well the Laforguian techniques he would use in the *Homage.* Finally, Pound quoted approvingly from *Prufrock.* Since he began his own Laforguian tribute in 1917, one surmises that

Pound saw in both Eliot and Yeats examples of how to modernize his anachronistic masks, and turn them from personal to more public themes.[9]

Besides the desire to contemporize his verse, another cause of Pound's irony in the *Homage* concerns his resentment toward crass publishers who enjoy the power of censorship. Poverty becomes the price a poet pays for preserving his own integrity: unless one's "ventricles palpitate to Caesorial *ore rotundos,*" the bookstall next to "Q. H. Flaccus'" will not be forthcoming. Moreover, Pound's attitude toward booksellers (i.e., Maecenas) within the poem helps explain the difficulties he had in getting it published.[10] Over the years Pound even came to see the *Homage* as something of a personal triumph over Fleet Street. In November, 1930, he claimed in reference to the poem's initial appearance in *Poetry* that Harriet Monroe "mutilated my 'Homage to Sextus Propertius' at a time when I had to take what I could get, and long after I had ceased to regard *Poetry* or its opinion as having any weight" (*The English Journal,* 19, 692). Two years later, after blasting both censorious publishers and an ignorant public, Pound conceded that the *Egoist* did publish in serial certain worthwhile things, and then it began to publish worthwhile books—among which was "*Quia Pauper Amavi* (containing 'Homage to Sextus Propertius')."[11] In 1933, after criticizing the "established printing business" of his London years, he implied by contrast his pride in the *Homage*'s contemporaneity: "My one modern volume issued by Mathews [*Lustra*] was sent to the ineffable printer before dear old Elkin had read it. He wanted a 'book by' me. In the case of *Quia Pauper Amavi,* he again wanted a book by me, and suggested that I omit the *Propertius* and the *Moeurs Contemporaines*" (*SP,* 197).

Since Pound began the *Homage* in 1917, and published it in 1919, a final pressure under which he worked, and a natural outgrowth of his reaction to publishing interests, was the war itself. Unlike his early aestheticism or his responses to pedants, poets, and publishers, all of which induce his poem's irony, Pound's reaction to World War I provided its major theme of shared anti-imperialism as well. Not only had Propertius lost a kinsman during the civil wars (1.22), but also Pound had recently lost Henry Gaudier-Brzeska in France (1915). The parallel heightens the speaker's determination in the *Homage* to sing of love, the subject of elegy, rather than war, the subject of epic, particularly given Propertius' own line, "Love is the god of peace, loving we venerate peace" (3.5.1). But in a sense, Pound overlooks the widespread convention in love-elegy of rejecting the traditional Roman sentiment for the patriot and man of action in favor of that for the lover and his mistress. For Propertius was moving—even as he said he would not—from the subject of love to that of war in his poetry. Propertius' anxiety about the direction of his career defines Pound's own identity crisis. For he, too, defends a Cynthia who is sick against a morally obtuse society; that is,

this is the point: the textual perversion now passes for a plausible parallel. At any rate, the many critics who have read the *Homage* more understandably than Hale perceive that it was never intended as a traditional translation. Here the field is roughly four times as numerous, and offers a variety of terms to describe what Pound was doing with his *Homage*—"paraphrase," "imitation," "creative translation." After Adrian Collins' early but measured review of *Quia Pauper Amavi* in *The New Age* (26.4 [Nov. 27, 1919], 62), which Pound liked enough to invite Collins to dinner, the list of enlightened critics reads like a who's who of Pound's friends for the next ten years: Wyndham Lewis, May Sinclair, Max Bodenheim, A. R. Orage, T. S. Eliot, and W. B. Yeats.[15]

J. P. Sullivan, with *Ezra Pound and Sextus Propertius,* has had the last word as spokesman for the enlightened camp. As a classicist, he wants to dispel the stereotype of the scholar knowing little about the classics as literature, and thus serves as an apologist for persons like Hale. Assimilating much of the criticism that has come before him, Sullivan reaches his conclusion that the *Homage* is an exercise in "creative translation" with equanimity. Preoccupied with how the poem relates to Propertius' Latin, Sullivan through his discussion of Pound's techniques helps redeem it on a line-by-line basis. But just so his lack of distance prevents him from pursuing the implicit *causes*—as opposed to the textual *effects*—of Pound's distortion. Sullivan's desire to be fair induces him to see too much Laforguian irony in Propertius, while the causes of the *Homage*'s irony lie more in Pound himself. More important, Sullivan's own romantic estimation that Cynthia was the center of Propertius' work leads him to accept at face value the idea that Pound chose Propertius as a mask primarily because of his ironic attitude toward the Roman empire and the whole Augustan ethos (Sullivan, p. 72). Sullivan lets Pound's assertion of shared anti-imperialism persuade him that "Propertius does not feel that he can sincerely and without mockery write the sort of court poetry so many Augustan poets wrote— and yet cannot ignore entirely the demands for it. The result is parody" (p. 76). But Propertius' problematic attitude toward empire is a red herring, for Pound's true inspiration in making Propertius his mask involves the unstated parallel between Propertius of books two and three evolving from conventional love-elegy to a more Callimachean kind of poetry, and Pound of the *Homage* and *Mauberley* dramatically maturing from the lyric (Catullan) poetry of *Personae* to the epic (Ovidian) poetry of the *Cantos.*

Having appreciated the contemporary pressures that induced the *Homage*'s irony, as well as the poem's reception that prompted Pound's defense of imitation, we can now turn to his troublesome conception of *logopoeia* (i.e., being ironic).[16] For through *logopoeia* Pound would link

Propertius' supposed with his own anti-imperialism, although he probably derived his notion of ironic wordplay through Eliot from LaForgue. Pound neither associated Propertius and LaForgue until 1922 (*L,* 178), nor attributed *logopoeia* to each until 1923 ("OCiG," 152).[17] But evaluating Pound's discovery of Propertian *logopoeia* simply involves contrasting how little irony he found in Propertius with how much he used in the *Homage*. More important, this procedure reveals a range of distortion that not only moots Pound's assertion of shared anti-imperialism, but also exposes his own poetic anxiety as the real reason he chose Propertius for his dramatic mask.

Pound's cited examples of Propertius' irony are few indeed. The first one (2.16.43–44) he did not initially read as such (see n.7, this chapter), the second (2.28c.59–62) depended upon a textual error (see "Prayer" above), and the third (4.8.11–16) resulted more from his sneer at Victorianism (see Mackail above). Pound's final example, at least, does seem the most plausible. After suggesting that Hale had "never understood anything but syntax and never seen the irony of Propertius" (*L,* 149), Pound affirmed his own development of a "germ" of Propertius that "the juxtaposition of the words 'tacta puella sono' and 'Orphea delinisse feras' might have revealed to any sensitive reader."[18] Hale and others had objected to Pound's use of "devirginated" for "tacta" in Propertius'

> Carminis interea nostri redeamus in orbem,
>   gaudeat in solito tacta puella sono.
> Orphea delenisse feras et concita dicunt
>   flumina Threicia sustinuisse lyra.[19]

> [Meanwhile let us return to the sphere of our song,
>   let my girl touched by my wonted music rejoice.
> They say that Orpheus tamed the wild beasts and
>   with his Threcian lyre stayed the rushing rivers.]

> And in the mean time my songs will travel,
> And the devirginated young ladies will enjoy them
>   when they have got over the strangeness,
> For Orpheus tamed the wild beasts—
>   and held up the Threician river....
>   (*Per,* 208)

Perhaps "devirginated" as the opposite of "intacta" ("chaste") is implied in "tacta puella sono," for in taming her through his Orphean song Propertius did make Cynthia his mistress. Certainly Pound clinched the anti-Puritan bias of his reading by setting the renegade against the establishment: "Propertius...brought a new and exquisite tone into Latin...that was not the stilted Horatian peg-work or Georgian maunder of Maro" (*The New Age,* 26.5, 83).

As textual comparison readily shows, the *Homage* is a *tour de force* that derives its vitality from Pound's zealous rendering of Propertius' wit. Hedging just a bit, Pound himself claimed that he could "snugly fit into the words of Propertius almost thirty pages with nothing that isn't S. P., or with no distortion of his phrases that isn't justifiable by some other phrase of his elsewhere" (*L,* 181); and later added that he "certainly omitted no means of definition...including shortenings, cross cuts, implications derivable from other writings of Propertius" (*L,* 231). But to appreciate Pound's irony for ourselves, we might as well begin with section I, where Propertius wrote: "I first enter from the pure font as a priest / to carry Italian mysteries among Grecian dances" (3.1.3-4). By using the English transliteration of "orgia," Pound has perverted Propertius' intent to write about Italian (not Greek) *customs* in the Greek style. Lines like "Out-weariers of Apollo will, as we know, continue / their Martian generalities, / We have kept our erasers in order" (*Per,* 207) as "enlightened para-phrase" owe little to Propertius' "Ah, away with whoever delays in Apollo's arms! / Let my verse flow polished with fine pumice" (3.1.7-8). Nor did Pound derive such compounds as "out-weariers" or "new-fangled" or "flower-hung" from the Latin. Unlike Propertius, he often explains the allusion of a line with the line itself, thus creating a mockingly pedantic effect: "the temple of Phoebus in Lycia, at Patara" (*Per,* 208) glosses "Lycia deo" (3.1.38; "Lycian god"), as "Taenarian columns from Laconia (associated with Neptune and Cerberus)" (*Per,* 208) glosses simply "Tae-nariis columnis" (3.2.11; "Taenarian columns"). As is clear from his con-temporary substitutions, much of Pound's ironic comment was not in Propertius at all. His

> Nor are my caverns stuffed stiff with a Marcian vintage,
> My cellar does not date from Numa Pompilius,
> Nor bristle with wine jars,
> Nor is it equipped with a frigidaire patent...
>   (*Per,* 209)

is based apparently on Propertius' single line, "Non operosa rigat Mar-cius antra liquor" (3.2.14; "nor does the Marcian water wet my artificial caves").[20]

That mount Citharon rather than Apollo "shook up the rocks by Thebes" (*Per,* 208) is minor compared to Pound's increasingly revealing distortions in later sections of the *Homage.* Using inverted commas, he casts an ironic shadow over Propertius' roll call of Roman deeds:

> "Of" royal Aemilia, drawn on the memorial raft,
> "Of" the victorious delay of Fabius, and the left-
>   handed battle at Cannae,
> Of lares fleeing the "Roman seat". . . .
>   (*Per,* 210)

Pound's "Martian generalities" are just that: In Propertius *Ameilius'* trophies were being drawn, and lares were *frightening* Hannibal from their Roman home (3.3.8, 11). While Propertius' Apollo says,

> alter remus aquas alter tibi radat harenas,
>   tutus eris: medio maxima turba mari est. . .
>   (3.3.23–24)

> [Let one oar skim the water for you, the other the sand,
>   you will be safe: the greatest crowd is in mid-sea. . .]

Pound's Apollo says, "'Let one oar churn the water, / 'Another wheel, the arena: mid-crowd is as bad as mid-sea'" (*Per,* 210). So Odyssean Pound would pursue neither, but the periplum instead. He fancifully ends Lygdamus' indirect report that Cynthia was greatly upset over Propertius' infidelity by saying, "And you expect me to believe this / after twelve months of discomfort?" (*Per,* 215). Propertius, by contrast, ended the elegy on a conciliatory note:

> [If my girl has lamented these things to you with true sincerity,
>   run back the same way, Lygdamus,
> and report with many tears my message that
>   anger but not deceit is in my love,
> that I too beset by a similar fire am tormented:
>   I will swear I have been chaste for twelve days.]
>   (3.6.35–40)

Of course, Propertius poetically procrastinated throughout the *Elegiae,* while Pound soon produced *Mauberley* and then the *Cantos.* Propertius' allusion to Marius' victories over the Cimbrians, "[I would sing neither]. . . nor the threats of the Cimbri and the good deeds of Marius" (2.1.24), relates to Pound's, "Nor of Welsh mines and the profit Marus had out of them" (*Per,* 217), only by the word "minas" meaning "threats" in Latin. But Pound's line does foretell of *Mauberley*'s "usury age-old and age-thick" (I.iv).

Pound tires of Propertius' catalog of myths exemplifying for the sick Cynthia that ease follows peril,

> Io versa caput primos mugiverat annos:
>   nunc dea, quae Nili flumina vacca bibit.

> Ino etiam prima terris aetate vagata est:
>   hanc miser implorat navita Leucothoen.
> Andromede monstris fuerat devota marinis:
>   haec eadem Persei nobilis uxor erat.
> Callisto Arcadios erraverat ursa per agros:
>   haec nocturna suo sidere vela regit...
>   (2.28A.17–24)

> [Io changed with respect to her head lowed through her first years:
>   she is now a goddess, who once as a cow drank the Nile's waters.
> Ino also wandered the earth in her youth:
>   the wretched sailor calls on her as Leucothoe.
> Andromeda was offered to sea monsters:
>   she likewise became the wife of noble Perseus.
> Callisto wandered as a bear through Arcadian fields:
>   she now rules nocturnal sails with her own star...]

as his facetious treatment of Propertius' examples reveals:

> Io mooed the first years with averted head,
>   And now drinks Nile water like a god,
> Ino in her young days fled pellmell out of Thebes,
>   Andromeda was offered to a sea-serpent and respectably married to Perseus,
> Callisto, disguised as a bear,
>   wandered through the Arcadian prairies
>   While a black veil was over her stars.
>   (*Per,* 222)

In view of his reverence for metamorphosis and Leucothoe in the *Cantos,* Pound's fun with the transformations of Io, Ino, and Callisto in Propertius' *exempla* illuminates his current comic and ironic intent.[21]

Pound's most revealing local distortion involves his satire of Propertius' admiration for Virgil. In the critical poem (2.34), Propertius first chided Lynceus for courting Cynthia, using the hypocrisy of his friend's passion to urge him to forego tragedy for love-elegy (2.34.41–42). Here mindful of his own poetic aspirations, he referred to the love poetry of Virgil, who would soon publish an epic greater than the *Iliad.* Propertius was implying that since Virgil matured from love-elegy to epic, someday he, too, might treat broader themes, if not in epic form. But Pound lets his own antipathy for Virgil vitiate Propertius' sincerity by suggesting to Lynceus that Virgil is a goose. Propertius' envious praise,

> Actia Vergilium custodis litora Phoebi,
>   Caesaris et fortis dicere posse ratis.
> qui nunc Aeneae Troiani suscitat arma
>   iactaque Lavinis moenia litoribus.
> cedite Romani scriptores, cedite Grai!

nescio quid maius nascitur Iliade...
(2.34.61-66)

[It pleases Virgil to sing the Actian shores of guardian Apollo,
  and the brave ships of Caesar,
Virgil who now brings to life the arms of Trojan Aeneas
  and the walls founded on Lavinian shores.
Yield Roman writers, yield Greeks!
  Something greater than the Iliad is born...]

becomes Pound's anxious parody:

Upon the Actian marshes Virgil is Phoebus' chief of police,
  He can tabulate Caesar's great ships.
He thrills to Ilian arms,
  He shakes the Trojan weapons of Aeneas,
And casts stores on Lavinian beaches.
Make way, ye Roman authors,
    clear the street, O ye Greeks,
For a much larger Iliad is in the course of construction
(and to Imperial order)
Clear the streets, O ye Greeks!
(*Per,* 228-29)

Casting a long shadow, Pound's immediate mockery measures not only his anxiety about beginning the *Cantos,* but also his abandonment of Augustan Virgil and Horace (see *Per,* 210) as establishment poets to England, while taking Catullus, Propertius, and Ovid as antiestablishment poets with himself to fascist Italy. "Make way," indeed, "for a much larger Iliad is in the course of construction (and to Imperial order)."

Thus, whereas Propertius would follow Virgil, Pound rebukes Lynceus for doing so. Of Virgil's love poetry, Propertius said,

[You make such song as the Cynthian god makes
  with his fingers placed on his learned lyre.
Yet your verses will seem unpleasant to none reading them,
  whether he be unlearned or skilled in love.
Nor here less in passion, though he be less in diction,
  has the melodious "swan" yielded to the unskilled
    song of the goose.]
(2.34B.79-84)[22]

Virgil had once (see *Ec.* 9.35-36) disparagingly compared himself to the poetaster, Anser, whose name in Latin means "goose." In effect, Propertius kept the pun, while praising Virgil. But not so with Pound, whose Propertius still lectures Lynceus, and apparently agrees with Virgil.

> Like a trained and performing tortoise,
> I would make verse in your fashion, if she should
>   command it,
> With her husband asking a remission of sentence,
>   And even this infamy would not attract
>   numerous readers
> Were there an erudite or violent passion,
> For the nobleness of the populace brooks nothing
>   below its own altitude.
> One must have resonance, resonance and sonority
>   . . .like a goose.
> (*Per,* 229–30)

This perversion of Propertius' regard for Virgil, in turn, elucidates Pound's misprision of Propertius' aesthetic malaise as if it were a moral one. For just as Pound ridiculed Propertius' Virgil, so he could not face because of his own poetic anxiety Propertius' desire, despite his conventional denials to the contrary, to be like Virgil by writing (albeit only in elegy) on Roman, historical, and epic themes. Propertius, in fact, wanted to write himself out of love-elegy, and eventually did so by employing the *topos, recusatio;* that is, by doing so even as he denies doing so. Hence his repeated assertions, particularly in his middle two books (from which Pound wrote the *Homage*), that he would write only love and not a more public kind of poetry were precisely the means by which he effected a transition from writing about Cynthia in book one to writing about Roman historical themes in book four. Moreover, in his protestations, Propertius was writing neither love nor war poetry but writing *about* love and war poetry. This is the true center of his work, and also the central debate of the *Homage:* arguing for love and against war poetry, rather than epitomizing either. But in Propertius, there was less "debate" than "evolution" from one topic to the other. Pound, by excluding the first and fourth books from his own poem, transformed the evolution into a debate. Of course, understanding why he did so unmasks his true motivation for writing the *Homage,* which characteristically concerns his own poetic maturation more than the problematical anti-imperialism of Propertius.[23]

In the *Homage,* Pound distorted the whole of Propertius' work, after all, by exclusion. Not only did he omit books one and four, respectively representing the extremes of amorous and martial matter, but of his twelve sections fully five of them (I, II, V, part of VI, and XII) are based on those of Propertius' poems (3.1 and 2; 3.3; 2.10 and 2.1; 3.4 and 5; and 2.34) that protest against turning toward more historical, or martial, Roman themes. Pound's focus on such a high number of poems that project Propertius' artistic debate—he even reversed Propertius' two central transitionary poems (2.34 and 3.1) by putting them at opposite ends of the *Homage*—when combined with his intense irony, presents Propertius as an overt anti-imperialist. Indeed, by focusing so on Propertius' debate, Pound himself sidestepped the issue of Propertius' anti-imperialism in that his focus reveals his real interest in Propertius' aesthetic crisis. This interest in Propertius' evolution from love-elegy toward a more Roman as well as Callimachean verse identifies Pound's own poetic crisis as the critical parallel between the two men. Propertius' poetic evolution propounds Pound's own maturation from the short, lyric, Catullan poem to the long, epic, Ovidian poem. Pound makes Propertius' debate his own because, as with Propertius at the time, at least half of his career lies before him. As it did with Propertius, the debate displays Pound's self-consciousness about the direction to be taken, the drama of poetic insecurity, in mid-career. Just as Propertius' partial success justified his anxiety, so Pound's anxiety anticipates what some would consider, ultimately, his own mixed success in the *Cantos.* The dramatic debate of the *Homage,* then, reflects the poetic crisis of Pound's career, even more so than his Pisan work, for which the die had long since been cast.

The *Homage* itself clearly exhibits Pound's anxiety about the future of his career. Not only does the poem progress linearly from one section to the next, but also it proceeds symmetrically by pairs toward its center.[24] The poem's end sections present its theme of love versus war poetry, while its two central sections settle the issue by first theoretically and then practically exemplifying the love poetry Pound's Propertius writes. In section VI he asserts that since death belies the warrior's vanity, at his modest funeral three books of elegy should confirm his choice of love over war; in section VII Pound presents Propertius' most erotic celebration of love with Cynthia, sounding a *carpe diem* (i.e., late-romantic) note that echoes Catullus' "Vivamus, mea Lesbia." In offering his books to Persephone (VI), Propertius would seek poetic immortality, which his recollection of love (VII) signifies. But for Pound the heart of the *Homage* represents his own Eleusinian rededication to a lyric love of the Hellenic past, a rite repeated in the *Cantos* especially by venerating Aphrodite. That section VII contains so few errors of translation signals Pound's solemnity; yet even here, as in the lynx song of canto LXXIX, Pound winks:

> "Turn not Venus into a blinded motion,
>   Eyes are the guides of love,
>   Paris took Helen naked coming from the bed of Menelaus,
>   Endymion's naked body, bright bait for Diana,"
>   —such at least is the story.
>   (*Per,* 220)

Paradoxically, Pound's comic irony suggests that he, like Propertius before him, was extolling the Catullan side of a career that was concluded, less to preserve it than to leave it behind. Thus, to romanticize the *Homage* would perpetuate the very myth of Propertius the love poet that an insecure but daring Pound was reacting against. For seeing Propertius as young Werther overlooks Pound's rejection of his own aestheticism in *Canzoni.* It also overlooks the various contemporary pressures (from pendants, poets, publishers, and the war) that induced Pound's intense irony. It overlooks—by accepting his assertion that Propertius' own anti-imperialism was the primary reason for choosing him as a mask—that, in fact, Propertius exhibited the same kind of identity crisis over the future of his career as Pound was undergoing in 1917.

In contemplating the *Homage* as the ironic result of Pound's search for a new speech, one invariably recalls Wordsworth's analogous interests in diction. Whereas Wordsworth in reacting to neoclassicism sought the natural speech of common men, Pound in rejecting Wordsworth's own romanticism sought the satiric speech of sophisticated men. Mindful of Hebraic Milton, Wordsworth was after all a "bleating sheep," but Pound we soon realize on reading the *Homage,* lacks *caritas.* Ever faithful to his lyric love of the past, Pound nevertheless sharpened his satiric skills against society. In the *Homage* Pound's Propertius still does most of the talking, of course to Cynthia and Lygdamus, but also to Apollo and Zeus (myth) as well as to Maecenas and Lynceus (history). Perhaps the greatest irony of the poem is that professing love, Pound next practices hatred in *Mauberley.* The *Homage*'s negative reception may have prompted the smokescreen of imitation, but also it provokes Pound into blasting the obtuse society that threatened his Hellenic program. How deeply Hale and the British reviewers hurt Pound when he was most vulnerable poetically can be measured by *Mauberley*'s vituperation. In penning his *ad hominem* attack on the milieu that had panned his *Homage,* Pound purged much of his poetic self-doubt, as indicated by the historicizing of his lyric ("EP") and satiric ("HSM") voices and by the ironic regulating of his rhythms to conform with society's tastes. With *Mauberley,* Pound made up his mind to "forge Achaia," and never again looked back. Once taken, this small step made Hellenizing an entire Hebraic tradition seem poetically possible. Pound even buried his insecure Propertian-Mauberleyan self as Elpenor, not once but twice (i.e., in *Maub.* 2.4 and in canto I), so as to insure that he would stay buried. He also met C. H. Douglas while serializing the *Homage* in Orage's offices in 1919, proclaimed from Paris the death of the Christian era on Halloween 1921, and published canto VIII (soon to become as canto II the programmatic metamorphosis of the *Cantos*) in May 1922. Five months later Mussolini marched on Rome, two years later Pound himself moved to Italy, and eight years later he finally published the first installment of his own Ovidian epic, timed to coincide, no doubt, *ex fano Caesaris* with the bimillennium of Virgil's birth.

4

Ovid as Epic Mask

"No Greek was so interested in
the magic instant as was Ovid"
("OCiG," 155).

As his criticism and early poetry show, Pound was familiar with Ovid's
work from the beginning of his career.[1] But Ovid emerged as Pound's preferred Latin poet only in the *Cantos,* where his epic influence although
derivative is both profound and pervasive. By relating Ovid in his criticism
to classical, medieval, and renaissance poetic tradition, Pound offers himself as the latest, modern translator of Ovid's own mythopoeic borrowings
from Greek poetry. By employing Ovidian mythology in his early poetry,
Pound conveys how he came to consider such "tales of old disguisings" as
masks with which to screen himself from a public skeptical of his own
anachronistic beliefs. Only in the *Cantos,* however, does Pound accommodate Ovid's great compendium, the *Metamorphoses,* into his own synchronic (i.e., anti-Virgilian) synthesis of myth and history. By redefining
Ovid's typical moments of physical metamorphosis as "magic moments"
of psychological metamorphosis, Pound conceived his own syncretic projections of the gods which serve both as private ritual and as public condemnation. In effect, Pound would use the poetic metaphor of the gods'
appearance in the poem's ideogrammic arena not only to sanctify his own
neopaganism, but also to prod the public into accepting his Hellenic reval-
uations of their essentially Hebraic tradition. Yet Pound's Ovidian desire
to mythologize history in the pre-Pisan sequence is frustrated by the rude
intrusion of history itself into the *Pisan Cantos.* Here Pound's elegiac
account of fascism's demise allows us to recognize how losing the only
audience amenable to his reactionary designs for polity aborts his dedicated quest for epic identity. Then confirming what has been the inherently
romantic nature of his classical search for self all along, Pound in the post-
Pisan sequence defers his dream of paradise by prophesying furiously for
the faithful. Thus, instead of singing *il Duce*'s bimillennial triumph as

Virgil *redux,* Pound was left to languish in St. Elizabeth's not unlike Ovid who for his own *carmen* and *error* "had it much worse" in Tomis.

In *The Spirit of Romance* Pound distinguished Ovid's "classic" verse from Apuleius' "romantic" prose, almost as if he were contrasting his own poetry with the modern novel. Before juxtaposing the simple tale of Daedalus and Icarus[2] with the complex one of Cupid and Psyche, Pound praised Ovid's sophistication and the clarity of his verse.

> "Convenit esse deos et ergo esse credemus."
> "It is convenient to have Gods, and therefore we believe they exist"; with all the pretence of scientific accuracy [Ovid] ushers in his gods, demigods, monsters and transformations. His mind, trained to the system of empire, demands the definite. The skeptical age hungers after the definite, after something it can pretend to believe. The marvellous thing is made plausible, the gods are humanized, their annals are written as if copied from a parish register; their heroes might have been acquaintances of the author's father. (*SR,* 15)

In describing Ovid, Pound is really previewing himself. The Latin attesting to a convenient belief in the gods is apparently Pound's, for it is not Ovid's. As the poet of images, vortexes, and ideograms, Pound himself would prize the "pretence of scientific accuracy," by means of which he includes history in his own epic. As a modern poet, Pound, too, lives in a "skeptical age" that "hungers after...something it can pretend to believe." For Pound the lapsed Protestant, this hunger is eventually satisfied by his aesthetic appreciation of Ovid's mythology about the gods and heroes in the *Cantos.* Ironically, while Ovid often satirized his gods by giving them mankind's foibles, Pound in redirecting his own puritan impulses would solemnize his pantheon not unlike the prudish Virgil.

Pound again honored Ovid's narrative abilities by relating him to Chaucer. In 1919 he saw Ovid's *Ars Amatoria* as the prototype of Chaucer's *Romaunt of the Rose* (*SR,* 84), and in 1917 he stated that "There is perhaps a good deal of Ovid in Chaucer" (*SP,* 356). Then in "How to Read" (1928), Pound made the important point regarding his view of Chaucer and Ovid: "English literature lives on translation, it is fed by translation; every new exuberance, every new heave is stimulated by translation, every allegedly great age is an age of translations, beginning with G. Chaucer, Le Grand Translateur...paraphraser of...Ovid, condenser of old stories he had found in Latin" (*LE,* 34–35). As a poet who deduces himself from the past, Pound also is blessing the beginning of his own Ovidian epic translation. Indeed, his final allusion to Chaucer as "the maker of a compendium comparable to Ovid" (*ABC,* 98) announces himself and the *Cantos* as well.

Pound initiated his discussion of Marlowe and Golding as renaissance translators of Ovid in "Notes on Elizabethan Classicists" (1917), he renewed it in *The ABC of Reading* (1934), and concluded it in *Confucius to Cummings* (1964). Limited mainly to "Notes" in 1917, Pound's passing interest in Marlowe's *Amores* relates to his interest in Propertius by highlighting how much the *Homage* concluded his lyric, Catullan period, even as it introduced his epic, Ovidian one. (Ovid himself began with love elegy but soon moved on to epic.) After suggesting that the "old versions of Ovid are worth more than a week's random reading" (*LE*, 230), Pound alluded to Marlowe's volume, consoled that it was "'printed abroad'":[3]

> Now ore the sea from her old Love comes she
> That drawes the day from heavens cold axletree.
> *Aurora* whither slidest thou? downe againe,
> And birdes for *Memnon* yearely shal be slaine.
> Now in her tender armes I sweetly bide,
> If ever, now well lies she by my side.
> The air is cold, and sleepe is sweetest now
> And birdes send forth shrill notes from every bough:
> Whither runst thou, that men, and women love not?
> Hold in thy rosy horses that they move not.
> Ere thou rise, starres teach sea-men where to saile,
> But when thou commest they of their courses faile.
> Poor travailers though tierd, rise at thy sight,
> And souldiours make them ready to the fight.[4]
> The painefull hinde by thee to field is sent,
> Slowe Oxen early in the yoake are pent.
> Thou cousenst boyes of sleepe, and doest betray them
> To *Pedants* that with cruell lashes pay them.
>   (Marlowe, 1.13.1–18)[5]

Besides surpassing the work of his contemporaries, Marlowe's poem also embodies the Propertian contrast between lovers and the world so appealing to Pound.[6] As an *aubade,* or lover's complaint against the coming of dawn (Pound had examined one by Flaminius in 1910 [*SR*, 229]), the poem effectively shows how "time is the evil" (30/147). Clearly "time," i.e., society and then history, increasingly distracts Pound from his lyric love of the past, whether symbolized by "Lesbia" or "Cynthia" or eventually Aphrodite herself, whose appearance in the great dawn song of the *Pisan Cantos* dramatizes how "what thou lov'st well remains," while "the rest is dross."

Pound's remaining selections from Marlowe in 1917 further support the *Homage*'s amatory note, forming a swan song to the early period of his career. After suggesting that Marlowe the translator had "beauties no whit inferior" to Marlowe the poet (*LE,* 232), Pound used some "anonymous rather unskilled work" in fourteeners—"Cyclops to Galatea the Water-Nymph" (*LE,* 233)—to foil his selection from Marlowe's 3.13 (*Amores,* 3.14). Pound's Cyclops speaks "too much in his own vein" while Marlowe was "much more dexterous" (*LE,* 234). Though Ovid was asking his mistress not to discuss with him her affair with another lover, Marlowe romanticized Ovid's cynicism by re-addressing his allusions to the lover to himself (see Marlowe, 3.13.19–26). Pound's Marlowe was more the poet of the "Passionate Shepherd to his Love" than the Ovid of *Amores* 3.14. Concluding his selections from Marlowe (and, in effect, the Catullan period of his own career), Pound turned "gratefully to Corinna (*Amores,* 1.5) in a long loose gown" (*LE,* 242; see Marlowe, 1.5.10–12). In fact, the poem, concerned with a noontime tryst between the poet and Corinna, is one of the most erotic poems of the *Amores* (indeed, an echo of *Prop., 2.15,* on which the erotic section VII of the *Homage* was based). Finally, Pound's "'C.M.' gets quality even in the hackneyed topic" (*LE,* 242; see Marlowe, 1.15.21–28). That Ovid's catalog of poetic predecessors (*Amores,* 1.15) echoes Propertius' in the final section of the *Homage* suggests how much Pound's own early work was now "hackneyed" to himself as well.

While Marlowe's *Amores* anticipated the love interest of the *Homage,* Golding's *Metamorphoses* proclaims the mythological content of the *Cantos.* Echoing his praise of Douglas, Pound admires Golding's "reality and particularization" (*LE,* 237), although this time Ovid is the outcast and his translator writes in English. Before presenting his seemingly incongruous selections about Proserpina, Atalanta, and the devotees of Bacchus (*LE,* 235–37), Pound asked, "Is there one of us so good at his Latin, and so ready in imagination that Golding will not throw upon his mind shades and glamours inherent in the original text which had for all that escaped him?" (*LE,* 235). After plucking Golding's "Proserpina" as if to underscore his own desire for Propertian, i.e., poetic, immortality, Pound selected his bolder view of Schoeneus' daughter:

> [...and Tegean Atalanta, the glory of the Lycaean grove:
> a polished buckle clasped the top of her robe,
> her hair was unadorned, gathered in one knot,
> hanging from her left shoulder resounded an ivory
> quiver of arrows, her left hand held a bow, too....]
> (*Metamorphoses,* 8.317-21)[7]

> And from the Citie *Tegea* there came the Paragone
> Of *Lycey* forrest, *Atalant,* a goodly Ladie, one
> Of *Schoenyes* daughters, then a Maide. The garment she did weare
> A brayded button fastned at hir gorget. All hir heare
> Untrimmed in one only knot was trussed. From hir left
> Side hanging on hir shoulder was an ivorie quiver deft:
> Which being full of arrowes, made a clattring as she went.
> And in hir right hand shee did beare a Bow already bent.
> (Golding, 8.426-33)[8]

Here Atalanta almost rivals Douglas' version of Venus as the maid "Harpalyca," and Golding's "brayded button" for the Roman "rasilis fibula" ("polished buckle") and his "gorget," or "wimple," for "summam...vestem" ("top of her robe") are very English. Golding displays imagination when rendering Ovid's "resonabat eburnea...telorum custos" ("resounded an ivory...quiver of arrows"): "Ivorie quiver...which being full of arrowes, made a clattring as she went." He even gives Ovid's Atalanta a bow "already bent" and for pictorial balance switches it to her "right hand." Through Pound we next encounter Golding's band with whom Atalanta hunts: Some men "pitched the toyles" (Ovid: "retia tendunt" ["stretched the hunting nets"]) and some "pursude the foyles [i.e., droppings] / In places where the swine had tract" (Ovid: "pressa sequuntur / signa pedum" ["followed the pressed signs of feet"]). Then Pound offers us Golding's Hippomenes, watching Atalanta race the wind with ribbons "whisking from her feete" and "ham," her "golden locks" tossing upon a back "as whyght as snowe," and her entire body flushing in exertion,

> [...not otherwise than when above white halls
> a crimson awning lends them borrowed hues.]
> (*Meta.*, 10.595–96)

> As when a scarlet curtaine streynd ageinst a playstred wall
> Dooth cast like shadowe, making it seeme ruddye therwithall.
> (Golding, 10.694–95)

In asking whether Ovid's Latin could "quite give us [Golding's] 'scarlet curtain'?" (*LE,* 235), Pound finally glosses his original metaphor concerning Golding's ability to project the "shades and glamours inherent in the original." Just as Hippomenes glimpses Atalanta blushing, so Golding captures Ovid in all his beauty, and so Pound would translate the Hellenic past through Ovidian metamorphosis in the *Cantos.* No wonder Pound chose Golding's gloss on "Tegeaea" as "*Atalant*...one of *Schoenyes* daughters" to describe Helen's voice in canto II (2/6). Atalanta's terms were "race to win my love or die," and Helen of Troy is but one of many incarnations of hazardous *eros* in the *Cantos* that the poet would pursue as his chief salvation from the world of time. Pound confirms that chasing the past as *eros* truly translates into seeking his poetic self by closing with "a bit of fun anent Bacchus" (*LE,* 237). For Golding's Bacchus who "into Sea didst send / The Tyrrhene shipmen" soon becomes Ovid's avenging god in whom Pound as Acoetes alone believes, the remaining "crew" being "mad for a little slave money" (2/7). So Pound would dissociate Hebraic history from an Hellenic mythos "back before dew was shed" in an Ovidian effort to discover his epic self.

Pound closed his initial discussion by emphasizing Golding's translator's interest in the *content* of his original; nor could he help mentioning Milton by contrast. "Golding," for Pound, "in the ninth year of Elizabeth can talk of 'Charles his wane' in translating Ovid, but Milton's fields are 'irriguous,' worse, and much more notably displeasing, his clause structure is a matter of 'quem's,' 'cui's,' and 'quomodo's'" (*LE,* 238).[9] After defending Golding's "constant use of 'did go,' 'did say,' etc." as less "fustian and mannerism [than] contemporary speech," Pound asserted that he was not saying "Golding is a greater poet than Milton," and that such comparisons are "odium" (*LE,* 238; though he did say in a footnote 12 years later that Golding's "*Metamorphoses* form possibly the most beautiful book in our language"). In short, Pound was not insisting on "Charles his waine" as the sole mode of translation, but did want to commend Golding's "endeavoring to convey the sense of the original to his readers. He names the thing to his original author, by the name most germane, familiar, homely, to his hearers. He is intent on conveying a meaning, and not on bemusing them with a rumble" (*LE,* 239). Moreover, for Pound, "Chaucer and Golding are more likely to find the *mot juste*...than were for some centuries their successors, saving the author of *Hamlet*" (*LE,* 239). For Pound, then, Golding "was a poet" (*LE, 241*), who "has never had due praise since his own contemporaries bestowed it upon him" (*LE,* 247).

As is clear from his increased selections in 1934, and again in 1964, Pound's admiration for Golding as a translator augmented with time. In *The ABC of Reading* (1934), notwithstanding an excerpt from the story of Persephone, Pound varied his selections to include the tales of Cadmus, Minyas' daughters, and Procne (*ABC,* 124–31). After the story of Cadmus, Pound noted Golding's ability to preserve Ovid's own "art of lucid narrative" (*ABC,* 126–27; see also, *CtC,* 322), and again praised Golding's translation as "the most beautiful book in the language" (*ABC,* 127). In *Confucius to Cummings* (1964), he provided his most extensive selections: including the complete tales of Acteon, Daedalus, Meleager, Philemon and Baucis, King Midas, the Cyclops, and Ovid's conclusion to the poem. By now Pound (or perhaps his co-editor) felt free to quote himself: "Ovid has been luckier than all other writers in the matter of translation. Golding translated the *Metamorphoses* in a volume that has been called 'the most beautiful book in our language'" (*CtC,* 37). The many footnotes on Golding's diction in 1964 reveal Pound's enduring interest in Golding's ability to find "the name most germane" to his readers. That he alluded to Golding as Shakespeare's Ovid—"one of the six great books which Shakespeare had read, as perhaps no other man ever will" (*CtC,* 66)—highlights his own reading as well. Thus, the final measure of Golding's significance for

Pound lies in his translation's influence on his work, especially the *Cantos.* Essentially, Pound's selections from Golding imply Ovid's *Metamorphoses,* which in turn implies the pagan mythology that so informs the *Cantos.* Divinities from Pound's Golding (Persephone, Atalanta, Bacchus, Cadmus, Procne, Acteon, Philemon and Baucis, and Midas), as well as many more from Ovid (Salmacis, Daphne, Danae, Somnus, Diana, Glaucus, Terminus, Syrinx, Arachne, Pomona, and Leucothoe), all recur in the *Cantos.* Of course, Pound's practice of emphasizing a god's attributes rather than the story in which he occurs characterizes his final concern less for Ovid himself than for the paganism he has preserved.

Even in his early poetry Pound treated Ovid derivatively, because he read the *Metamorphoses* less as a source than as a translation itself of Greek mythology. Besides, he was too unaccomplished to incorporate Ovid's great compendium in any serious way into his work. Pound's Ovidian technique did mature, however, from the personal and passive — pretending to be a tree in *A Lume Spento* (1908) and a fisherman friendly to Glaucus in *Personae* (1909) — to the impersonal and active — witnessing the gods returning as hunters in *Ripostes* (1912) and soldiers departing as gods in *Lustra* (1916). In short, his Ovidian juvenalia represent Pound's search for the appropriate mask through which to voice his own love of the Hellenic past to a skeptical modern world. Not surprisingly, then, do we see a spate of criticism in *Pavannes and Divisions* (1918), *Instigations* (1920), and *The New Age* (1921) that not only justifies Pound's flirtation with mythology thus far, but also declares his debut in canto II as the epic poet who paradoxically seeks the return of the gods to men's gardens for the sake of his own salvation.

Almost too candidly, Pound confessed his paradoxically selfish love for the past in an early theoretical poem called "Masks" (*ALS,* 52). Such "tales of old disguisings" are "strange myths" from souls "that found themselves among / unwonted folk that spake an hostile tongue." This not only characterizes Pound's view of Ovidian myth, but also hints at his motivation for seeking out Ovid in the first place, namely persecution in the present. Escaping into the past, the lad who would be poet discovers himself by spinning a tale about singing "carnate with his elder brothers... / Ere ballad-makers lisped of Camelot." That young Pound would repeatedly adopt the guise of old singers, painters, poets, and wizards underscores how much the sad silent pondering "o'er earth's queynt devyse," which he defensively imputed to them, was his own. More important, the reflexive lesson of "Masks" cautions us to beware that in proclaiming his neopaganism through Ovid as his epic mask in the *Cantos,* Pound the apostate Protestant is not propagating religious belief so much as pursuing poetic identity. That is, developing into a great epic poet has become his personal salvation, and the gods are a means to that end.

Perhaps Pound's best early "strange myth," or example of Ovidian translation is "The Tree" (*ALS,* 1908), where in preserving Ovid he changes his account of Apollo and the laurel bow by identifying with Daphne herself:

> I stood still and was a tree amid the wood
> Knowing the truth of things unseen before,
> Of Daphne and the laurel bow
> And that god-feasting couple olde
> That grew elm-oak amid the wold.
> 'Twas not until the gods had been
> Kindly entreated and been brought within
> Unto the hearth of their heart's home
> That they might do this wonder-thing.
> Nathless I have been a tree amid the wood
> And many new things understood
> That were rank folly to my head before.
>
> (*ALS,* 54)

If one reads Ovid's myth (*Meta.* 1.452–567) as a metaphor for poetic inspiration, i.e., the harvesting of sexual for poetic energy, then Daphne becomes Pound's first feminine incarnation of the Hellenic past and the poem dramatically reveals itself as a plea for poetic, i.e., pagan, inspiration. Certainly this is no laughing matter, and yet the near-androgynous tale sets Pound among "folk with a hostile tongue" because becoming a tree in 1908 is absurd, right? As we sensed with Pound's Propertian ravings, "The Tree" is a self-fulfilling prophecy: He escapes into the past to discover himself with a mask that only elicits more hostility, and therefore determination, indeed dedication, to "do better" the next time until he has written his own compendium. Moreover, Pound's query, after an unsuccessful career of trying to reform our Hebraic culture—"Laurel bark sheathing the fugitive, / a day's wraith unrooted?" (110/779)—sadly reveals the root of his Hellenic inspiration.

Thus, having entreated and brought the gods, including the mortals Baucis and Philemon who are themselves transformed into trees late in life for befriending Jupiter and Mercury (*Meta.* 8.610–724), "within / unto the hearth of their heart's home" (*ALS,* 54), Pound now feels secure enough to plant "The Tree" as the programmatic opening poem of *Personae* (1909). And he promptly honors this volume's motto—"Make strong old dreams lest this our world lose heart"—by propounding his paganism in "An Idyl for Glaucus" (*Meta.* 13.904–68). While Pound soon deleted the poem, with its nineties diction and its static situation, it does dramatize "The Tree"'s own lyric dissociation between "many new things understood / That were rank folly to my head before" (*ALS,* 54). This time the speaker of "Idyl" lives among fishermen who "mock" him for admiring the "strange" Glaucus. Despite the fishermen's contempt, the speaker feels that Glaucus and his new-found crew "That ride the two-foot coursers of the deep, / And laugh in storms and break the fishers' nets..." (*SPs,* 179) yet mock him more. Hence he insists that though the fishermen try to keep him "hid within four walls," he will continue instead to seek the magic grass. At least, in yearning to be a sea-god, Pound has moved closer to his Odyssean manner in the *Cantos* of mythopoeically projecting the gods so as to inspire his Hellenic revaluation of Hebraic history.

As if consolidating his approach to Ovidian mythology so far, Pound in 1910 remarked that, "Greek myth arose when someone having passed through delightful psychic experience tried to communicate it to others and found it necessary to screen himself from persecution" (*SR,* 92). Significantly, Pound here has neglected to mention his original motivation for seeking out the past: self-discovery prompted by escapism has become a "delightful psychic experience." Communicating this temporary recovery of psychic integrity to one's insensitive audience requires adopting the poetic mask or persona "to screen" oneself from persecution. Thus, poetry for Pound, i.e., mythically explicating his mood, means screening himself from his audience. Or as he said in reference to "The Tree," "I know, I mean, one man who understands Persephone and Demotes, and one who understands the Laurel, and another who has, I should say, met Artemis. These things are for them *real*" (*SR,* 92). Such is the knowledge, the feminine incarnation of Hellenic beauty, indeed the reality of self, that Pound as Odysseus would soon sail after. Of course, the Corn Mother and Maiden of Eleusis would provide Pound with the vegetatie, sexual, and economic feeder roots traceable to the taproot of his poetic virility. Similarly he would enshrine Artemis, the Arician huntress who represents the pagan values of stoicism and "clean killing," in his own Nemian grove, the *Cantos.*

Capitalizing on his image of Artemis as huntress, Pound in *Ripostes* (1912) published "The Return," wherein the gods appear as hunters. More impersonal than "Idyl," the poem neatly reports, "See, they return...", and so represents our clearest indication yet of Pound's inevitable poetic program to redeem the gods for mankind. Moreover, Pound has now historicized his former contrast between the fishermen and Glaucus, although "The Return"'s movement from present to past to present accents Pound's own ambivalence about paganly appealing to a contemporary audience. The gods have returned all right, but with "tentative movements," a "troubled pace" and "uncertain wavering," and "fear" to a hostile because modern world. In its middle section the poem triumphantly testifies to what the gods once were, and by implication could be again at least in Pound's poetry:

> These were the "Wing'd-with-Awe,"
>   Inviolable.
>
> Gods of the winged shoe!
> With them the silver hounds,
>   sniffing the trace of air!
>
> Haie! Haie!
>   These were the swift to harry;
> These the keen-scented
> These were the souls of blood.
>   (*Per,* 74)

Kenner (*Era,* p. 190) has well shown how, in a poem fraught with unstable meters, an emphatic rhythm dominates this section. The vitality of Pound's venatic image, so appropriate to his vision of an ideal past, contrasts sharply with the poem's return to the real present, wherein the hounds are "slow" and their masters "pallid." In effect, Pound was pledging himself to the dead, and soon he would honor that vow with gods who would be only too "swift to harry" a fallen world.

Pausing once again to ponder Ovid's other myth concerning poetic inspiration, Pound in "Arnold Dolmetsch" (*New Age,* XVI, 1915) portrayed his friend playing a recorder as the god Pan, who made his music by kissing Syrinx as a reed (*Meta.* 1.689–746). As Pound said, "The undeniable tradition of metamorphoses teaches us that things do not remain always the same" (*LE,* 431): neither Ovid's Syrinx nor the tale itself as recreated by Pound. But only "when men began to mistrust the myths and to tell nasty lies about the Gods for a moral purpose," Pound added, did "these matters become hopelessly confused," and "some unpleasing Semite or Parsee or Syrian began to use myths for social propaganda," and "the Gods no longer walked in men's gardens" (*LE,* 431). Clearly, Pound racially resents all obfuscation of Hellenic mythology because it impedes his own aesthetic progress toward selfhood. Moreover, his allusion here to the end of Catullus 64[10] predicts how he would employ the returning gods in the *Cantos* to inspire his own quest for epic identity. Revising his earlier account of Greek myth in *Spirit,* Pound again translates his own myth-making from the Homeric age: his "delightful psychic experience" becomes"'nonsense,'" i.e., "some very vivid and undeniable adventure"; his mask, "The Tree," becomes "a myth—a work of art that is—an impersonal or objective story woven out of his own emotion"; and his nascent epic ambitions become the story that, "perhaps, then gave rise to a weaker copy of his emotion in others, until there arose a cult, a company of people who could understand each other's nonsense about the gods" (*LE,* 431).

Here Pound anachronistically melded his own Calvinistic upbringing into an account of myth's bastardization by history, and even Plato becomes Hebraic:

These things were afterwards incorporated for the condemnable "good of the State," and what was once a species of truth became only lies and propaganda. And they told horrid tales to little boys in order to make them be good; or to the ignorant populace in order to preserve the empire; and religion came to an end and civic science began to be studied. Plato said that the artists ought to be kept out of the ideal republic, and the artists swore by their gods that nothing would drag them into it. That is the history of "civilization," or philology, or kultur. (*LE,* 432)

So once history allows Pound to describe "Bolshevism" as the height of mankind's anthropocentricity, we may peel right back (Catullus' verb in 58.5 *was* "glubit") through the Protestant Reformation, the Catholic Church, classical Rome, and Athens of the fifth century B.C. to the pip itself of Eleusis in the late archaic age (pre-600 B.C.). Perhaps because his *Cantos* would include this Hellenic view of history, Pound returned in the essay to his metaphor of musical, i.e., poetic, inspiration: "It reduces itself to about this. Once people played music [but now] we have come to the pianola [and] something is lacking" (*LE,* 433). Pound himself believed "that a return...not necessarily of 'old' music, but of pattern music played upon ancient instruments, is, perhaps, able to make music again a part of life, not merely a part of theatricals" (*LE,* 435). Could an Hellenic epic, wherein the gods theatrically return, presage a fascist reality? Noting that "'everyone knows Dolmetsch who knows of old music, but not many people know of it,'" Pound asked in 1915, "Is [this] a judgment on democracy?" (*LE,* 435-36).

While in "The Return" the speaker merely describes the gods, in Pound's imagiste "The Coming of War: Actaeon" (*Lustra,* 1916) a god actually comments upon mankind's folly. Pound used the story of Actaeon, a hunter devoured by his own dogs (*Meta.* 3.143-252), to foreshadow the fate of soldiers in war.

> An image of Lethe,
>   and the fields
> Full of faint light
>   but golden,
> Gray cliffs,
>   and beneath them
> A sea
> Harsher than granite,
>   unstill, never ceasing;
> High forms
>   with the movement of gods,
> Perilous aspect;
>   And one said:

> "This is Actaeon."
>   Actaeon of golden greaves!
> Over fair meadows,
> Over the cool face of that field,
> Unstill, ever moving
> Hosts of an ancient people,
> The silent cortege.
>   (*Per,* 107)

The poem's "fields," its "gray cliffs," and "sea," imply the English country-side, the cliffs of Dover, and the English channel, even as "Hosts of an ancient people" describes the British soldiers. Pound's knowledge of Ac-taeon's end subtly colors the poem's scene: "Lethe" suggests that, if not already in hell, at least the troops have forgotten their endeavor's historical repetitiveness, and "silent cortège" that they are moving toward their own doom. Pound achieves tragic majesty with his allusion to divine authority: "High forms / with the movement of gods, / Perilous aspect." But the one who speaks in a moment of higher awareness does not judge so much as characterize man's presumptuous behavior before him. Pound, by con-trast, is judging through his aesthetic rhetoric: if only we remembered who Actaeon was. Thus, "Actaeon" announces the upcoming "war" of the *Cantos,* wherein the recurrence of Pound's gods and Hellenic heroes seems impartially intended to save us from ourselves.

After *Lustra,* Pound grew preoccupied with the *Homage,* the initial cantos, and *Mauberley,* but still found time to sharpen his speculations about the relationship of myth and poetry. With "Religio: Or a Child's Guide to Knowledge" (*PD,* 1918), Pound leaves little doubt as to how he would soon proceed. While this missal's juvenile subtitle allows him an out, Ovidian Pound, as Michael Alexander concedes of "The Tree," seems "to be in good earnest."[11] For the childe who would sail after self-knowledge, a god is an "eternal state of mind," whose existence depends on the constancy of human consciousness itself. When Pound intuitively "becomes a god," he enters a mood that is mythic rather than historical, and generic rather than individual. Moreover, this mood of immortality can be known by its "beauty," the cult of which Pound had juxtaposed with the delineation of ugliness as early as 1913.[12] He further remarked in "Religio" that most people's disbelief in the gods, in fact, forewarns us "to be ready to look." For while appearing "formlessly" to intuition, the gods can also appear "formed" to one's vision, or presumably other senses, as when a god "stands behind" and causes one to consider "what god it may be." Although accessible through "hearsay," the gods are better perceived more directly, and so Pound would impart his "knowledge" of a given god to us in the *Cantos* by describing before naming him, if he names him at all. The gods that we should honor in this ritual of formed appearance include a "reasonable number," and those listed here recur in the *Cantos:* Apollo, Helios, Diana, the Cytherean, Kore, Demeter, and several elemental creatures. Significantly, "it bodes well for us that they should be pleased to appear," since their return to men's gardens would signal epic success for the poet and Hellenic paradise to his audience.

Mustering a final fusillade of criticism before doing battle as Ovid in the *Cantos,* Pound published "Genesis" (*In,* 1920), "Axiomata" (*New Age,* XVI, 1921), and a "Calendar of the New Era" (*Little Review,* VIII, 1922). He impugned the veracity of Genesis by citing ostensibly parallel tales from the *Metamorphoses:* e.g., the creation (*In,* 269), the fall (*In,* 275), and the flood (*In,* 278). Ending this foray, he quoted Lucretius on the superstitions of mankind:

> O miseras hominum mentes! O pectora caeca!
> (*In,* 285)
>
> [O wretched minds of men! O blind hearts!]
> (*De Rerum Natura* 2.14)

In "Axiomata," Pound did posit the existence of a non-human "intimate essence" or "*Theos*" of the universe, but added that "we have no proof that this God, Theos, is one, or is many, or is divisible or indivisible, or is an ordered hierarchy culminating, or not culminating, in a unity" (*SP,* 49). In summing up this position, Hugh Witemeyer (*Poetry of Ezra Pound,* p. 26) says, "What emerges most clearly from Pound's 'Axiomata' is the high value he places upon states of consciousness themselves as the ultimate knowable truths." When characterizing his heretical calendar, Pound pronounced, "The Christian era came definitely to an END at midnight of the 29–30 of October (1921) old style.... There followed the Feast of ZAGREUS" (*Little Review,* 8.2, 2). In *The Dial* of May, 1922, Pound published the "Eighth Canto," which quickly reappeared as canto II, his epic's programmatic Ovidian metamorphosis of Dionysus, and a clear indication of the poet's determination to achieve epic selfhood by heralding the advent of a neopagan polity or paradise.[13] This intention, Massimo Bacigalupo rightly notes, "will make the *Cantos* both formidable and tragic."[14] In short, through Ovid as his epic mask Pound would mythopoeically Hellenize the historically Hebraic heritage of Western civilization. "I consider," he informed Harriet Monroe from Paris in July, 1922, "the *Metamorphoses* a sacred book, and the Hebrew scriptures the record of a barbarian tribe, full of evil" (*L,* 183).

Under Ovid's influence in the *Cantos,*[15] Pound sought his epic self by employing the gods to verify his role as a *vates,* who would revaluate our

Hebraic history in order to lead us toward Hellenic polity. Besides obviously manifesting this vatic identity, Pound's gods that recur in "magic moments" as projections of his own consciousness generate a more comprehensive mythology for the poem. Their return to men's gardens becomes a prerequisite for paradise, and in seeking the selfhood paradise would confer Pound is compelled to Hellenize society so that his gods can return. Hence, the poet reifies his own metaphor, or the myth metamorphoses the man. Moreover, his neopagan pursuit of *eros* eventually proved irreconcilable with what amounts to the poem's demand for Christian *agape*. Charity is needed not because paradise is an exclusively Hebraic notion, but because epic requires tribal approval and the tribe in this case is largely Judeo-Christian. By bestowing scientific credibility upon his mythical (as well as historical) adventures, the ideogram almost allowed Pound to secure our poetic if not political approbation. Indeed, his pre-Pisan poetry (e.g., cantos II, XVII, XXVII, XXX, XXXIX, XLV, and XLVII) promotes the mythical outlines of an Eleusinian ideal, which Pound then located historically by redacting from de Mailla's *Histoire Generale de la Chine* and from Adams' *Life and Works of John Adams*. Who knows how he would have proportioned his paradise had World War II not overwhelmed him?

We do know, however, that armed with Legge's Confucius and Mathews' Chinese dictionary, Pound reverted to his gods in the *Pisan Cantos*. Although their profuse return (especially in cantos LXXIX, LXXXI, and LXXXIII) represents the temporary triumph of Ovidian metamorphosis over Catullan loss, not even the guards take notice. In fact, the intrusion of real history into the poem at Pisa, i.e., the fall of fascism, invalidated Pound's hope for Hellenic polity, and therefore epic success. In the post-Pisan poetry Pound revisited China and then America in a final effort to found paradise (e.g., canto XC). But really he required Leucothoe's bikini more, while streaking through Byzantium, China, and England in order to document his grain rite (e.g., canto CVI) for the future. Thus, the poet has unrepentantly but romantically deferred his dream, confessing only at the end his utter disorientation of self: "That I lost my center / fighting the world" (117/802).

As a point of departure from Ovid, canto II programmatically announces not only Pound's epic role as a *vates* of the gods, but also his reading of history as a struggle between the few who espouse the mysteries and the many who espouse money.[16] Pound recalls the historical rape of Helen and the mythical one of Tyro to introduce his version of Ovid's tale about the Tyrrhenian sailors, which forms part of the larger legend of Bacchus' cruel and harsh punishment of Pentheus for his impiety. In focusing just on the tale within Pentheus' story, Pound stands reverently with

Acoetes while implying Penthean dismemberment for those who do not.[17] Cutting to the center of Ovid's account,[18] Pound condemns the crew's greed "for a little slave money" ("So blind was their desire for booty," *Meta.* 3.620) as "god-sleight," thereby emphasizing the divinity that Acoetes witnesses and minimizing the metamorphoses of the crew that so delighted Ovid.

After briefly setting the scene, Pound fondly pauses over Ovid's transformation of the boy into the god:

> [...the ship stood in the sea
> not otherwise than if a dry dock held her.
> They marveling redouble their thrashing of oars
> and make sail and try to run with double aid:
> Ivy impedes the oars and with curved knot
> creeps and decorates the sails with heavy clusters.
> The god himself with his brow girt with clustered grapes
> shakes his wand covered with vine-leaf fronds;
> about whom tigers and empty images of lynxes
> and the wild bodies of spotted panthers lie.]
>   (*Meta.* 3.660–69)

> Aye, I, Acoetes, stood there,
>   and the god stood by me,
> Water cutting under keel,
> Sea-break from stern forrards,
>   wake running off from the bow,
> And where was gunwale, there now was vine-trunk,
> And tenthril where cordage had been,
>   grape-leaves on the rowlocks,
> Heavy vine on the oarshafts,
> And, out of nothing, a breathing,
>   hot breath on my ankles,
> Beasts like shadows in glass,
>   a furred tail upon nothingness.
> Lynx-purr, and heathery smell of beasts,
>   where tar smell had been,
> Sniff and pad-foot of beasts,
>   eye-glitter out of black air.
> The sky overshot, dry, with no tempest,
> Sniff and pad-foot of beasts,
>   fur brushing my knee-skin,
> Rustle of airy sheaths,
>   dry forms in the *aether.*
> (2/7–8)

Having begun with an apostrophe to "King Pentheus," and then the aurally insistent "Aye, I, Acoetes," (whom the god "stood by"), Pound legitimizes the lad's report, which his subsequent description verifies. The

Ovidian echo, "ship stock fast" and "ship like a keel in ship-yard," frames Pound's hypostatization itself, illuminating the moment of incarnation when all earthly or natural motion must cease. Then, true to his earlier prescription for knowing a god indirectly—"think what god it may be" (*PD*, 24)—Pound appeals to four of the five senses in describing the cats by which Bacchus is known:

> hot breath on my ankles,
> Beasts like shadows in glass,
>   a furred tail upon nothingness.
> Lynx-purr, and heathery smell of beasts....
>   (2/8)

He would suggest the insubstantiality and hence the divine origin of his image: "Rustle of airy sheaths, / dry forms in the *aether*" (2/8).

Pound has broken with Ovid's chronology in order to stress the magic moment when his boy-god dramatically speaks. Where Ovid's god merely commented to Acoetes after the metamorphoses of the sailors, "Banish fear from your heart and hold for Naxos" (*Meta*. 3.689–90), Pound ritualizes his revelation by having "Lyaeus" explain how he might henceforth be recognized:

> ..."From now, Acoetes, my altars,
> Fearing no bondage,
>   fearing no cat of the wood,
> Safe with my lynxes,
>   feeding grapes to my leopards,
> Olibanum is my incense,
>   the vines grow in my homage."
>   (2/8–9)

Promptly concluding his version with a summary of what happened to "Lycabs" and "Medon," and with a warning to Pentheus (whom Ovid calls "contemptor superum" [*Meta*. 3.514]; "scoffer at gods") Pound closes with Acoetes' own religious testament:

> I have seen what I have seen.
>   When they brought the boy I said:
> "He has a god in him,
>   though I do not know which god."
> And they kicked me into the fore-stays.
> I have seen what I have seen....
>   (2/9)

Thus, in criticizing civilization, i.e., the sailors' greed for "slave-money" that results in "god-sleight," Pound through Acoetes asserts the inviolability of having "seen what I have seen," which line he has added to the original. Mindful of Pound's own epic pursuit of polity, we might recall that Cadmus, who warned Pentheus about his irreverence (2/9), built Thebes with the help of Amphion's lyre; he also fathered Ino, Dionysus' aunt by virtue of his second, historical birth, who as Pentheus' mother led the throng of Bacchantes in tearing him apart, but who also as Leucothea-Leucothoe would rescue Pound rudderless after Pisa for having steadfastly witnessed what he "had seen."

Pound closed his tale about the Tyrrhenian sailors with his own myth concerning the rape of "Ileuthyeria, fair Dafne of sea-bords" (2/9). In apparently conflating "Eileithyia" (the goddess of childbirth) with "eleutheria" ("freedom"), he determines the Daphne-like opening (reminiscent of "The Tree") of canto XVII. In a letter (#745, Yale Collection) Pound referred to this canto as "a sort of paradiso terrestre," and as such it completes the progression from hell (cantos XIV and XV) through the purgatory of various contemporary wars (canto XVI). Moreover, he had written to his father in April, 1927, of the cantos' fugal pattern: *nekuia,* repeat in history, and "'the magic moment' or moment of metamorphosis, burst thru from quotidien into 'divine or permanent world.' Gods, etc." (*L,* 210). Since canto XVII initiates *A Draft of The Cantos 17–27* (1928), the second installment of his quest for epic success, we might expect Pound's ritual invocation in the form of becoming a vine for having venerated "ZAGREUS! IO ZAGREUS" (12/76), and also the return of his other gods to Venice as a Renaissance approximation of polity. Even the opening "So that" of canto XVII echoes the closing "So that:" of canto I. Besides Bacchus and his telltale panthers, Diana appears in Pound's paradisal landscape, in her role as *venatrix* with her "white hounds" and "the oak-woods behind her," which promptly metamorphose into the "marble trunks" of the "palazzi" of Venice (17/76). The city itself, or perhaps its Cathedral of St. Mark,[19] Pound describes as "Cave of Nerea, / she like a great shell curved" (17/76), thereby associating Venice as a daughter of the sea (Nereus) with Venus' own birth as depicted by Botticelli in *La Nascita.* Venice symbolizes Aphrodite for Pound because he yearns nostalgically for another great cosmopolitan vortex of East and West wherein men of craft like the glassmakers of Marano, "i vitrei" (17/78), may find a haven for peaceful productivity from the sterile and loveless world of war. Hermes arrives as a messenger of the gods capable of leading the Aenean hero to Elysium, and Athena advances as the goddess of wisdom, patroness of peace, and guardian of cities. The condottieri we have encountered before in the Malatesta group, all militarists (i.e., *venatores*) who in their day struggled to protect Pound's Venetian ideal of polity. Carmagnola (1380–1432) would have become Malatesta's father-in-law had he not been executed instead "between the two columns"; Borso de Este (1413–1471) was a patron of the arts, a peace-maker, and Malatesta's friend, shot at with "the barbed arrow"; and Sigismundo never ceased to struggle for a Hellenic revival against Pius II and then Paul II, even "after that wreck in Dalmatia" (17/79). The line, "'In the gloom the gold / Gathers the light about it'" (17/78), first referred to Pandolfo himself hailed as a hero (11/51); now it betokens Pound's own heroic pursuit of a Venetian paradise known by its aesthetic (neo-platonic) "light not of the Sun" (17/77). Eleusinian Kore's apostrophe, "For this hour, brother of Circe" (who was Aeetes, keeper of the golden fleece), would seem to bode well for Pound's epic program of Hellenic revival. Although as with his beloved Malatesta, the poet may yet be besieged for his beliefs, feeling at this "evening," or "hour," or "sunset" of history somewhat like "the grasshopper flying" (17/79) errantly in the wind (*ventus*).

Exfoliating from earlier references to "Cadmus" (2/9) and "Cadmus of Golden Prows" (4/13), from Lincoln Steffens' remarks regarding the Russian Revolution (cantos XVI and XIX), and from the "Sero, sero. . . / Nothing we made, we set nothing in order" passage of canto XXV, canto XXVII closes *A Draft of The Cantos 17–27* (1928) as Pound's Cadmaean complaint on the difficulties of refounding Thebes. In supplying its symbolism of men as grain, Cadmus' story (see *Meta.* 3.1–130) suggests that dragon's teeth can indeed, when planted, produce the Sparti. Pound's search for epic selfhood involves imitating Cavalcanti who would form "di disio nuova persona," while avoiding other possible fates: "One man is dead, and another has rotted his end off / Et quant au troisième / Il est tombé dans le / De sa femme" (27/129). Tribally, too, the struggle toward polity often requires a country like England during World War I to adopt the expedient measures of refurbishing an old "Cruiser," of declaring the "goddamned Porta-goose" an ally, and of mandating that her troops be properly "fed and relaxed" (27/129). Sailing after knowledge for the sake of his modern epic, Pound sympathizes with the risks involved in Dr. Spahlinger's tubercular or Pierre Curie's radioactive research (27/129). So much for the Cadmaean hero, but of his troops in the twentieth century: "England off there in black darkness" (Anglicanism), "Russia off there in black darkness" (the Revolution), and France now cynically entertaining Brisset's theory of man's descent from the frog (27/129). Pound honors the "golden bark" of the Bucentoro in pursuing his Cadmaean vision of the new Europa, but by 1920 only the old washerwoman sings "Stretti!" in a "cracked voice," and in 1927 the "Two young ladies" have betrayed their erotic heritage altogether by confessing to being "commercianti" (27/129–30). Unlike the music publisher who "Took out Floradora in sheets, / And brought back a red-headed mummy," Pound returns for inspiration to the

Middle Ages (i.e., pre-Reformation) when "et universus quoque ecclesie populus, / And rushed out and built the duomo" in vital imitation of the Sparti themselves. And at least the French Revolution began well ("Brumaire..."), which is more perhaps than Pound could say about the Russian Revolution, where *tovarisch* again "rose, and wrecked the house of the tyrants," but also "talked folly on folly," being "cursed and blessed without aim" (27/131). Thus, we have come not to the *Mensheviki,* but to the *Bolsheviki,* not to "Petrograd," but to Leningrad. Even the archetypal *tovarisch,* always capable of individual as well as racial metamorphosis, seems aware of his historical loss of will:

> I neither build nor reap.
> That he came with the gold ships, Cadmus,
> That he fought with the wisdom,
> Cadmus, of the gilded prows. Nothing I build
> And I reap
> Nothing; with the thirtieth autumn
> I sleep, I sleep not, I rot
> And I build no wall.
>   (27/132)

On the one hand, Pound is stressing the difficulties of instigating an Hellenic revolution through the *Cantos;* the "wall of Eblis / At Ventadour" (27/132), after all, was in ruins when he visited there in 1919. On the other, however, the poet is confessing his own doubts about achieving epic success with the poem itself; like *tovarisch* who returns to earth in his "thirtieth autumn," Pound as "E.P." also "passed from men's memory in *l'an trentiesme / De son eage,*" having presented "No adjunct to the Muses' diadem" (*Per,* 187). Still, grain-like both *tovarisch* and E.P. are capable of rebirth, for the eucharist of Eleusis suggests that thanks to the "Xarites, born of Venus and wine" (27/131), they can be "Baked and eaten...And up again" (27/132). Pound's paradise may yet metamorphose from "The air...into leaf," his thorny Mediterranean "acanthus" may yet flower, and his "down" with Persephone's aid may yet prove to be "up" (27/132). Even so, we must not forget the lesson in Cadmus' own end (see *Meta.* 4.563–603): for daring to slay the holy serpent prior to civilizing the dullwitted Boeotians, the Theban himself in old age was transformed into a snake.

Representing the clearest statement yet of Pound's mythopoeic intent to achieve epic success by Hellenizing society, canto XXX aptly concludes *A Draft of XXX Cantos* (1930). In this canto the poet addresses the problem of redeeming time (or mortality), which in Christian tradition has prompted society sentimentally to extol pity as a virtue. Pity suggests an accommodation with evil, and the development of an apocalyptic conscience (*caritas*); Diana the rejection of evil, and the development of a metamorphic consciousness (*eros*). Counterpointing Chaucer's own "compleynt" that pity is dead and cruelty rules, Pound projects his own frustration at being an outcast for his neopaganism onto Artemis in her role as huntress:

> Now if no fayre creature followeth me.
> It is on account of Pity,
> It is on account that Pity forbideth them slaye.
> All things are made foul in this season,
> This is the reason, none may seek purity
> Having for foulnesse pity
> And things growne awry;
> No more do my shaftes fly
> To slay. Nothing is now clean slayne
> But rotteth away.
>   (30/147)

Not only does Artemis lament her inability to rid society of its evil; mythically, Venus would give her love to that "doddering fool," Vulcan, rather than to "young Mars" (30/147). To Pound, "Time is the evil" (30/147) both for the pity it induces in others, and for its passing on himself, who at age 45 has roughly two-thirds of an epic to go and whose synchronic structural method Yeats had just panned in *A Packet* because the romantic poet did not know "a fugue from a frog" (*L,* 293). Pound's allusion to the story of Pedro and Inés has often been read as an example of the king's inability to accommodate himself to time. And so it is: While Pedro out of extreme self-pity set his wife's corpse to banquet, Francesco Gonzaga would assist his wife Isabella d'Este in patronizing masters like Leonardo, Titian, and Montegna (see 3/12). Yet as Michael Bernstein correctly notes, there is a "curious homologue" between Pedro's necrophilia and Pound's own epic manner of digging up "the illustrious dead."[20] In ur-canto II (1917), the poet rehearsed Camoens' own comparison of "*linda Ignez,*" long invoked by "maidens in Mondego," to "Proserpine" (*Poetry,* 10.4, 187). Inés is a vestigial incarnation of Pound's erotic ideal, which through his poetry (Sappho-Lesbia, Cynthia-Artemis, Venice-Aphrodite) he would redeem. As he asked of Browning's ghost at the beginning of ur-canto I (1917): "Is't worth the evasion, what were the use / Of setting figures up and breathing life upon them, / Were't not *our* life, your life, my life, extended?" (*Poetry,* 10.3, 115). In other words, resuscitating the Hellenic past through a poetry of classical association (rather than romantic imagination) constitutes the *penetralia* where in 1930 Pound's epic, Ovidian self was struggling to be born, and which if still-born would thus have confirmed the tragically reactionary identity that most of the public already sensed they saw.

But Pound, ironically full of Frazer's Calvinistic notions about scape-goats and the sacred marriage, still hoped to be king of the grove by accommodating himself to time with epic success. In canto XXX his hero becomes the pitiless Caesare Borgia who, though certainly a murderer and a pimp, arranges the match between his sister Lucrezia and Isabella d'Este's squeamish kid brother Alphonso for the sake of extending the power of the Borgia family and of the Papal States. To what end? Because the Borgia's, like the Gonzagas (and Pound), would use their power to instigate the Renaissance as an anodyne to the Dark Ages, by hiring humanists like Hieronymous Soncinus (a Jew) to create a vortex of learning with printers like da Bologna and classical scholars like Manutius (30/148). In printing Petrarch's *Rime* for Caesare in 1503, Soncinus acknowledges he took his text from a codex of Lorenzo de Medici, founder of Florence's Laurentian Library and the man who commissioned Botticelli's *Venus* (ca. 1485), and from a codex "once of the Lords Malatesta" (30/148-49). Moreover, Soncinus, "here working in Caesar's fame" (30/148), established himself in the church, once a shrine or triumphal arch to Augustus, of Fano, now part of Caesare Borgia's territory, but "olim de Malatestis" (see 9/34). Two years after Soncinus began in 1501, "Il Papa mori" (30/149), and Caesare in 1507, thus promptly ending the Borgias' efforts to advance art, spread culture, and unify Italy. While the pope died in Augustus' month, Pound would continue to disseminate aureate letters by enrolling his own Goldingesque codex of Ovidian metamorphoses on the bimillenium of Virgil's birth. "Explicit canto XXX" (30/149), then, also reiterates the first 30 cantos, as well as promises greater adventures to come. Thus, in teaching the Boeotians the use of letters, Cadmus of the "golden prows" has become the Tyrian of "golden prose."

Feeling the economic and political strain of his Italian self-exile, Pound in canto XXXIX (1934) rededicates himself to his quest for epic identity by returning to Odysseus' conquest of Circe and then affirms his Hellenic progress toward *eros* by celebrating his own rite of spring. The poet whom Yeats watched feeding Rapallo's stray cats sacred to Dionysus opens this canto with a lament, "Desolate is the roof where the cat sat, / ...the iron rail that he walked / And the corner post whence he greeted the sunrise" (39/193). Pound associates the "thkk, thgk" of Rapallo's looms with the sound of Circe's, and thus Elpenor's testimony concerning the "fucked girls" and "fat leopards" of the witch's hall emphasizes Pound's own recurrent bouts with *abulia* in waging his heroic struggle. With references to Circe's smooth-stoned house, her wolves and mountain lions, and dreadful drugs (see *Ody.*, X.211-13), to Polites exhorting his companions on Circe's threshold (see *Ody.*, X.227-28), and to the crew's menu before and after their transformation into swine, Pound intensifies Homer's picture of Odysseus' dilemma. The glance at Ovid's Hecuba, Priam's queen, speechless in grief over her last child slain at Troy (39/194), highlights Pound's own (as well as Odysseus') psychic predicament. But just here we encounter perhaps the most important advice of the *Cantos:* Circe's injunction to Odysseus that in order to return to Ithaca he must first sail to the realm of Death and pale Persephone to hear the prophecy of Tiresias (see *Ody.,* X.490–94). The witch's advice confirms Pound's own poetic practice of deducing himself from the classical past. Moreover, the canto's disjunctive account of Homer's book X demonstrates her advice as well: What follows her advice (Pound's Homeric allusions, from Eurylochus' report to Circe's request that Odysseus stay with her) originally preceded it, and within this second sequence Circe's recognition or naming of Homer's hero originally preceded her amorous plea. In short, for Pound, achieving selfhood involves interrupting, indeed reversing, the Homeric chronology of events: the hard-earned naming precedes the seduction; both of which as Odysseus' encounter with the witch precede her advice; both of which as the Circe episode, in fact, precede the *nekuia* of canto I. Pound requires all of those who would progress with him toward paradise to regress into the past, which has got to be one of the most original, not to say bizarre, innovations in American literature since Twain penned *Huckleberry Finn.* Here time is the evil, i.e., a "fall" into time and a redemption through time, or history. Pound would develop not conscience but consciousness, achieved synchronically through an un-English or periodic sense of Latin, through the Ovidian mythopoeic highjinks of the *Cantos.* Clearly Hathor, the Egyptian goddess of beauty, and Dante, viewing the splendor of paradise, are more favorable omens than Glaucus foiled in his pursuit of Scylla (39/194). But now that Odysseus knows (rather than imagines) who he is, he will not give up the journey like Ovid's Macer (39/194). As the sorceress says: "feel better when you have eaten.... / Always with your mind on the past...." (39/195). Odysseus weeps because he has endured much upon the inhuman sea and upon the land from hostile men; Circe can feed and rest him, restoring the heart behind his ribs. So Pound, in this first notably Eleusinian canto would feed upon the grain-hoards of the Homeric past, gaining the courage to note that no man has ever "Been to hell in a boat yet" (39/195), both an acknowledgment of his pilotlessness and an affirmation that he as "noman" would persist in pursuing the illustrious dead so as to get home, despite the one-eyed cyclops in his way.

What follows the Circe episode of canto XXXIX that chronologically precedes it and thus Pound's *nekuia*? The litany to love closing canto XXXIX previews Pound's answer by metaphorically demonstrating his determination to continue his epic adventures. Since Kore as corn-maiden also rules in hell, the poet who metamorphoses the literary and historical past is mysteriously performing a sacrament intended to rejuvenate himself and his readers. Pound's recreation becomes a rite of spring, a secular eucharist, whereby in "feeding" (i.e., writing his *Cantos*) he assumes something of the aura or fire of the life-force that pervades nature. The tradition of associating Eleusis and sex dates back to the polemics of Clement of Alexandria (whom Pound put in hell; see 14/62) and other Church fathers, is echoed in the *fin de siècle* work of Frazer, Farnell, and Foucant, and made much of in Pound's own poetry by Leon Surrette. Yet sex, for Pound, is not some sort of Circean end in itself, but rather a metaphor for art. While sexual ritual (*hieros gamos*) constitutes a kind of vegetative renewal, Pound's interest in *eros* or Venus (de Gourmont, Provence, love elegy, Homer) symbolizes his love for the Hellenic past, uniting with which produces the offspring that is his poetry. Pound reveres the agricultural cult of Eleusis because without grain, there can be no civilization, and therefore no culture, and therefore no poet who, as the farmer cultivates the earth, would cultivate the past to produce his own poetic harvest. Thus, Pound's gleanings from Catullus, Ibycus, and the fourteenth-century lyric *Alysoun,* as well as references to Flora, Aphrodite above Terracina, and the *Pervigilium Veneris* compose a celebration of *eros* in that the poetry is charged with the metamorphic energy of vegetative renewal. The poet mounts not Circe but Circeo, he cries not "fuck" but "fac," and he makes not "spring overborne into summer" but just "spring" (a Cummings pun). Nassar (p. 55) is right to see cantos XXXIX and XLVII as "not about coitus, but about art." For the "coitus" of cantos XXXVI, XXXIX, and XLVII, and especially at Pisa, is really a coming together, or convocation, or intercourse of the illustrious dead so as to illuminate the sense of Hellenic beauty celebrated in Pound's poetry, which in turn solemnizes his own sense of epic selfhood. That the poet sees only "their eyes in the dark," besides the plentiful puns ("Aye, I, Acoetes"; the eyes of canto LXXXI; "aere perennius"; I, Ray...), implies that ultimately he is referring to the "coetus" (Cat. 64.402) of the gods whose departure Catullus lamented and whose return Pound would proclaim as an Ovidian *vates.* Like the absent cat referred to at the beginning of the canto, Pound's Hellenic *theos* in contrast to Christianity's never returns to earth; this poet can see only the apparition of faces in a crowd, "not the bough that he walked on" (39/195). Yet in harnessing the erotic energies of spring through his art, Pound plays the god-role; that is, he has "eaten the flame," while his bride, herself an example of sexual renewal and therefore an inspiration to the poet, has "nested the fire" (39/196).

With *The Fifth Decad of Cantos XLII-LI* (1937) Pound further refines his sense of selfhood: to complete his Ovidian epic, to express certain humanitarian desires (notwithstanding the ominous fascist and anti-

Semitic implications of the sequence), and to register his revulsion for Protestantism. Noticeably inciting Pound's Hellenic satire in canto XLV and his Hellenic lyricism in canto XLVII, T. S. Eliot published *After Strange Gods* in 1934,[21] partly to expiate for his own preconversion infidelity to Christianity and partly to chide modern writers such as Yeats, Lawrence, Joyce, and Pound, who would substitute poetic for religious belief. Eliot attributes such literary heresy to not having been raised in a "living and central tradition," and in Pound's case to an individualistic and libertarian "post-Protestant prejudice." He also notes that Pound was attracted to the Middle Ages for the wrong, i.e., non-religious, reasons and that he found Cavalcanti more sympathetic than Dante (despite their respective merits as poets) because Guido was likely a heretic. Not incorrect as far as he goes, Eliot from Pound's point of view does not go far enough. One might quibble that St. Louis (Boston) could have offered little more culturally than Hailey (Philadelphia), that Possum was not quite the "Yankee" he wished to seem before his Virginia audience, or that Eliot's curiously insular remark regarding "free-thinking Jews" circumscribes the notions about tradition. At least, Pound's notion of "usura" in canto XLV includes the entire Hebraic tradition from Deuteronomy 23:20, through the Church's medieval equivocations discouraging Christians but encouraging Jews to lend money, to Calvin's sanctioning of interest and the modern industrial rise of capitalism, socialism, and even Marxism. Most of this tradition is monotheistic, all of it historically or temporally oriented, and thus associated in the mind of a modern, post-Protestant, poet in exile like Pound with the "profit motive." Thus, while Pound is indeed a heretic from Eliot's limited Christian perspective, Eliot in turn is part of a greater, even more heretical movement that has long threatened Pound's tradition of Eleusis and that in 1937 threatens to "stoppeth the spinner's cunning"; that is, increasingly to prevent Pound from completing the "deductum carmen" that would allow him at last to discover himself. Ironically, running out of time in his quest through time simply sharpens Pound's protest against time in canto XLV.

Alexander accurately notes that canto XLV critiques the modern industrial world, but I think misleadingly adds that "its positives are medieval and Quattrocento" (p. 179). Pound, in fact, catalogs medieval architecture and early renaissance painters and sculptors to suggest that the light from Eleusis still shown prior to the Reformation. Jean Seznec (*The Survival of the Pagan Gods*)[22] is helpful here, in suggesting that although often bastardized or metamorphosed by Christianity, paganism thereby flourished in medieval and early renaissance art. Browning makes a similar point in his monologues, and so, too, Pound in canto XXX. Pound himself would link the profanation of the mysteries with Protestant morals, usury tolerance, and the vulgarization of sex (*GtK,* 50). The mysteries of Eleusis originally attested to Greek gratitude for the adequate food supply upon which society depends: agriculture indeed has freed mankind from being nomads or hunter-gatherers. That culture comes from agriculture was, for Pound, last demonstrated by pre-Reformation art, which bountifully celebrated the point in preserving the Hellenic past. Gonzaga was a great patron of art, Duccio worked on the Tempio, with "La Calumnia" Botticelli allegorized Pound's own struggle against the world, Adamo the craftsman typifies *tovarisch* hailing from Cavalcanti's and Catullus' Verona, St. Trophime exhibits its cloistered peristyle for all to see, and so does St. Hilaire its romanesque proportions. The Quattrocento was the last time, Pound seems to be saying, that western society had time for art. In effect, rejecting our time, where time is money, Pound nostalgically reveres a time where artists were respected and themselves celebrated the Hellenic principles responsible for that respect. Pound's anti-Semitic remark that "civilization entered [Arles] before L[eon] Blum and Co. got control" (*L,* 303) reveals the primitivistic, i.e., concrete rather than abstract, coloring of his "elliptical" (*L,* 303) Eleusis, wherein artists but not bankers would be allowed to manipulate natural symbols. In such a guild-oriented world, the bread would be made of "mountain wheat" and "strong flour"; the "stone-cutter" could work "his stone," the "weaver...his loom," and the "maid" her "needle"; the "line" of painting would be finely drawn; and the poet in exile would finally be able to "find site for his dwelling" (45/229), or root himself through poetic re-creation. Moreover, such life would be open to all—not just men, but women, children, slaves, even foreigners—so long, of course, as they spoke Greek. Of those proscribed from these rites, Pound implies, we need only denounce them as usurers who would prevent our coetus with "Azure" ("sky's clear"), "cramoisi" ("night's sea" blooded by spring freshets), and "Emerald" ("green of the mountain pool") (45/230 and 81/520). For "Usura," deriving its use from *money lent* in *time* (which triple-headed abstraction Pound vehemently denies), aborts the natural cycle of *Eros:* "Usura slayeth the child in the womb / It stayeth the young man's courting / It...lyeth / between the young bride and her bridegroom" (45/230). Sexually speaking, modern man loves for pay; the natural act, "coition" (*L,* 303), must now be sanctioned, licensed, and taxed, "going to a fatbuttocked priest or registry office" (*L,* 230): "They have brought whores for Eleusis" (45/230). Aesthetically, for celebrating his moveable feast of metamorphosing the illustrious dead, the hierophant is made again to feel like young Pedro: "corpses are set to banquet / at behest of usura" (45/230). Thus, prompted by his rootlessness into heresy, and egged on by Eliot's moral posturing, Pound sought the magic herb of Eleusis that would transform his poetry into prayer.

Having answered Eliot satirically in canto XLV, Pound now answers him lyrically in canto XLVII by illuminating the *Hiera* (food, sex, art) of his syncretic Eleusis, as best he ever does before the war effectively confines his notions about paradise to "the wilds of [his] mind only" (*GtK,,* 52). Such is not a bad fate, however, for the poet who would emulate Tiresias, "Who even dead, yet hath his mind entire!" (47/236). Pound has been practicing Circe's advice about going "the road / to hell" (47/236) to glean from the illustrious dead the way home to epic selfhood since canto I, if not since *A Lume Spento*. In time what he has learned or "knows" will be added as the "shade" (or prophecy) of his "shade" (or epic mask) communing with that of the blind seer in Persephone's bower of the classical past. For what, after all, does Tiresias "know"? The metamorphic knowledge of "'Shalt return through spiteful Neptune, over dark seas, / 'Lose all companions'" (1/5) contrasts strikingly with the apocalyptic imagination of Anchises concerning Rome. The Eleusinian knowledge of canto XLVII, what Tiresias has to say, so to speak, involves discovering how to reverse time in order to live in time, which implies less transcendent imagination, as M. L. Rosenthal suggests,[23] than associative memory. Such knowledge anticipates the "full knowing" of canto LXXXI, where "*eidos*" (81/520) means "seeing" in the perfective sense of "having seen"; even as it recapitulates the knowledge of canto II, where Acoetes testifies to having "seen what I have seen" (2/9). The climax, we recall, of the *epopteia* at Eleusis involved the *deiknymena* ("things shown"), "when the Hierophant standing in front of the Anaktoran and in the midst of a radiant light exhibited the Hiera to the initiates" (Mylonas, p. 273).

After his Homeric opening in canto XLVII, Pound blends references to the Adonia, to woman's constant intention, and to Hesiod's prescriptions for plowing with a grim reflection, a richly rhetorical question, and a magic moment plus coda in his effort to "reconstitute Deuteronomy" (Alexander, p. 180). The vegetation (corn) god Adonis (Tamuz),[24] born of the myrrh-tree, beloved by Proserpine and Aphrodite (Dione), was slain by a wild boar at harvest time, i.e., in the spring, near Byblos. Subsequently, his death and rebirth were celebrated annually throughout the Mediterranean, especially during the spring rains that stained the river Adonis with his blood. With "The small lamps drift in the bay" (47/236) and "Wheat shoots rise new by the altar" (47/237), Pound refers to Christianized vestiges of the pagan practices of carrying the god's image to the sea (St. John's Eve) and of raising gardens of Adonis (Maundy Thursday). The rites of Adonis, like those of Eleusis, were intended to promote a successful harvest and thus occurred "in time," that is, in natural as opposed to calendar time. So, too, woman as an embodiment of *eros* is mindful of both the menstrual cycle and the nine month period of human gestation (i.e., two times five or ten sidereal months): "Two span, two span to a woman, / Beyond that she believes not. Nothing is of any importance" (47/237). Aside from the chauvinistic implications of this view, Odysseus, too, is governed by the same sexual desires and but for Hermes' magic herb, "Molu," would be like the moth "called over mountain" or the bull who "runs blind on the sword" (47/237). Instead, he is thereby "freed from the one bed / that [he] may'st return to another" (47/237), which is both a blessing and a challenge for Pound, whose true Penelope is reunion with self, a psychic reintegration possible only on successfully completing the *Cantos*. Thus, the modern poet at odds with calendar time who also lacks a natural internal clock reverts to the natural external clock recommended by Hesiod in *The Works and Days*. In associating from sex to agriculture, Pound returns to Eleusis, for plowing (and sowing) in November, "when the Pleiades go down to their rest" and "when the cranes fly high" (47/237), initiates the chief agricultural season of Attic Greece that ended with the harvest of winter wheat in May. As Nilsson (pp. 42–64) carefully clarifies, Eleusis was an autumn rite celebrating the reunion of the corn mother with her daughter when the seed corn is planted and rises as the new winter crop. The rub comes when we realize that Adonis dies, the Pleiades lie hidden, olive blossoms fall, martins appear, and almond trees bloom all in the spring, while Pound with time running out at age 52 must yet ponder his winter plowing, his one constant intention.

Espousing natural time yet unable to partake of the joys of spring, Pound beholds the falling olive stars and the martin's wing-print disappearing with his cry, and becomes cognizant of his own and therefore history's "forked shadow" falling darkly across his "terrace" (47/237–38). Sensing the tragic frailty of his Ovidian self so rooted in the classical past, Pound perceives in 1937 that his epic quest for polity—Ecbatan (4/16), the stars, the olive branch, the terrace (47/237), and "to build the city of Dioce whose terraces are the color of stars" (74/425)—is jeopardized by the Martin bombers of war, especially one describable in Hellenic versus Hebraic terms. The poet's personal vulnerability prompts him to note how much poetically, at least, he has "gnawed through the mountain" (47/238) in building his own *Via Gardesana* (110/778) or interstate to paradise. Such insecurity also prompts the polysemous, Jonsonian question concerning "nest," "rest," "deeper planting," "swifter shoot," and entering "more deeply the mountain" (47/238). Despite the inclination of several critics to read Pound's answer in sexual terms as a "no, nothing softer,"[25] clearly the poet intends to affirm his devotion to the Hellenic past, i.e., to grain, and *eros,* and art, which lost helps make him lord ("adon") over all nature in his search for self-fulfillment:

> The light has entered the cave. Io! Io!
> The light has gone down into the cave,
> Splendour on splendour!

By prong have I entered these hills:
That the grass grow from my body,
That I hear the roots speaking together,
The air is new on my leaf,
The forked boughs shake with the wind.
Is Zephyrus more light on the bough, Apeliota
more light on the almond branch?
By this door have I entered the hill.
(47/238)

Aesthetically, Pound's Hellenic efforts to recover paradise, i.e., himself, have made him feel like the god for a time. So, the break and the switch from "darkness" to "light," and from "thou" to "I"; so, the Catullan marriage cry of "Io" Hymen and the Dionysian-Eleusinian one of "Io" Bacchus-Iacchus; so, the Whitmanian puns on "grass," and "roots," and "leaf"; and so, the metamorphic emphasis on flowering anew in the wind like an almond branch, as only the speaker of "The Tree" knew he would. Through this "door," or "cave," or "hill" into the past, redemption lies, and not unlike Roethke, whose father was a fish, Pound fancies he can "hear the roots speaking together" (47/238), as indeed he can. Thus, for the poet who would fall like Adonis, and thereby sprout (Whitman's verb) again in time, Pound must ponder his winter plowing most when the Pleides rest, almonds flame, and new shoots are brought to the altar (47/238–39). For contemplating the past can lead to renewal, to a knowing by memory and association that rivals seeing by vision and imagination, "that hath the gift of healing, / That hath the power over wild beasts" (47/139). "KAI MOIRAI' ADONIN" (47/139), then, implies bread, and love, and poetry, and also the peace to enjoy them all. Sadly enough, however, the Adonia were rites back before dew was shed, and though Pound would reintroduce them to our time, they were not right for 1937.

In his *Works and Days* Hesiod also spoke of justice, which has prompted Nilsson in discussing Eleusis to derive Greek piety from agriculture, which entails peace, justice, brotherhood, and a belief in "the eternity of life in the sense that life flows through the generations which spring from each other" (p. 60). Only later, during the fifth century heyday of an industrialized and commercialized Athens that had forgotten the agricultural foundations of civilization, was man "no longer content with the immortality of the generations but wanted immortality for himself"; so the mysteries "promised even this in a happy life in the underworld" (p.64). Labeling this later Athenian notion of resurrection as Hebraic and the earlier archaic one as Hellenic, we see that Pound would celebrate the metamorphic renewal of life through agriculture, through the generations, and through poetry. Justice for Pound, of course, means self-justification through his *Cantos,* or making his Eleusinian ideal spring anew in the verse of subsequent poets even as he has germinated in the work of predecessors, thereby giving them new life.

Thus, neopagan Pound is still answering Christian Eliot when in 1938 he says,

> I offer for Mr. Eliot's reflection the thesis that our time has overshadowed the mysteries by an overemphasis on the individual. R. L. Stevenson, whom no mystic has, so far as I know, ever mentioned, had more emotional wisdom than most men (*Virginibus Puerisque*). Eleusis did not distort truth by exaggerating the individual, neither could it have violated the individual spirit. Only in the high air and the great clarity can there be a just estimation of values. Romantic poetry, on the other hand, almost always requires the concept of reincarnation as part of its mechanism. No apter metaphor having been found for certain colours. I assert that the gods exist. (*GtK,* 299)[26]

Pound's reference to *Virginibus Puerisque* (1881) is telling, for Stevenson therein defends "marriage" as meant for men with faith, not boys with hope;[27] and falling in love as "the one illogical adventure, the one thing of which we are tempted to think as supernatural, in our trite and reasonable world" (57). Stevenson closes with a question that underscores Pound's heroic determination not to desert his Hellenic cause in time of crisis: "And how many loves have perished because, from pride, or spite, or diffidence, or that unmanly shame which withholds a man from daring to betray emotion, a lover, at the critical point of the relation, has but hung his head and held his tongue?" (73). In short, the "marriage" Pound would adhere to before Eliot is his own to the tradition of Aurunculeia, i.e., to the Hellenic tradition of Ovid's gods and Eleusis that he desires we accept in his *Cantos.* "What thou lovest well remains" (81/520) and "Here error is... / all in the diffidence that faltered" (81/522). Pound's remark, then, about "romantic reincarnation" can be seen to include Hebraic notions about Life-after-Death, Resurrection, the Second Coming, and Apocalypse, but especially the secularization thereof in high romantic poetry wherein the speaker visionarily transcends the bonds of the flesh before returning to a more mundane state. Pound is saying, it appears, that he can transcend reality, too, not romantically but classically, by becoming "a god for a time." So he concludes by asserting "that a great treasure of verity exists for mankind in Ovid and in the subject matter of Ovid's long poem, and that only in this form could it be registered" (*GtK,* 299).

The obvious problem with Pound's justification is that his long anticipated coition of the returning gods is threatened by the war; the peasant's fields are burned and his olive trees cut down, as it were; Odysseus' raft is overturned. The "Pact of Steel" (May 1939), therefore, precludes the poet's progress onto "questions of BELIEF" (*L,* 328). Instead of returning permanently to the states in 1939, Pound reverts to broadcasting for Rome Radio during the war, scandalously vilifying Roosevelt, the Jews, and all Protestant usurers for jeopardizing his poetic project of self-justification. Circe (*Ody.*, 12.113ff.) had advised Odysseus that in order to escape "Scylla's white teeth" (47/238) he should row on and not look back, and so Pound did, producing 20 new cantos in three years. No wonder he turned to extolling Confucius as the Hesiod of the East and the agrarian ideal of the Chinese peasant, and then to John Adams as the chief post-Puritan hero of the American Enlightenment. He might, in addition, have read Woolman on the evils of slavery and worse. At any rate, by 1944 Pound as epic poet found himself without even an audience of one, caught upon the barb of time. Yet even Pisa poses irony: for having thought so long about death, he now like Whitman in "Lilacs" also has the opportunity to feel it for himself, which suffering almost allows him in *propria persona* for perhaps the only time in his poetry to achieve a vision of sorts, or at least to complete his Catullan coetus with the gods. While Pound would doubtless have preferred to celebrate Mussolini's martial triumph after the fact, as did Virgil Augustus', he had to settle for defiantly restating his Hellenic belief as represented by the encounter with Aphrodite in canto LXXXI. Ironically, this coition under pressure, almost leading to fusion, only appears to represent the poet's adoption of romantic aesthetics. Through suffering, then, Pound was nearly led to love, to *caritas,* but as he says in retrospect, he "cannot make it flow thru" (116/797). We might, nevertheless, recall Lowell's lines from "Ezra Pound" (1969): "'When I talked that nonsense about Jews on the Rome / wireless, Olga knew it was shit, and still loved me.'"[28]

Written from 14 July to 8 October 1945, while Pound was in the DTC near Pisa awaiting his fate, the *Pisan Cantos* (1948) represent some of the most remarkable poetry of our time. In them Pound appears at the nadir of his epic ambitions, and yet at the zenith of his poetic powers, as if through falling his salvation lies. How can this be? As an Ovidian *vates* Pound was supposed to be celebrating the triumph of Hellenic polity in a manner rivaling Virgil's epic vindication of Octavian's victory at Actium in 31 B.C.; instead he must confront not only the death of "Ben" and the destruction of their Fascist dream, but also the severe obstruction of his quest for justice or psychic integrity or selfhood. In returning so profusely, as the seer has long forecast they would, the gods signify not the millennial marriage of myth and history on achieving earthly paradise, but Pound's desperate effort to demonstrate that his case for "coetus" has not been tragically interrupted. Moreover, complicating our interpretation of this central Ovidian theme, which climaxes with the momentary trinity of garden ritual (canto LXXIX), ecstatic chant (canto LXXXI), and cognitive calm (canto LXXXIII), other motifs involving the poet's memory, his respect for Confucius, and a new awareness of nature underscore the incredible emotional richness of this vortex. Perhaps the most important complementary motif of the *Pisan* sequence, however, is history, i.e., our awareness of the historical reality of events that have led Pound to his Pisan predicament (as opposed to the Alexandrian or Confucian exempla that he statically catalogs as history elsewhere in the *Cantos*). While landing Pound in the death cells (the Cyclops' cave, Circe's liar, the inundated raft) historical reality also for the only time in the poem prompts him to speak in *propria persona* ("ego scriptor") to the "gentle reader." Thus, Pound's fictively autonomous (i.e., dramatic in Joyce's sense) discourse made possible by the ideogram is given an air of bona fide objectivity that his mythopoeic manipulation of myth and history both before and after Pisa simply lacks. In short, the premier poet of Latin masks almost unmasks himself in that DTC tent. More important still, the resultant verity of emotion in these cantos should not, as it already has many commentators, tempt us into viewing the sequence as Pound's belated discovery of love. His candor, a comparative absence of anti-Semitism, and our own mix of admiration, pity, and forgiveness do not imply *agape* or *caritas* or loving-kindness on the caged panther's part. For to impose the romantic paradigm of vision born of suffering leading to love on "Old Ez" would be to make him sacrifice to a spirit not his own, a sycophancy of which he has never been guilty, especially not in the famous epiphany of Aphrodite.

Pound's unusually free association comes as something of a shock after his chronological redactions from de Mailla and C. F. Adams. The feverish poet of *Cantos LII–LXXI* and the Rome broadcasts has come a cropper and must now rely for sanity's sake upon the elegiac fragments of his memory. Of course, this is not quite accurate: Pound yet had Legge's *Confucius* (and Mathew's dictionary) for support, as well as a Bible and occasional copies of *Time* magazine, and Speare's anthology, "found on the jo-house seat" (80/513). But even so, the poet sifts through a host of recollections concerning writers, artists, musicians, philosophers, politicians, teachers, friends, and family, most long since "to earth o'ergiven" (74/432). Recasting the international periplum of the pre-Pisan cantos, Pound recounts the people, places, and events of his own lifetime. "So that leaving America I brought with me $80 / and England a letter of Thomas Hardy's / and Italy one eucalyptus pip / from the salita that goes up from Rapallo" (80/500). Impressively, he also includes several "luminous details" from the half-dozen or so languages that have been part of his own poetic maturation over the years. Pound's panic wandering seems intended less to justify his wartime behavior (although there is some of this) than simply to ease the pain of the present moment, of feeling "the loneliness of death" (82/527), for example. After all, he had begun so well, knowing Yeats, Eliot, Joyce, Ford, Lewis, Frost, Cummings, Williams, and Hemingway, with Swinburne his "only miss" (82/523). Gone are the days of good conversation over dinner with friends in the restaurants of Europe. Gone, indeed, is the good food in a camp where "the wild birds wd not eat the bread" (74/428). In diminution the poet of Eleusis seems resigned to the current state of culinary affairs: "'Some cook, some do not cook / some things cannot be altered'" (81/518). In forte, on the other hand, this same poet of grain, *eros,* and art notes that "nothing matters but the quality / of the affection— / in the end—that has carved the trace in the mind / dove sta memoria" (76/457). Marvelously enough, such counterpointing works, our confusion vanishes like the mists over Mt. Taishan, and after some difficulty we glimpse Pound's sense of "beauté" (80/511). This is not to say he always succeeds in staving off his "DAKRUŌN" (83/532), nor are his tears Hebrew or Christian, but Greek, as Alexander (p. 199) has noted. Consequently, our sadness, in turn, comes from witnessing the spectacle of a great poet, who has carefully built his career on discovering himself from the recorded past, reduced at last to repeatedly sifting through his own past in order to discern his immediate future. As to mortality, the intellection of Homer's *nekuia* has yielded to the emotion of Whitman's "'O troubled reflection / 'O Throat, O throbbing heart'" (82/526). In this sense, the self-exiled American poet truly has come home.

The roots of Confucius at Pisa are deep. Discounting the Fenellosa material that became *Cathay* (1915), we note that canto XIII (1925) is a pastiche from the *Lun Yü* (the Analects), Pound translated from the *Li Chi* (Book of Rites) in 1928, and he rendered *The Analects* in 1937. For the Chinese cantos (1940) he relied on de Mailla and Lacharme, but by Pisa on Legge's version of the *Ssu Shu* (Four Books), three of which (*The Analects, The Great Learning,* and *The Unwobbling Pivot*) he had translated by 1947. Thus, Pound had long since accommodated Confucius to his Hellenic approach to reality.[29] Pound's static approach to history till now has been a mixture of Alexandrian recitation by catalog and, through de Mailla, the *Shu Ching* (History Classic), and the *Ch'un Ch'iu* (Spring and Autumn), Confucian redaction whereby dynasties either adhere to or deviate from the *T'ien Ming* (Mandate of Heaven). Here it should be noted that merely pursuing material retributive Justice belies the Hebraic notions of time, evil, and theodicy. Deriving his ideogrammic method from both Ovidian association and the Chinese ideograph has allowed Pound to mask or objectify in epic his Hellenic belief as if he were speaking for the public at large. But more important still, Confucius himself has set Pound a critical example. Orphaned, genteelly poor, once a keeper of granaries, largely

self-educated, a compiler of court records, living in an age of political turmoil, espousing the people's virtue over their rulers' corruption, hoping to
win some influential government post, and writing in the cryptic, *wen-yen*
style that requires serious study and the use of commentaries, Confucius
had taught Pound by 1945 to cease worrying about winning over the audience or tribe that he as a writer of epic was traditionally supposed to have.
"To study with the white wings of time passing / is not that our delight /to
have friends come from far countries / is not that pleasure / nor to care
that we are untrumpeted?" (74/437). The point is, however, that Pound's
arrest by the partisans and subsequent internment at Petano afford him the
opportunity to ponder his neglect in cultivating *tao,* or the pathway to
heaven, by not practicing the supreme Confucian virtue of *jên* (benevo-
lence, human heartedness, *caritas*) more.

"Free speech without free radio speech is as zero" (74/426), cries
the poet mindful of his own versus the BBC's wartime broadcasts. Yet he
remains insensitive to the shocking incongruity between *chêng ming,* which
Confucian correspondence of conduct and language he had often espoused
in cantos LII–LXXI, and his subsequent performance *sans* masks over
Rome Radio. Nor does Pound's preoccupation with Confucius and language in the *Pisan Cantos,* his examination of conscience, as it were,
wherein he implies we should concentrate on the poetry rather than on his
radio speech, constitute even a full admission of his *error.* From the poet's
point of view he is "Wanjina" (i.e., Wondjina), or "Ouan Jin" (i.e., *wen
jen*), "the man with an education," whose father removed his mouth because he spoke too much, naming too many things and "thereby making
clutter" (74/426-27). Having lost his microphone, the poet would end his
satire of the world and concentrate only on the lyric beauty he knows and
loves so well, invoking for his "paraclete" or comforter "the verbum per-
fectum: sinceritas" (74/427). This attitude is appealing—Pound seems gen-
uinely sorry—especially when we realize that Wondjina is a rain god capable of insuring fertility, plentiful crops, and health, and it does "rain"
later in this sequence. Yet beneath Pound's apparent contrition, there lies a
fundamental inability to understand why he remains so far and yet came so
close to realizing his life's ambition of epic success: "from the death cells in
sight of Mt. Taishan @ Pisa" (74/427). Although understandable enough,
Pound can only reaffirm his reverence for the same spirit of Hellenic *eros*
that, when obstructed by the world around him, incited him to the very
scurrility responsible for his present predicament. In this light, his emphasis
on Confucius' concept of *ch'êng* (the word made perfect)—"better gift can
no man make to a nation" (76/454)—becomes important indeed, but we
are still speaking of the candor of Lesbia's foot rather than of real repent-
ance. Moreover, part of such honesty involves seeing penitence, the poet

implies, as *fei ch'i kuei erh chi chih ch'an yeh* (sacrificing to a spirit not one's own, or sycophancy) (77/467); and part involves *tz'u ta* (saying exactly what one means) (79/486), even if this means *ch'êng* or invoking Zagreus (cf. canto II) to "bringest to focus" (77/475). Hellenically speaking, then, Pound's plea for the candor of *ch'êng* (words plus to perfect) centers on "the sun's lance coming to rest on the precise spot verbally," which with *hsien* (sun over silk plus the running eye: to manifest, to be illustrious) and *ming* (sun plus moon: bright, clear intelligent) he would associate with the medieval philosophers of light; Erigena ("omnia, quae sunt, lumina sunt") and Grosseteste ("lux enim [per se in omnem partem se ipsam diffundit]") (83/528). As early as 1934 Pound had associated the "plura diaphana" of light immanent in nature's "panta rhei" (83/529–30) with Cavalcanti's paean to *eros:* "Where memory liveth, / [love] takes its state / Formed like a diafan from light on shade / [that] shineth out / Himself his own effect unendingly" (36/177). Pound's essay on Cavalcanti appeared simultaneously in *Make It New* (1934), a slogan as title in whose ideogram for new (*hsin*) Pound spied the fascist axe,[30] all of which should give us pause as we appreciate "Snag" throughout the *Pisan Cantos* trying to recover like "noman" (*mo*) his *chung,* or pivot, or axis.

Besides employing personal memory in an effort to determine his fate, and Confucius in an effort to recover his sincerity, Pound also discovers nature and thus the romantic virtue of becoming an ignorant man again. In a world of earth, flowers, grass, a midge, ants, a spider, beetles, a cricket, a lizard, a wasp or two, a butterfly, birds, a cat, a dog, an ox, a swineherd-ress, "ego scriptor" himself, his tent, fellow prisoners, the guards, their towers, Mt. Pisa, the wind, and rain, and clouds, and sun, and moon, and stars, "knowledge" per se seems somewhat beside the point. More important, because the learned poet has been brought down to earth, to the "facts" of a real landscape Alexander (p. 195) would say, there enters a newer, fresher, more chastened, potentially visionary quality into his work. At times this new humility almost leads Pound to absolution, to an awareness through suffering of the charity that binds us all as brothers: as with Mr. Edwards of the Baluba mask, "doan you tell no one / I made you that table" (74/434), out of a medical corps crate no less. Rediscovering his Wordsworth the hard way—"For I have learned / To look on nature, not as in the hour / Of thoughtless youth; but hearing oftentimes / The still, sad music of humanity, / Nor harsh nor grating, though of ample power / To chasten and subdue"[31]—Pound at Pisa has the opportunity to uncover the revolutionary miracle of the commonplace that could indeed set him free by leading him to love (*agape*). The kind of innocent seeing, an almost child-like attention to detail, can be found in his reference to the mint that "springs up again / in spite of Jones' rodents / as had the clover by the gorilla cage / with a four-leaf" (83/533). Pound is very delicately suggesting his own resilience through images of the mint that smells all the sweeter when trod upon and the clover that is a lucky omen. His, "when the mind swings by a grass-blade / an ant's forefoot shall save you / the clover leaf smells and tastes as its flower" (83/533), just hints at Whitmanian transcendence, until we recall the associations between poetry and the centaur and the ant and Pound, whose attenuated music aesthetically implies a redemptive ritual of acquiring nature's vitality by sampling its flower.

The faintly Eleusinian scent of these seven lines has interrupted the poet's preoccupation, while dreaming of Arthur's heroism in Bracelonde (i.e., Broceliande), of the Pisanos' synthesis of myth and history on Perugia's Fontana Maggiore, of old Bulagio's cat that could easily escape with a "well timed leap," and of Mr. Walls (DTC) who "must be a ten-strike with the signorinas," with "Brother Wasp" who is himself "building a very neat house" (83/532). Suddenly, "in the warmth after chill sunrise / an infant, green as new grass" sticks its head out of "Madam La Vespa's bottle" (83/532,33) and Pound's preferred mode of escape, his Eleusinian rather than Wordsworthian use of nature, becomes clearer:

> The infant has descended,
>   from mud on the tent roof to Tellus,
>   like to like colour he goes amid grass-blades
>   greeting them that dwell under XTHONOS   XΘONOΣ
> OI XΘONIOI;   [to carry our news]
>   εις χθονιους   to them that dwell under the earth,]
> begotten of air, that shall sing in the bower,
>   of Kore,   Περσεφόνια
> and have speech with Tiresias, Thebae.
>   (83/533)

The modern poet of *nekuia* transforms the wasp's descent from tent roof to earth into a mythopoeic re-enactment of his own lifelong but maturely Odyssean (cf. cantos I and XLVII) quest for meaning (selfhood) from the spirits of the dead. In going "amid grass-blades / ... / ...to carry our news / ...to them that dwell under the earth, / begotten of air, that shall sing in the bower / of Kore,... / and have speech with Tiresias," Pound conceives an emblem of his own beginning and, doubtless as well, of his end.

But for the ultimate implications of Pound's Hellenic treatment of nature, we must return to the close of canto LXXXII, which concerns the poet's "mysterium" of Eleusis. Leon Surrette reads Pound's "connubium terrae" as a vision involving death-copulation between the poet as victim or couch-mate and the goddess *Gea Terra,* all of which is "Eleusinian in inspiration if not in detail" (p. 214). Surrette's curiously Christian preoccupation with hell and sex, however, besides distorting Eleusis into an explicitly chthonic cult, obscures Pound's own distinction here between death as *nekuia* (the figurative descent) and death as an end ("the loneliness of death"). Certainly, Kore can be associated with dread Persephone (*Odyssey,* XI), but it is Virgil (not Homer) who via fifth-century Athens and Hellenistic Alexandria locates the Elysian fields in the underworld (*Aeneid,* VI). Thus, Pound's interest in the rebirth, immortality, or paradise to be achieved through *nekuia* has concerned his poetic practice of deducing himself from the past, his epic ambition of proclaiming polity, and his ultimate hope of joining the seers of the past by being interrogated in the work of future poets — none of which are otherwordly concerns. Eleusis, for Pound, signifies a natural rite of agricultural, sexual, and above all aesthetic cultivation; it celebrates the evolution of life, not the eschatology of death.

The considerable impact of canto LXXXII, then, lies in its revelation of the humbled poet, remembering Swinburne, Yeats and Ford, and Whitman in an effort to resolve his own highly ambiguous end: "Terreus!" yields to "TERRA" and "Terrae," and then to "terror" (82/525–26). Pound identifies with Swinburne for his paganism, his passion for liberty, and his adherence to belief, despite the impending tragedy that clouded his career: "When the French fishermen hauled him out he / recited 'em / might have been Aeschylus / till they got into Le Portel, or whatever / in the original" (82/523). Pound next recalls Yeats and Ford, wistfully aware of how in his *Cantos* he had been trying to employ Ford's sense of the prose tradition (i.e., the novel, realism, and history) in an effort to move poetry beyond the lyric purity of Yeats and the symbolists:[32] "and for all that old Ford's conversation was better, / consisting in *res* non *verba,* / despite William's anecdotes, in that Fordie / never dented an idea for a phrase's sake / and had more humanitas" (82/525). Pound's use of "Jên," here, confirms the bias in his sense of *humanitas* as implying an aesthetic or static view of history rather than a moral or dynamic one, emphasizing Hellenic culture rather than Hebraic redemption through time. Pound remembers Whitman, in turn, recalling how a German instructor at the University of Pennsylvania had noted the good, grey poet's popularity in Europe but ignominy at home: "'Fvy! in Tdaenmarck efen dh' beasantz gnow him,' / meaning Whitman, exotic, still suspect / four miles from Camden" (85/526). With "Out of the Cradle," his beautiful parable about why the "he-bird" sings, Whitman presents his own version of death as the mother of beauty. Yet Pound's allusion to the end of the bird's aria — "'O troubled reflection / O Throat, O throbbing heart'" (82/526) — betrays his doubts about the method of *nekuia* while conducting one last mystery rite ("drunk with

ICHOR of CHTHONIOS"). Marriage with "GEA TERRA" was supposed to have brought "wisdom" — vegetative, sexual, and aesthetic renewal. As many commentators have pointed out, Pound hints at the paradise that was to have been and that he hopes still someday may be: "Where I lie let the thyme [time] rise / and basilicum [church] / let the herbs [city] rise in April abundant" (82/526). But under the circumstances Pound has difficulty preventing the "fluid CHTHONOS" from becoming simply his own "dakruon" (82/526-27), because death for him now ("at 3 P.M., for an instant") means an unnatural end to his quest for selfhood, epic success, and poetic immortality. The memory of Swinburne shouting Aeschylus has become an image of Agamemnon dead.

In examining the impact of history (i.e., contemporary events) on the *Pisan Cantos,* we should bear in mind how Pound's elegiac memory, his Confucian desire for sincerity, and his newfound awareness of nature have stirred our sympathy. This affective quotient is heightened further with the intrusion of real history, which in destroying Pound's dream of epic success encourages him to speak in his own voice, thereby seeming to unmask and help lead him to love. These cantos just brim with an emotionally wide range of personal remarks that restore a much needed credibility to the poetry: "in Tangier I saw...," "methenamine eases the urine," "I surrender neither...," "the two largest rackets are...," "they suddenly stand in my room here," "'Hey, Snag, wot are...,'" "as a lone ant... / ...ego scriptor," "say to La Cara:amo," "the Pisan clouds... / ...splendid... as any I have seen," "I heard it in the s.h.," "the donne intorno alla mia mente," "'ah certainly dew lak dawgs, / ah goin' tuh wash you' (no, not to the author," "Old Ez folded his blankets," "I wonder what...," "Whitman liked oysters / at least I think it was oysters," "put me down for...," "so that leaving America," "you cannot yet buy..., "je suis au bout de mes forces," "as I lay by the drain hole," "there came new subtlety...," "Swinburne my only miss," "it comes over me that...," "that day I wrote no further," "my lids," "oh let an old man rest," "my old great aunt," "out of all this beauty something must come." Thus, for once Pound seems to be conversing with, rather than lecturing at, us, and by now we have all been waiting to meet the wizard behind the machine at Oz. Paradoxically, even the caged panther's deep-throated snarls for fascism and against the allies seem almost acceptable in this personal context as the convictions of a Job, an Old Testament prophet, or even Christ ("with Barabbas and 2 thieves beside me"), being martyred for his steadfast belief, a rather beguiling paradigm for most Hebraic readers.

Pound makes his political sympathies immediately clear by hailing Mussolini as his "twice crucified" (i.e., first shot and then hanged upside down in Milan's Piazzale Loreto by the partisans) leader, a dubious Hellenic distinction wherein history complements myth: Dionysus himself was "DIGONOS" (74/425). Similarly, the poet closes the Pisan sequence with an even more troublesome farewell: "Xaire Alessandro / Xaire Fernando, e il Capo, / Pierre, Vidkun, / Henriot" (84/539). Pavolini and Mezzasoma were fellow fascists caught while fleeing with Mussolini, Laval, of course, was Premier of Vichy France, Quisling the Norwegian Nazi collaborator, and Henriot Petain's minister of propaganda; all had been summarily executed by war's end. In between Pound still tells time by the fascist calendar, numbers "H." and "M" among the few who "did anything of any interest," remembers Von Tirpitz's plea that il Duce "get rid of" his son-in-law Ciano, admires the style of Mussolini's *Program of Verona,* appreciates the Boss' willingness to consider his economic ideas, and after pondering the "jactancy, vanity, peculation to the ruin of 20 years' labour" (77/470) excuses "Benito" himself with, "the problem after any revolution is what to do with / your gunmen" (80/496). Pound repeatedly declaims against altering the value of money and usury, makes an anti-Semitic remark about Léon Blum (premier of France in 1936–37), and exhibits his animus for Churchill and Roosevelt. Moved by the charity of Army prisoners toward him, Pound notes that "petty larceny / in a regime based on grand larceny / might rank as conformity" (74/434). We glimpse Pound's Hellenic view of the allies ("hoi barbaroi") primarily through his characterization of the guard's often ironic vulgarity. Their view of their commanders: "all them g.d.m.f. generals c.s. all of 'em fascists"; of the D.T.C.: "the a.h. of the army" (74/436,37). One NCO in particular felt that "the Fuehrer had [not] started it / [but] that excess population / demanded slaughter at intervals" (76/457). After noting that "the army vocabulary contains almost 48 words" (78,471), that the "american army" (i.e., Medical Corps) uses the caduceus of "Mercury god of thieves" (77/471), and that the guard's opinion of the army "is lower than that of the prisoners" (80/514), Pound prophesies, "woe to them that conquer with armies / and whose only right is their power" (76/463), and reminds us from the *Ch'un Ch'iu* that "there / are / no / righteous / wars" (78/483). So much for Eisenhower's *Crusade in Europe.* As for distinctions in clarity, the poet leaves us with a Dantean interrogation of his daughter (Stock, *Life,* p. 524) in "neutral" Italian, wherein when asked to compare the Germans with the Americans she replies, "uguale" (84/540), which conversation fairly considered seems rather more self-serving than sincere.

Thus, besides shocking Pound into speaking in his own voice, history, because it puts the poet in clearer perspective, ironically reveals this voice as just another *persona,* or shadow ("Only shadows enter my tent"), or half-mask on the road to selfhood. Entangled like Arachne in his own ideogrammic web, Pound through his incarceration gains more distance on himself than he has had in years, and consequently these cantos are more comic (i.e., humorous, self-depreciatory, and charitable). But when he should have been celebrating the marriage of myth and history at the dawn of a new era, the poet finds himself instead repelled by events back into the past. Apropos of one seeking himself from the past, Pound in 1938 had asserted, "A man does not know his own ADDRESS (in time) until he knows where his time and milieu stand in relation to other times and conditions" (*GtK,* 93). In 1910 with uncannily prophetic irony he had said, "An epic cannot be written against the grain of its time: the prophet or the satirist may hold himself aloof from his time, or run counter to it, but the writer of epos must voice the general heart" (*SR,* 228). Besides the ruin of his epic ambition, Pisa proves how much Pound stands against his time, how much his "address" in time remains out of time (*achronos*), for the only marriage he can celebrate is the private, mythical one with his gods. While such a rite of "coetus" ironically sanctifies Pound's Ovidian power of mythopoeia, it also illuminates his lifelong "search for 'sincere self-expression'" (*GB,* 85) as a tragedy of truly heroic proportions: betraying his final inability to reconcile a candid adherence to Hellenism with an ever elusive sincerity born of *caritas,* a dignified psychic integrity, and genuine selfhood.

Just as the ideogram until Pisa has masked Pound's Hellenic approach to history, so it has tended to impersonalize his projections of the gods. Coerced into his own voice, however, the poet now defends his belief with new conviction, literalizing the gods as deities to whom candor compels he bear witness. Nor should we view Pound here as Job, insisting upon his righteousness before God; rather he is Ovid, reasserting his veneration of Aphrodite. As we might suspect, Pound again recalls Botticelli (especially his *Birth of Venus*) because he, too, in his painting sought to express the gods as viable spirits, and to enrich his understanding of Venus and her fellow Olympians through careful redaction from classical and contemporary texts, thus epitomizing the essence of the Renaissance itself. Pound's profound "coetus" of the returning gods, climaxing with the momentary trinity of garden ritual, ecstatic chant, and cognitive calm, ironically vindicates his youthful ambition to "write paradise" in the *Cantos,* a temporary triumph of Ovidian metamorphosis over Catullan loss. Indeed, the libretto, "magic moment," and chant of canto LXXXI demonstrate conclusively that Job has not cornered the market on integrity. Nevertheless, because the gods have always lacked historical (as opposed to poetic) significance ("which means that nothing will happen that will / be visible to the sargeants"), they also suggest the shortfall between Pound's *eros* and the *agape* needed for legitimate Virgilian synthesis. In his tent the humbled poet finds the courage to turn his satire on himself, then continues to love the past, but he never quite brings himself to love the world, wherein halfway is not always good enough.

Pound's invocation of the gods begins gradually, focusing on Aphrodite through Botticelli but also including other divinities, in preparation for both the lesser ritual and the greater chant. Thinking of the war's end, Pound recalls Micah's prophecy of Jerusalem's triumph when the warring nations shall beat their swords into ploughshares and every man shall sit under his fig tree or "walk each in the name of his god" (4:5); for himself Pound would honor Aphrodite by restoring her statute above the sea at Terracina, and recognize the goddess "by her manner of walking" as had Anchises in the Homeric Hymn (74/435). Nor would Pound as a type of blind Tiresias in hell forget Koré (74/442, 80/494). Soothed by the sea breeze of Coltano Pound considers how "this air brought her ashore a la marina / with the great shall borne on the seawaves / nautilis biancastra" and how his own Botticellian experience has been "By no means an orderly Dantescan rising" (74/443). Nevertheless, "'Spiritus veni' / adveni / not to a schema" (or Aquinas map) but a la Whitman and Eleusis "as grass under Zephyrus" (74/443–44). In this world "Time [*chronos*] is not, Time is the evil" and Venus as the morning star becomes "Brododaktylos" beloved of "the hours"; here the poet would "carve Achaia" in an *aubade* that ritually rivals Caesar: "Venere... / vento..., veni" (74/444). And of "the wind under Taishan / where the sea is remembered / out of hell," this "liquid" or clarity (with Catullan associations of limpidity and evanescence) ultimately becomes a neoplatonic property of the mind, "nec accidens est [sed] est agens." As Jonson said of Charis, "Hast 'ou seen the rose in the steel dust / (or swansdown ever?) / so light is the urging, so ordered the dark petals of iron" for the poet having "passed over Lethe" (74/449). After highlighting the recurrent birdsong of his poetry with a musical score from Arnaut, Jannequin and Da Milano, Gerhart Munch, and Olga Rudge, and after discerning Amphitryon's Alcmene, various hamadryads, Landor's Dirce, Malatesta's Ixotta, and Botticelli's Primavera "on the high cliff" of a cloud bank, Pound notes "that they suddenly stand in my room here" (76/452). Soon, in the re-creative world between mind and sea, Cythera (Cytheria) *potens,* Koré, and dread Delia appear: "the sphere moving crystal, fluid, / none therein carrying rancour / Death, insanity / suicide degeneration"; and so, too, appear "ferae familiares / ...with fawn, with panther" (76/457). While his landscape is "of Dione," the poet carefully reminds us: "nor is this yet *atasal* / nor are here souls, nec personae / neither here in hypostasis" (76/458). Still Pound himself feels the imminence of the moment: "spiriti questi? personae? / tangibility by no means *atasal* / but the crystal can be weighed in the hand / formal and passing within the sphere: Thetis, / [Maia, Aphrodite]" (76/459). The seer also sleeps next to Demeter "copulatrix" (77/470) and beseeches Zagreus to "bringest to focus" (77/475); but after pondering the inefficacy of Botticelli's marriage chests, the futility of Tami Koumé's career aspirations since he died prematurely "in that earthquake" (*L*, 282), the incompleteness of Sigismundo's Tempio bas reliefs, the "great Ovid / bound in thick boards,"[33] and his own Odyssean "care in contriving," Pound tearfully testifies that Aphrodite while "richly enthroned" and "immortal" can also be "saeva" (76/462). Nor should we forget that in asserting through Baudelaire "Le Paradis n'est pas artificiel," the poet humbly concedes his own lack of charity, "J'ai en pitié des autres / probablement pas assez, and at moments that suited my own convenience" (76/460); yet he continues through Lope de Vega to insist upon the selfishness of *eros:* "No hay amor sin celos / sin segreto no hay amor" (78/483).

Having appealed to Athena, who sprung from the head of Zeus as goddess of sophistication, intelligence, and self-possession, to "sustain me" (78/479), and then noted humorously that Odysseus' protectress "cd / have done with more sex appeal" (79/486), Pound proceeds with the "lynx song" (Emery, *Ideas, pp. 145*–47) of his garden ritual in canto LXXIX. Not unlike Acoetes (canto II) the poet commands the compound cat, his "lovely lynx," to guard his wine pot "till the god come into this whiskey" (79/488). Surprised to have invoked "Khardas, god of camels," and recalling Circe's injunction to Odysseus, "'Prepare to go on a journey'" (see cantos XXXIX and XLVII), Pound can only paraphrase Confucius: "How is it far if you think of it?" (79/488). At sunrise the poet requests his lynx to "wake Silenus and Casey," to "shake the castagnettes of the bassarids" on the "hill of the Maelids" in the "garden of Venus," to "set wreathes on Priapus," Iacchus, and Cythera, "Io!", and to "keep watch on my fire" that is the fire of tradition (79/488–89). After again hailing Iacchus with the cry of Roland courageous in defeat, "AOI," Pound breaks into a continuous, insistent, ritualistic invocation of his paradisal garden of the gods (79/490–92). The grain of Pound's rite is the pomegranate (melagrana), which Koré was punished for eating in the underworld, and which he must eat beneath the sun and moon. Here the fruit symbolizes the orchard or grove of his *Cantos,* inhabited by the returning gods, that the lynx must guard against Demeter's furrow, or death.

> This fruit has a fire within it,
>   Pomona, Pomona
> No glass is clearer than are the globes of this flame
> what sea is clearer than the pomegranate body
>   holding the flame?
>   (79/490)

Besides the "sphere moving crystal" of canto LXXIX, we are reminded of the eucharist of canto XXXIX, as well as of the "unconquered flame" of canto LXXXI, for to eat of its seed is to partake of its fire, which is to revere the gods, including the attendant deities of this canto, as an Ovidian *vates.* Pound's grove is not without evil, in the form of "clicking crotales," Circean "acorns," and "thorn leaves," which merely reaffirm its "reality." But now that "the Graces have brought ᾿Αφροδίτην" (79/491), the seer can end his song by petitioning the "Goddess...born of sea-foam," whose metaphysical dominion over Koré (hell), Delia (earth), and Maia (heaven) encourages our consent that "aram nemus vult" (79/492).

The interlude between Pound's garden ritual and his ecstatic chant properly prepares us for receiving the supreme climax of the *Cantos,* and probably of the poet's career. A bittersweet triumph, or anticlimax, it is. Having directed our attention through Frazer to Nemi with "the huntress in broken plaster keeps watch no longer" (76/453), the *rex* of the grove underscores how much his epic integrity has been at stake by asking, "who will have the succession?" (80/495). Pound's comforter is less the Holy Spirit of Saint John (14:16), for receiving which we are to obey His commandments (14:16), including that of loving one another (13:34), than she who "At Ephesus...had compassion on silversmiths / revealing the paraclete / standing in the cusp / of the moon" (80/500–01). Thus far "Cythera egoista" has been less sympathetic to the plight of "Actaeon of the eternal moods," whose modern renaissance that was to have begun "in Fano Caesaris" (see canto XXX) appears to have faltered from insufficient "wan," "caritas," and "CHARITES" (80/501). The poet himself queries of the morning star riding above the crescent moon "Cythera, in the moon's barge whither?" (80/510), but characteristically he is inclined to blame others. "Les hommes" in general, and often artists in particular, fear beauty (Venus). As Beardsley knew, "Beauty is difficult," and so he copped out because he "knew he was dying and had to make his hit quickly" (80/511). Challenged, instead, by Yeats' more heroic example, Pound cannot give up, and in quoting from Symons' "Modern Beauty" (1899)—"'I am the torch' wrote Arthur 'she saith'" (80/511)—he indicates his willingness to step forth as "the moth that still dares die."[34] Paradoxically, of course, his Hellenic persistence will be rewarded with a confirmation of "all that Sandro knew, and Jacopo" (80/511) who "knew out the secret ways of love" (*Per,* 73); that is, with an audience before "Cythera deina" of the "pale eyes as if without fire" (80/511). Apropos of Ovid and Marlowe, the magic moment comes at dawn "before sunrise," while "Zeus lies in Ceres' bosom / Taishan is attended of loves," and the poet has recalled Padre Elizondo's remark delivered *voce tinnula* that "'Hay aqui mucho catolicismo—(sounded / catolithismo) / y muy poco reliHion'" (81/517).

Canto LXXXI, the poet's ecstatic chant, presents the quintessential Poundian dichotomy between the ideal past and the real present, here expressed as an antithesis between freedom and imprisonment. Underlying the canto, which divides conveniently at the libretto (history versus lyric reprise, magic moment, and chant), are the verse from Ecclesiastes, "Remember thy creator in the days of your youth" (12:1) and the notion that all worldly endeavor, including the poet's own lifelong epic ambitions, is vanity. Surveying the error, or in his view the wreckage, of his ways, Pound would return to basics; Aphrodite (at least the spirit of divinity) appears less in celebration than in sorrow. While hypostasis implies no public vindication of righteousness, redemption of integrity or selfhood, or final gesture toward synthesis or love (*agape*), Pound's self-satire and his vulnerable retreat from proclaiming epic to singing lyric success allow this supreme swan song to *eros* its tragically pathetic appeal. Emphasizing what has been his Hellenic or atemporal orientation all along, Pound opens like Ovid (*Am.* 1.13) with a mythological "dawn song" wherein Zeus (heaven) lies in Ceres' (earth's) arms with Cythera (love) reigning "before sunrise" (81/517). Lest we miss Pound's focus, through Elizondo he stresses that his topic will be "religion" rather than "Catholicism," and also that "Kings will. . .disappear" (81/517). The good father was thinking of Spain and the monarchies of Europe, but Pound is pondering his own *heroic* struggle against the *demos* that began "in 1906" (Catullus as lyric mask), progressed through "1917" (Propertius as dramatic mask), and has continued into 1945 (Ovid as epic mask).

As usual history for Pound signifies war between the forces of Eleusis and "the world," and from the sound (music) of this canto—its initial sibilants, the speech of Elizondo, Santayana, and Mussolini, the prosody of the libretto, and the *leggier mormorio* of its magic moment, all reminiscent of the "sound slender, quasi tinnula" in canto XX and the "voce tinnula" in canto III that becomes the *ventus* of Venus at Pisa and the "wind" of "paradise" in canto CXX—Eleusis as only in an aesthetic recreation of life is going to "win," Pyrrhicly at least. Dolores ("grief") had advised that young Pound eat his bread, and Sargeant had painted her before he "descended" to thumb sketches of Velazquez, whom Pound considered ignorant of Botticelli's Renaissance knowledge. In those days "books" and the "brass candlesticks" to read them by were affordable. "Later" C. G. Bowers, the American ambassador to Spain (1933–1939) noted that the communists so hated Franco that they would actually support him the better to create political and social turmoil. Moreover, as not in 1945, in Alcazar de San Juan (ca. 1906) the young poet of the past was told to "go back" from whence he came "to eat" (81/517), but even then he should have taken more to heart the "goat bells," the hostess' unchaste remark, "Eso es luto, *haw*! / mi marido es muerto," and the "black border half an inch or more deep" around the paper she gave him to write on (81/ 517–18). Cabranez' "egg broke. . . / thus making history," indeed (81/518). Of his time Bunting could remark, "they beat drums for three days / till all the drumheads were busted / (simple village fiesta)," while Eliot could observe that "the local portagoose folkdance / was danced. . . / in political welcome" (81/518). And more pessimistically yet, the French-Zionist poet, André Spire, speaking of the nepotism within the government's Agricultural Bank: "'You will find. . . / that every man on that board (Crédit Agricole) / has a brother-in-law" (81/518). Jefferson may have feared "the one," but John Adams feared "the few," and Pound in his sphere the tyranny of "the pentameter" (81/518). Joseph Bard, the English essayist (b. 1892), could characterize human antagonism as if it were "baker and concierge visibly" or "La Rouchefoucauld and de Maintenon audibly"; Pound mindful of Mencken's own iconoclasm toward Americans recalls the earthiness of Malatesta's ongoing feud with Urbino (see canto X), "'Te cavero le budella' / 'La corata a te'" (81/518). Eleusis can almost be reduced to the maxim, "'some cook, some do not cook,'" and the poet would agree with Theocritus' maiden, seeking to charm her faithless lover into returning (81/518). "What counts" is how culture arises from agriculture, i.e., Benim's "table ex packing box" that will "'get you offn th' groun'" (81/518–19). Santayana, who could write of idealism and the German mind, kept off Boston's "shoddy / . . .quais" with "high buggy wheels," and womanizing Mussolini employed "grief" as "a full act / repeated for each new condoleress / working up to a climax" (81/519). G. H. Lorimer, editor of the *Saturday Evening Post,* helped "'get Beveridge'" for the Senator's anti-Hamiltonian opposition to private banking, by "assailin' him at lunch breakfast an' dinner," but "my ole man went on hoein' corn" (81/ 519). So Pound's *vers libre* springs by association, espousing Eleusis against his time, not unlike the "vacant lot" George Horace crossed, "where you'd occasionally see a wild rabbit / or mebbe only a loose one" (81/ 519). "AOI!" cries the undefeated but doomed knight, aware that his love song is but "a leaf in the current," and assuming prematurely "at my grates no Althea" (81/519).

The "grace quasi imperceptible" (81/519) of recent Eleusinian history promptly resolves itself into song with the libretto, the text of an opera (*opus*) or other dramatic musical work (the Italian diminutive of *libro,* from the Latin, *liber:* the inner bark of a tree, the old Italian agricultural diety associated with Bacchus, and free as in verse or spirit, if not in body). The core of Pound's reprise concerns not only the Renaissance musicians Lawes, Jenkins, and Dowland (all capable of adding song to speech) and the modern instrument maker Dolmetsch (Pound's "god Pan"), but also such Renaissance lyricists as Richard Lovelace ("When I lie tangled in her hair / and fettered to her eye, / The gods that wanton in the air / know no such liberty."), Ben Jonson ("Do but look on her eyes; they do light / All that Love's world compriseth!"), and Edmund Waller ("Bid her come forth, / Suffer herself to be desired, / and not blush so to be admired.").[35] Pound's allusions to Lovelace, then Jonson, then Waller suggest that in order to achieve his moment of ecstacy he must characteristically *go back* in time: "To Althea, from Prison" he deals with here in canto LXXXI (1949), "The Triumph of Charis" he dealt with first in canto XLVII (1937), and "Go, Lovely Rose" he had dealt with in the "Envoi" of *Mauberley* (1919). The poet "descends" not only personally, but also in terms of literary history. In returning from Althea (the "healer"), Charis (one of the Graces), and Waller's Rose to the beginning of Chaucer's triple rondel to "Merciles Beaute" ("Your eyen two wol sleye me sodenly / I may the beauté of hem not susteyne"), Pound describes his Shakespearean dedication to the Hellenic tradition of lyric love poetry: "And for 180 years almost nothing," until the magic moment transforms "This thou perceiv'st, which makes thy love more strong, / To love that well which thou must leave ere long" (11. 13-14, Sonnet 73) into "What thou lovest well remains..." (81/520). In imitating Renaissance song and dance measures, Pound's text is replete with ascending iambic and anapestic rhythms, with a syncopated first foot in the lines of his refrain, and a somewhat various rhyme scheme. As if anticipating the dramatic climax to come, Aphrodite arises "Born upon a zephyr's shoulder" through the "aureate" or sunrise "sky" (81/519); she inquires whether the poet ("he") has "tempered" his instrument in order "to enforce both the grave and the acute" accents of his verse (81/520), a matter of "curving" the "bowl of the lute" or annealment through "luto"; and then she puts the Eleusinian question so as punningly to answer itself: "Hast 'ou fashioned so airy [manner, melody] a mood / To draw up leaf [poetry] from the root [tradition]?" (81/520). Thus "airy" alone refines so much: "air," "wind," "breath" (*aer*); "appearance," "place of origin," "threshing floor" (*area*); and "aria" (*aera*). Or again the goddess inquires of the "cloud so light [bright]" it seems "neither mist nor shade," which soon becomes the numinous aura so illuminating it casts "shade beyond other lights" (81/520). Finally, this catechistic progression from "I" to "he" to "thou" harmonizes into "Then resolve me, tell me aright / If Waller sang or Dowland played" (81/520), which may be translated, "Since Waller sang and Dowland played, hypostatize me by recounting a rite." So the poet narrates his union with divinity; here at last *in coetu inluminatio*.

The magic moment of canto LXXXI constitutes the emotional and intellectual climax of the *Cantos*. And in what must be a most telling metaphor for the poet of Latin masks ever in search of himself, Pound describes the presence of Cytherian divinity as eyes suddenly unmasked.

> Ed ascoltando al leggier mormorio
>   there came new subtlety of eyes into my tent,
> whether of spirit or hypostasis,
>   but what the blindfold hides
> or at carneval
>   nor any pair showed anger
>   Saw but the eyes and stance between the eyes,
> colour, diastasis,
>   careless or unaware it had not the
>   whole tent's room
> nor was place for the full ειδως
> interpass, penetrate
>   casting but shade beyond the other lights
>   sky's clear
>   night's sea
>   green of the mountain pool
>   shone from the unmasked eyes in half-mask's space.
>   (81/520)

We begin by "listening to the light murmur" (an imitative root itself miming the heartbeat of divinity) of Venus' wind in Pound's own (*not* Dante's) Italian. "Subtlety of eyes" arises not only from the libretto's emphasis on seeing, but also from earlier passages like, "I have seen what I have seen" (2/9), "with the Goddess' eyes to seaward" and "Can you see but their eyes in the dark" (39/195), and previews later ones like, "from a fine old eye" (81/522), and the Yeatsian "proide ov his oy-ee" and Horatian "aere [I Ray] perennius" (83/534), as well as "the eyes, this time my world" (83/535). For the nonce their "subtlety" is "new," with implications of "thin" and "fine" as in "under a web" (*sub tela*) or masks ("I'''s). "Spirit" (breath, breeze) evokes the earlier "Spiritus veni"..."Venere... / vento...veni" (74/444) and "hypostasis" the earlier "not...yet *atasal*" or "hypostasis" (76/458). "Hypostasis" ("hypo" [under] plus "histanai" [cause to stand, as in "stasis" or standing]) implies a kind of Plotinan tertiary encounter between the soul and an individual, where Cytherian divinity descends into the poet's tent. "What the blindfold hides / or at carneval" suggests an unmasked presence, but "carneval" ("carne" [flesh] plus "levare" [to raise or lift up]) also suggests that this will be an enlightening or uplifting experience for Pound. Moreover, the poet is humble before the forgiving presence of divinity: "nor any pair showed anger." Seeing "but the eyes and stance between the eyes" figuratively measures Pound's new humility, wherein he can contemplate not only the masks of his career (Catullus, Propertius, Ovid), but also the shortfall or distance between the lyric success he celebrates here and the truly epic success he had hoped to celebrate. "Colour" suggests "light" of this world, and "diastasis" ("dia" [apart] plus "histanai" again) much more than just the dilation of and separation between "eyes." "Diastasis" also involves the last stage of diastole in the heart, the rest phase occurring prior to contraction wherein the ventricles fill with blood. Here one cannot help but consider Pound's live or blood tradition, as when Tiresias informs Odysseus that whoever he allows to approach the blood-filled fosse will speak to him without error (*Ody.,* XI. 146–49). Diastasis as diastole further implies the figure from Greek and Latin prosody, whereby a normally short syllable is lengthened.

Now we can appreciate the break between "carneval" and "nor" in Pound's verse, which is *free* of the metronomic rhythms of traditional English verse, and which continuously metamorphoses itself syntactically in one long sentence, in its effort to preserve or prolong the good moment wherein divinity appears, i.e., wherein the poet gains *new* distance on himself. We are talking here not just of "hypo-" or "dia-" but of *ex-* (out-) *stasis,* where Pound does what he has been trying to do all his life and does it better than he has done before or will do again, where he stands outside himself and looks back (of course) on himself with a sense of near complete integrity. More important, this lovingly extended Hellenic moment has very little to do, finally, with apocalyptic notions of vision, or mental action, or process,[36] and thus it sets the poet *apart,* as well, from the predominantly romantic aesthetics of his and our time (ΑΧΡΟΝΟΣ). Indeed, the very aposteriori (or post-lapserian) unconcern that constitutes his greatest vice, Pound would transform into divinity's most majestic virtue: "careless or unaware it had not the / whole tent's room / nor was place for the full ειδως" This word has often enough been interpreted to signify vision, but it means "knowing" (as in "sailing after knowledge") or "seeing" in the perfective sense of "having seen" ("I have seen what I have seen" and the *deiknymena* of Eleusis). In addition, the poet concedes that his tent is not the place for the "full knowing," which is the knowledge Odysseus sought when in seeking to go home (i.e., find himself) he first had to return into the past (i.e., descend into the underworld and query the dead), the knowledge of seeking to know one's self implicit in rooted olive trees, the rooted marriage bed, and the rooted poet of oral or formulaic tradition. Thus, in conceding his having erred, Pound will not forsake the essential rightness of his Hellenic position, expressed through the erotic injunctions "interpass" and "penetrate" to a light so bright that it projects shadows beyond lesser lights. Such illumination emanates from Pound's poetry itself, resulting from the coetus or gathering together of shades from the dead, and hence Pound becomes the "light" capable of "casting but shade beyond other lights [poets]." His brightness (*candor*) or wisdom (knowledge), then, is ethically, if not theologically, important because it offers not an otherworldly enlightening but one defined exclusively, humanistically, in terms of this world: "Sky's clear / night's sea / green of the mountain pool / shone from the unmasked eyes."[37] One might only add that since the world has interrupted Pound's epic search for self, thus determining this highly aesthetic confession of "wrong without losing rightness," his ecstatic projection of emotion as if it were divinity yet occurs in the "half-mask's space." Foiled just short of achieving selfhood, the poet understandably "cannot make it [charity] flow through" (116/797).

Triggered by his psychic encounter with divinity, the lyric-satiric chant that closes canto LXXXI measures both how far Pound has come and how far he has to go toward love (*agape*). These lines even share something of the plain style insistence of Pound's other great but earlier antiwar poems in *Mauberley:* "What thou lovest well..." recurs five times, then yields to "pull down...," which recurs ten times, then yields to the final sequence of "to have..." (three times), "this is not..." (twice), and "here error..." (once). Perhaps the key to this chant, apart from its tripartite, lyric-satiric-lyric pattern, lies with its pronouns, which suggest that from a higher, more mature, and almost integrated perspective the poet can lecture himself about the value of Hellenic tradition and about his own vanity, although he never does reach out in love to others. "What thou [the poet] lovest well," which "remains" and "shall not be reft from thee [the poet]" and "is thy [the poet's] true heritage" (81/520–21), signifies the Hellenic tradition of Eleusis and Aphrodite (*eros*) that Pound as Ovid has been struggling to celebrate in epic but that certainly persists in lyric poetry. We are pointedly informed, by contrast, that "the rest is dross" (81/521). The one question of the entire self-confident chant, "Whose world, or mine or theirs / or is it of none?" (81/521), occurs in this first lyric section. Besides prefiguring the poet's later disorientation ("That I lost my center / fighting the world"), the question contrasts past ideality ("mine") with present reality ("theirs"), even suggesting that the allies have prevented the poet from realizing his dream ("none"), but significantly it offers nothing about sharing or compromise ("ours"). "First came the seen, then thus the palpable / Elysium, though it were in the halls of hell" (81/521) implies the tangibility of this canto's hypostasis, Venus precipitating to the bottom, as it were, but also Pound's Ovidian ambition to surpass Virgil by locating paradise on earth rather than in the Elysian fields of the underworld. As matters stand, of course, the poet's blueprint for polity remains an idea only (not unlike Plato's Republic) presumably to be realized later by his followers.

The most interesting section of this chant, however, is the middle, satiric one wherein the poet at odds with the non-Hellenic world turns, for once, his invective in the tradition of Ecclesiastes on himself. Pound becomes the ant mythopoeically conceiving of himself as "a centaur in his dragon world" (81/521); nor was it "man" (neither Job nor Odysseus) who "made courage, or made order, or made grace" (81/521). As he has done at Pisa through his new awareness of nature, the poet lessons himself to "Learn of the green world what can be [his] place / In scaled invention or true artistry" (81/521); Pound as Paquin would become unaccommodated man again, aware that the "green casque has outdone [his] elegance" (81/521). To learn from nature suggests the poet has been sufficiently humbled through his suffering to identify with the "beaten dog" and the "swollen magpie"; sounding like Confucius but, in fact, paraphrasing Chaucer (1. 6 from "Truth"), the poet must learn to "'Master thyself, then others shall thee beare'" (81/521). Life's business of mastering one's self, ironically, is easier said (or quoted) than done, and here lies the disadvantage of the classical approach, as the poet well knows, or has discovered the hard way. Nevertheless, he has traveled far enough to excoriate his "hates / fostered in falsity," and his inclination to be "Rathe to destroy" and "niggard in charity" (81/521). Hence, without perceiving how much his kind of love has been itself his limitation, he at least can lesson himself: "Pull down thy vanity, / I say pull down" (81/521).

We know the wounded poet has not bridged the gap between *eros* and *agape* because at this crucial juncture where intellectually and emotionally he could (should) reach out to the opposition (i.e., to the rest of us who live in the world of dross and would reft what the poet loves from him), Pound instead reverts out of habit rather than imagination into the past. In this final lyric section of the chant, "to have done instead of not doing" and "To have, with decency, knocked" that the anti-imperialist, pro-Islamist, minor Victorian poet W. S. Blunt,[38] whom Pound visited with Yeats and other aspiring "Rhymers" on January 18, 1914, "should open" is assuredly "not vanity" (81/521–22), but neither is it the hoped for (if not expected) synthesis with Hebraism that has failed to develop dialectically from the antithetical self-satiric section. "To have gathered from the air a live tradition or from a fine old eye the unconquered flame" (81/522) reminds us especially of the Ovidian metamorphosis of Aphrodite or of the Hellenic poet himself who has *eaten* the flame. But who, finally, is to say? Perhaps in celebrating his greatest classical virtue, Pound, too, with supreme irony confesses to the lack of charity that has become his greatest romantic vice: "Here error is all in the not done, / all in the diffidence that faltered..." (81/522). Ah, such a wink this were!

After the ritual of canto LXXIX and the ecstatic chant of canto LXXXI, Pound in canto LXXXIII achieves a cognitive calm of sorts. We must remember, however, that Pisa has interrupted the poet's epic designs, and so makes impossible the kind of complete integrity or selfhood he had been seeking through his Latin masks. Marred by his own past folly,

Pound's peace of mind in this canto is, nevertheless, remarkable for the Hellenic self-confidence it helps him project. The day began with a hard rain, which has left the sun to filter through clouds and mist: thus the opening prayer to "HUDOR et Pax" (83/528). The contemplation of water and light prompts Pound to recall his favorite neoplatonists: first Gemistho who "stemmed all from Neptune / hence the Rimini bas reliefs" (83/528), where Duccio carved Plethon's gods amid the water imagery of Sigismundo's Tempio; then Robert de Grosseteste, for whom "lux" by its very nature diffuses itself and for whom "ignis est accidens" of light (83/528); and then Scottus Erigena, praised by Migne for his "*hilaritas,*" who was "in fact an excellent poet," and who claimed that "omnia, quae sunt, lumina sunt," for which heresy Pound liked to believe "they dug up his bones in the time of De Montfort" (83/528). Perceiving the emanations of light from the *nous* immanent in the scene before him, Pound has difficulty accepting the approach of romantic Yeats who "paused to admire the symbol / with Notre Dame standing inside it" (83/528). By contrast, Odyssean Pound would admire Pietro and Tullio Lombardo's sirens within Venice's Santa Maria Dei Miracoli, carved as no one has been able to carve them since (83/529, 76/460). The poet also complements his neoplatonic appreciation of Pisa after rain by recalling the ethics Confucius derived from water: "the sage / delighteth in water / the humane man has amity with the hills" and "as he was standing below the altars / of the spirits of rain / 'when every hollow is full / it [water] moves forward'" (83/529–30). Although identifying with the ants who "seem to stagger / as the dawn sun has trapped their shadows" (*hilaritas*), Pound serenely appreciates how divine light transmits itself through the "plura diafana," he beholds "the brightness of '*udor,*'" and moralizes that "this breath [mist] wholly covers the mountains / it shines and divides / it nourishes by its rectitude / does no injury / overstanding the earth it fills the nine fields / to heaven," further testifying that "Boon companion to equity / it joins with the process" inherent in nature (83/530–31).

However, though "in the drenched tent there is quiet / sered eyes are at rest" (83/529), all is not well as Pound gazes outside at the grass of the DTC, pondering the ruin of his epic ambitions. With "as the grass grows by the weirs" (83/529), he recalls Yeats' "Down By the Salley Gardens": "She bid me take life easy, as the grass grows on the weirs; / But I was young and foolish, and now am full of tears."[39] "Consiros" parenthetically invokes Daniel (i.e., Pound as *il miglior fabbro*) in Purgatory: "Contritely I see my past folly."[40] "The grass on the roof of St. What's his name / near 'Cane e Gatto'" reminds Pound of the line from a German art song about love, "soll deine Liebe sein" (83/529), and then the Sienese Polio (horse-races), an ironic trope for European nationalism before World War II.

Perhaps the poet's daughter, Maria, having come to comfort her father, becomes the "Dryas" whose "eyes are like the clouds over Taishan / when some of the rain has fallen / and half remains yet to fall" (83/530). But her presence avails little, for "in the caged panther's eyes: 'Nothing. Nothing that you can do...'" (83/530). We are reminded: "Nor can who has passed a month in the death cells / believe in capital punishment / No man who has passed a month in the death cells / believes in cages for beasts" (83/530). And that despite the vital breath of the mist shrouding the landscape before him, still "the stockade posts stand" (83/531). Hence the purgative rain of Gemisto and Confucius metamorphoses into the "DAKRUŌN" of Pound, wondering if he will ever see Venice again (83/532).

But, then, amazingly enough, bursting through the sheaves of his neoplatonism and his Confucianism, and watered by the tears of his grief, Pound's Hellenic confidence in Eleusis and Aphrodite proudly reasserts itself. As the poet himself says, "When the equities are gathered together / as birds alighting / it springeth up vital" and "If deeds be not ensheaved and garnered in the heart / there is inanition" (83/531). The Hellenic animus of Pound's heart, his dream of polity through poetry, is previewed by this canto's earlier lines, "The roots go down to the river's edge / and the hidden city moves upward / white ivory under the bark," which echo his former desire to re-create a Venice of Venus in canto XVII, if not his youthful desire to become himself "The Tree." Here he jests "simply" (*hilaritas*): "(have I perchance a debt to a man named Clower)" (83/531). George Kearns (following Jowett) astutely perceives Pound's allusion to Socrates, but fails to pursue the implication of Pound's remark.[41] Socrates, we recall, had spent the last day of his life discussing with Phaedo and others various "proofs" of the soul's immortality. Socrates finally suggests that the soul is immortal because it perceives truth, goodness, and beauty, which are eternal; that man can know God because he has in him something similar to the eternal that cannot die. He then cautions his audience that this description is only an approximation of the truth, drinks the poison, and suggests to Crito he ought to offer a cock to the divine healer, Asclepius. Thus, Socrates' last words show better than all the arguments what he believed, for as was the Greek custom on recovering from an illness, his offering indicates that to himself he was not dying but entering into life more abundantly. Now Clower (Clowes) was the man who censored but printed *Lustra* (1916), Pound's most Catullan volume, which in effect represents the beginning of his lifelong pursuit of selfhood through his Latin masks. Bearing in mind that "death" has always been "life" for Pound, we might also recall that Koré's bird is the peacock, and note that Pound's anecdote about Yeats (whose anecdotes Pound always valued) composing "The Peacock" is imminent.

Pound, in short, enshrining and garnering his Hellenic achievement in his heart, would "eat of the barley corn / and move with the seed's breath"; he would emerge from this rainy day like the "sun as a golden eye / between dark cloud and the mountain"; and, contrary to old Giovanna's advice ("non combattere"), would persist to the end. For he like "Brother Wasp" with his poetry "is building a very neat house" (83/532), and like "the infant" he "has descended" repeatedly into "the bower / of Kore" to "have speech with Tiresias, Thebae" (83/533). In this sense, "fatigue deep as the grave" offers some consolation to Pound, who knows that the "kakemono" of his *Cantos* "grows in flat land out of mist" and who witnesses how the "sun" of his verse "rises lopsided over the mountain" (83/533). Garnering Hellenism in his heart excites Pound to recall "the noise in the chimney":

> as it were the wind in the chimney
>   but was in reality Uncle William
> downstairs composing
> that had made a great Peeeeacock
>   in the proide ov his oiye
>   had made a great peeeeeeecock in the...
> made a great peacock
>   in the proide of his oyyee
>
> proide ov his oy-ee
> as indeed he had, and perdurable
>
> a great peacock aere perennius.
>   (83/533-34)

Aside from the hilarity of this anecdote about a very great poet, how like the poet of *personae* to seize upon a minor poem of someone else to make a major statement about himself. For through Yeats ("What's riches to him / That has made a great peacock / With the pride of his eye?"),[42] the poetry of Pound's Latin masks has become a "great peacock" that he would offer as his gift to Persephone. The repetition of "oiye...oyyee... oy-ee" makes one aware of Pound's established and punning preoccupation with "eyes" ("I"'s), but the snipet "aere perennius" from Horace who composed a monument more lasting than bronze (*Od.* 3.30) confirms as we shall soon see in more detail Pound's belief that "I Ray" shall live on forever through his poetry, itself composed in the best imitative, classical, and Hellenic tradition as seeds from the past that will themselves sprout in subsequent verse, thereby triumphing over time and death. Such is the metamorphic process of life (agricultural, sexual, and aesthetic) that Pound would celebrate in his verse. So much for "the advice to the young man to / breed and get married (or not) / as you choose to regard it" (83/534).

Of this same winter with Yeats at Stone Cottage, Coleman's Hatch, Sussex, in 1914, Pound jokes that the Irishman insisted on "reading nearly all Wordsworth / for the sake of his conscience" but preferred the German "Ennemosor on Witches" (83/534). Nor does "conscience" or the Hebraic notions of a fall into and redemption through time (history) have much to do with Pound's own Ovidian, mythopoeic, and Hellenic sense of epic: "did we ever get to the end of Doughty: / The Dawn in Britain? / perhaps not / Summons withdrawn, sir.) / (bein' aliens in prohibited area)" (83/534). Such ironic recollection is not funny, only because Pisa has made it so sad.

Yet cognitive calm allows not for sadness, and so the poet's outburst of Hellenic self-confidence leaves us with a view of his incomplete self, or the "unmasked eyes" of canto LXXXI, restored behind his "half-mask's" visage:

> A fat moon rises lop-sided over the mountain
> The eyes, this time my world,
> > But pass and look *from* mine
> > > between my lids
> > > > sea, sky, and pool
> > > > alternate
> > > > pool, sky, sea....
> > > (83/535)

If the war (time) has made the "sun" of Pound's verse that includes history "lop-sided," so, too, it has made the moon that bore Aphrodite to him at dawn in canto LXXXI both "fat" and "lop-sided." Here the after-image of that encounter reveals that now the speaker's own eyes reflect the landscape that signifies the "full knowing." The image, however, suggests not beatific eyes that shine like a lamp, or even the union of self and nonself, as Pearlman (pp. 289–90) has argued, but rather eyes that simply mirror the scene before them. The divinity of canto LXXXI has been re-internalized, where it was all along prior to projection as Aphrodite. More important, peering into the poet's eyes ("I"'s) we are screened yet again from his innermost self by elements of the earthly world of *eros,* out of which, of course, he has habitually made his poetic self. This static state of present repose by a poet of the past perennially seeking his future identity Pound characterizes again in terms of the Ovidian *aubade:* "morning moon [the ideal] against sunrise [the real] / like a bit of the best antient greek coinage" (83/535). Such a frontal view that is ever the view in profile Eleusinian Pound would recommend as the coin of his realm. Maria (or someone else) tells the poet in German that the ladies think him an old man; the Greek lyric poet Anacreon, known for not taking himself or others too seriously, is said to have choked in old age on a grape-pip (83/535). Pound himself "learned in the Tirol" that a "Madonna novecento / cd / be as a Madonna quattrocento," and would compare the German he once heard in Bolzano to how "in my mother's time it was respectable, / ... / to sit in the Senate gallery / ... / to hear the fireworks of the senators" (83/535–36). For himself he heard the debate "in Westminster... / and a very poor show" it was; "but if Senator Edwards cd/ speak / and hope his tropes stay in the memory 40 years, 60 years" (83/536), perhaps the *ignis qui est accidens lucis* could occur again. "In short / the descent" (whether Pound's poetic technique or the West's Spenglerian decline) "has not been of advantage either / to the Senate... / or to the people," for "the States have passed thru a / damn'd supercilious era" (83/536). Yet, "Down, Derry-down / oh let an old man rest" (83/536), also confirms the vanity of always using "down" to achieve one's "rest."

In his provocative theorizing about Pound's epic intentions, Michael Bernstein unmasks the inherent contradiction of Pound's poetic program to discover himself from the past—what Bernstein (p. 95) calls "the limitation of his mythological vision as a means of finding meaning in history"—but then spoils this important insight by insisting that Pound was indeed trying to compose his *Cantos* according to the romantic notions implicit in such an Hebraic model of epic. Bernstein's own discussion of Confucian historiography clarifies how Pound was using the ideogram to mask his own Hellenic (static) approach to time as history, until, of course, Pisa as real history gives him the lie. Pound was playing Ovid by composing a metamorphic compendium that would have celebrated the new Italian Revolution as Virgil had sung the old Roman one. Unlike Virgil's, Pound's revolution was aborted; like Ovid in Pontus, Pound earns "exile" in St. Elizabeths for his efforts. In effect, Bernstein has made Pound's personal dilemma that of his own book, for if criticizing Pound's mythology because it fails to justify history does not beg the question, at least it underscores the deficiency of *agape* in Pound's Hellenic epic. Tragically enough, epic success was merely the latest means (mask) to the more important, Jobian goal of self-justification and consequent public acceptance that achieving genuine selfhood and psychic integrity would entail. In this sense, events (history) doomed Pound to failure, and the implications of what would have allowed him to claim success are too frightening to contemplate. "History" would have begun in 1945, had it not already started in 1922 (Mussolini's march) or in 1930 (Virgil's bimillenium), should the allies have lost the war. Had the fascists won, where would Pound have stood? Thus, history almost had a different "meaning" in 1945, and to answer Bernstein (p. 92) further, "why the gods have withdrawn from most men's range of vision" and "why the decline in social equity" seems inherent in

Pound's mythopoeic approach to history at least since canto II, or since the end of Catullus 64, or even since Plato banished the imagists ("knowledge the shade of a shade") from his Republic, whereupon "the artists swore by their gods that nothing would drag them into it" (*LE,* 432). Pound's gods, then, especially Aphrodite, return to Pisa not in triumph, but in spite of evident failure, almost as if to acknowledge the persistence (if not justice) of the poet who had long been aiming to write for the new Republic his own foundation myth, not a noble lie but a magnificent story soon to be vindicated, of the kind Plato previewed and Virgil produced. Having already written off Virgil's hero as a "priest," Pound was also aware that Plato himself had Hebraically condemned the anthropomorphism of Homer's gods and the immorality of his heroes as well, in particular Homer's descriptions in the *Odyssey* of life in hell (including that of Pound's archetypal seer Tiresias). After all, what young man would enlist (and Plato's Athens needed recruits) if he thought that once dead he would flit around like the shade of a shade? No wonder Eleusis (and Plato) began to promise individual immortality to Athenians in the fifth century B.C. (*not* to be confused with the pagan immortality Pound expects for having honored Eleusis in his poetry). But interestingly enough, just as the Peloponnesian War, Athen's political turmoil, and Socrates' death impelled Plato away from the poets toward a more theological idea of justice, so his own suffering near Pisa compelled Pound to adopt a more humane attitude about himself in relation to others. Yet both men, the philosopher and the poet, finally prefer fascist control (however benevolent) to democratic compassion. Plato, at least, had an excuse: he knew neither about Judeo-Christian love nor about American representative government. Pound, by contrast, should have better appreciated the impossibility of redemption apart from the community (*geopolis*) at large.

While Pound's gods appeared with individual significance in the pre-Pisan cantos, and returned with collective intensity in the *Pisan Cantos,* they never quite disappear altogether in the post-Pisan cantos. One could well enough chart how Pound's scheme to make the gods walk again in men's gardens concludes, examining the altar he finally builds for the grove of his poetry in canto XC, the last grain rite he celebrates in canto CVI, the homecoming he achieves in canto CX, and the envoi he leaves in canto CXVI. Certainly commentators like Wilhelm, Flory, and Bacigalupo have done important work on this late poetry, although Terrell has yet to provide us with the second half of his indispensable *Companion* for our assistance. But in reading *Rock-Drill* (1955) and *Thrones* (1959), one senses that Pound's desperate survey of various world civilizations lacks the method of his pre-Pisan work, reflects the more fragmentary nature of his Pisan poetry itself, and most of all constitutes one last effort less to found that new republic than to amass more evidence for those disciples who someday might realize the dream. This view, of course, derives from our belief that Pisa permanently proscribed the seer, who in spending the last quarter of his career behind bars at St. Elizabeths was disinclined to forgive or forget this fact. Thus, rather than bear witness to such a disappointing dénouement (something of a whimper after all) by following Pound further into the furze bushes, we should after bidding Ovid farewell seek another, more appropriate, albeit heuristic resolution that verifies our estimation of Pisa's abortive impact on Pound's progress by demonstrating how the poet himself came to conclude that he had not rivaled Virgil as planned. This Pound does in settling for the second best solution of estimating his achievement by outboasting Horace, who becomes his demimask precisely because he cannot face his own epic inadequacy.

Pound's conflation of Homer's Leucothea[43] with Ovid's Leucothoe (*Meta.* 4.542) underscores his need for help in the last stages of his journey; but also his reference in the same context to Ovid's *Fasti,* a poetic calendar of the Roman year left incomplete at the time of his exile, reiterates Pound's now tragic role as a *vates* of the gods.[44] Pound first referred to Leucothea as Leucothoe in canto XCV (95/644). Knowing of Ovid's sea-goddess, Leucothoe, Pound associated her with Ovid's other Leucothoe, who was buried alive by her father, King Orchamus of Babylon, for her unchastity, but transformed by Apollo into a frankincense bush (*Meta.* 4.196–255). After Leucothea-Leucothoe has given her magic veil to Pound as Odysseus (96/651 and 98/684), he refers in "Heraclitan parenthesis" to both Leucothoes, as well as to the Salt Commissioner of Shensi, who translated K'ang Hsi's *Sacred Edict* into more colloquial Chinese:

> And that Leucothoe rose as an incense bush
> —Orchamus, Babylon—
>   resisting Apollo.
> Patience, I will come to the Commissioner of the Salt Works
>   in due course.
> Est deus in nobis. and
>   They still offer sacrifice to that sea-gull
> est deus in nobis
>   Χρηδεμνον
> She being of Cadmus line,
>   the snow's lace is spread there like sea foam
> but the lot of 'em, Yeats, Possum and Wyndham
>   had no ground beneath 'em.
>   (98/685)

Having landed in Phaeacia and dropped Leucothea-Leucothoe's veil, the speaker repeats his conflation in canto CII (102/728), this time including,

"But with Leucothoe's mind in that incense / all Babylon could not hold it down" (102/729-30). Moreover, Leucothoe as Ino, besides being Cadmus' daughter, was also Pentheus' mother and the aunt of Dionysus, for whom "olibanum is my incense" (2/9). No wonder the white goddess assists the poet who has "seen what he has seen," unlike Yeats, Eliot, or Lewis who never rooted in Eleusis, a ground sufficiently fertile to sustain not only Pound's monetary but also his other Hellenic concerns (be they agricultural, erotic, aesthetic, political, economic, or Confucian).

After recalling that "Queen Bess translated Ovid" (85/543), Pound took consolation from Sir Francis Drake's unhappy end, whom he fancied as having seen the fire in Elizabeth as Aphrodite's eye:

> Light & the flowing crystal
> > never gin in cut glass had such clarity
> That Drake saw the splendour and wreckage
> > in that clarity
> Gods moving in crystal
> > ichor, amor.... (91/611)

In canto XCIII Pound contrasted the waning fire of his own eye ("I") with the other half of Ovid's line, "there is a god in us; *with him stirring we grow warm*" (*Fas.* 6.5; my italics): "The autumn leaves blow from my hand, / agitante calescemus... / and the wind cools toward autumn" (93/628). In his role as outlawed soothsayer, Pound often insists that, "The temple ||| is holy, / because it is not for sale" (97/676ff.) and invokes the "Manes Di, the augurs invoke them / per aethera terrenaeque / are believed to stay on / manare credantur" (97/682). Alluding to the futility of Buchanan's efforts to avert the Civil War, and obviously mindful of his own struggle to "build the temple" and "restore the state," Pound in St. Elizabeths recalls Ovid's exile at Tomis on the Black Sea:

> that men have sunk to consider the mere material value
> > of the Union
> a grant from States of limited powers
> > nec Templum aedificavit
> > > nec restituit rem
> but not his fault by a damn sight.
> > Winter in Pontus distressing
> > but still at Sulmona the lion heads....
> (103/736)

For Pound, "Ovid [had it] much worse in Pontus" (104/742), and the hundred-odd lion heads overlooking the reflecting pool at Sulmona (Ovid's birthplace) symbolize how the poet's work of metamorphoses endures in stone. "From Sulmona / the lion-fount— / must be Sulmona, Ovidio's" (105/746) itself becomes "At Sulmona are lion heads. / Gold light, in veined phylotaxis. / By hundred blue-grey over their rock-pool" (106/ 754). And yet who today, with Pound's fascist friends gone, despite the "stones'" ability to stand against time, appreciates the principles of their arrangement? "The holiness of their courage forgotten / and the Brescian lions effaced. . ." (110/780).

In the final fragments of the *Cantos,* Pound wavers without forsaking his belief. Considering the clash between his "amour" and the "world" (117/802) that had been his lifework, he could say, "And who no longer make gods out of beauty / Θρηνος this is a dying" (113/786). Sadder still, the poet comes full circle in rebuking Metastasio and himself for subscribing even to the possibility of paradise on earth (canto I, *Poetry,* 1917): "The gods have not returned. 'They have never left us.' / They have not returned" (113/787). Yet Pound persists to the very end, beseeching the gods and those he loves, but no one else, to forgive what he has made (120/ 803). So tragic and moving, such verse seems almost ancillary after Pisa for the chief pagan of modern poetry who had already done his best to interpret the light from Eleusis for his time. Through Ovidian moments of metamorphosis, but once in special, he had continually re-created his *Cantos.* If building this monument that is a bridge in verse eventually isolated Pound from reality, we must remember that even in ancient Rome the pontifex stood apart from the populace he sought to instruct. How fitting, then, that only by distancing himself from his own work could the poet of *personae* through Horace's *Odes* 3.30 measure his bittersweet achievement. Just so, by distancing ourselves from the remaining cantos we can better appreciate how in outboasting Horace, Pound was really admitting his own failure to have matched Virgil in epic. In short, he was finally conceding his own inability to discover at last himself.

5

Horace as Demimask

"Horace is a tessellation of
bits, fitted into each other"
("OCiG," 154).

Pound's Horace was primarily the poet of the *Odes,* who like Virgil in epic
was an establishment poet in lyric whose Augustanism Pound associated
with British neoclassicism and imperialism. But within his antipathy for
Horace's Hebraic didacticism (similar to Virgil's Puritanism), Pound
always admired Horace's boast about his lyric achievement in *Odes* 3.30,
thus underscoring his own abiding preoccupation with poetic fame and
glory that was to have culminated in epic success and the discovery of
himself in his otherness. In this sense Horace, the old man's poet,[1] serves
well as the Latin mask of Pound's old age. In other words, after studying
him in college,[2] Pound critically measured Horace in the *Criterion*
(January 1930), increasingly appreciated him in both the short poetry and
the *Cantos,* and then honored him greatly in his late translations of *Odes*
1.11 (1963), and 1.31 and 3.30 (1964). Of course, Pound outboasts Horace
because he is really praising himself, in judging his own career; that is, he
had endeavored to be an epic poet, hence not Horace's rival but Virgil's.
Here his speaking through Horace conveys a confidence about having out-
sung the lyricist, while not speaking through Virgil accents his anxiety
about having matched the Mantuan. Since Pisa blocked his ambition to
achieve selfhood through Hellenic epic, in effect denying him the *quies* or
peace of mind he so persistently sought, Pound's boast rings hollow
("...velut aes sonans, aut cymbalum tinniens") as an estimation of his epic
achievement, yet true enough ("voce...tinnula") as a testament to the lyric
traces therein. In short, the poet sadly remains half masked, because in the
long anticipated moment wherein he was to hold forth as a fully integrated
self, he is compelled to dissemble, less to us than to himself (a bitterly
ironic fate), as a conceited man frustrated in his magnanimous quest for
honor.

Pound's earliest Horatian criticism, in *The Spirit of Romance* (1910), remarkably previews his concern for his own achievement as expressed in the late translations. Alluding to *Odes* 3.30, Pound first misquoted Horace:

> "Magna pars mei," says Horace, speaking of his own futurity, "that in me which is greatest shall escape dissolution": The *accurate* artist seems to leave not only his greater self [upon his art, but] some living print of the circumvolving man, his taste, his temper, and his foible.... We find these not so much in the words—which anyone may read—but in the subtle joints of the craft, in the crannies perceptible only to the craftsman.[3]

In fact, Horace had written not "magna" but "multa" (*Odes,* 3.30.6), not "that in me which is greatest" but "a great part of me," and Pound's slip gauges his subsequent valuation of poetic immortality. Naturally the imagist would extol accuracy, but that he also respected the traces of personality an artist leaves on his work indicates his own "circumvolving" search through masks for himself. Indeed, Pound's momentary personality inheres in the "subtle joints of [his] craft," that is, in the way he fits the various "parts" or "bits" of his poetry together. His using Horace to define "that in me which is greatest" as craftsmanship explains well how Pound reads Horace and, more important, why he eventually chose 3.30 to evaluate his own work.[4]

Pound's other important comment on Horace in 1910 anticipates his late translation of *Odes* 1.31, which distinguishes between the simple life and the pursuit of worldly riches. Referring to the Renaissance Latinist, Aurelius Augurellus, Pound said that "his 'aegrum vulgus,' or 'diseased rabble,' is one degree more contemptuous than the 'profanum vulgus' of Horace" (*SR,* 239). Witemeyer (*Poetry of Ezra Pound,* pp. 112–13) also spots Augurellus' expression in "Au Salon" (1911). Writing to Harriet Monroe on March 30, 1913, Pound referred to the public of his own day as the "aegrum and fiercely accursed groveling vulgus" (*L,* 18). Clearly, he appreciated the disdain implicit in Horace's distinction between his own role as poet or soothsayer and that of the common or uninitiate crowd. In 1932 Pound refined his reading of "Odi profanum vulgus et arceo" (*Odes,* 3.1.1; "I hate the common crowd and keep it away") by suggesting that snobs would "accentuate the 'vulgus.' Let's put it on the 'profanum.'"[5] The point is that while Pound would publicize (*vulgo*) eros, Christian society would *vulgarize* it. The poet's own poetic diligence in providing a shrine for the populace explains his final preference in 1964 for translating 1.31, with its specific allusion to the "lyre" amid the simplicities of a healthful old age.

Between 1910 and 1930 Pound's remarks show his ambivalence toward Horace. Having listed Horace among the Latin poets "who matter," Pound presciently, if not ironically, informed Iris Barry in July, 1916, that "Horace you will not want for a long time" (*L*, 87). In 1923 he felt Horace to be "mediocre" ("OCiG," 148), adding in 1928 that he was "the perfect example of a man who acquired all that is acquirable, without having the root" (*LE*, 28). Given his own Eleusinian reverence for "roots," what does this say about Pound's secret estimation of himself in the late translations? Suggesting as well in 1928 that one could study the development of British verse by studying the translations of Horace having poured from the British press since 1650 (*LE*, 35), Pound not only forecast the method of his essay in 1930, but also revealed why he long associated Horace with the British neoclassical view of him. After perusing the British Museum's collection of Horatian translation, Pound wrote "Horace" (*The Criterion*, Jan. 1930), in which he considered the poet himself, related him to his peers and to subsequent European tradition, and surveyed various seventeenth-century translators of the *Odes*. Pound began by satirizing, in stylistically imitative fashion, both Horace and the English appreciation of him.

> Neither simple nor passionate, sensuous only insofar as he is a gourmet of food and of language, *aere perennius,* Quintus Horatius Flaccus, bald-headed, potbellied, underbred, sycophantic, less poetic than any other great master of literature, occupies one complete volume of the *British Museum Catalogue* and about half the bad poetry in English might seem to have been written under his influence, but as almost no Englishman save Landor has ever written a line of real criticism this is not perhaps very surprising.[6]

For Pound, Horace's own "jokes" were no less obvious and his "verbal arrangement" was "a dilettantism" ("H," 218-19).

Pound thought Horace "the devil to translate" ("H," 224), because of the discordant and abstract qualities of his poetry. He described as an example of discordance Horace's ability "to insert such lines as 'inter ludere virgines / et stellis nebulam spargere candidis...' [*Odes*, 3.15.5-6] in the middle of a poem whose general tone is that of a smoking-room snicker, without breaking the homogeneity of his medium." [7] One suspects that Pound, mindful of Botticelli, was objecting to Horace's willingness to characterize Chloris (i.e., Flora, the Roman goddess of flowers and spring in Ovid's *Fasti* 5.193-214) as an old hag (*vetula*). Of Horace's abstraction, Pound suggested that *Odes* 1.4.1 ("Sharp winter is dissolving with the pleasant change of spring and Favonius") "has a week's work in it for any self-respecting translator, and needs inspiration on at least one day of the seven" ("H," 220). Contemplating this poem's dance of Venus leading the Graces and the Nymphs (*Odes*, 1.4.5-7) through Botticelli's "La Primavera," we acknowledge Pound's point. Pound felt that Horace was "so full of matter which is not direct presentation of objects, or even direct statement of anything, that no method developed to meet the demands of such directness will serve to translate him" ("H," 225). Moreover, much of Horace's abstraction derived from his moralizing, especially in *Odes* 3.1–6, which prompted Pound to call him "such a humbug" ("H," 225). Alluding to Horace's patriotic poetry, and echoing his own anti-imperialistic reading of Propertius, Pound claimed that "Horace lived under that crapulous presbyterian Caesar Augustus and carried his camouflage with all the unction of an adulterous Methodist deacon" ("H," 226). Such apparent hypocrisy, however, probably reveals more about Pound's own post-Protestant sensibility than it does about Horace's pre-Christian morality.

Besides judging Horace's syntax, discordance, and abstraction, Pound briefly, and ambivalently, compared him to Catullus, Propertius, and Ovid. Pound labeled Horace a pompous liar for claiming "to have been the first to bring in the 'Aeolic modes,' for Catullus preceded him, and Catullus wrote better Sapphics."[8] But while Horace most often used the Alcaic and the Sapphic meters, Catullus himself wrote no Alcaics and only two poems in Sapphics, which together as we have seen Pound admired for their lyric-satiric contrast. Pound continued to discuss Horace, whose earlier odes were often translations, as if he were discussing himself: "Horace lifts passages; incorporates lines; I doubt if he improves on Alcaeus" ("H," 217). While Catullus and Ovid contributed "something to world poetry," Horace at his best is "sometimes more, sometimes less than a translation, [though] there is a definitely Horatian art" ("H," 217). Moreover, "apart from Catullus [Horace] was the most skillful metrist among the Latins, Propertius excelling him in but one habitual meter" ("H," 217). For Pound, against Catullus' "passion," and Ovid's "magic [and] sense of mystery," Horace had but little "poise and no stronger emotion than might move one toward a particularly luscious oyster" ("H," 218), although we should remember that "Whitman liked oysters" (80/495) and the sea, from whose foam (*aphros*) Aphrodite arose riding perhaps an oyster shell. Horace's "jibes at old women are like petty personal fusses"[9] that lack the "impersonality" of Catullus 39 ("H," 218), which makes great invective out of Egnatius the Spaniard's (i.e., non-Roman's) own indecorous behavior. While Pound missed the precision of a poem like Catullus 46, which recounts how Catullus in returning home from Bithynia during the season of Zephyrus detours to visit the famous cities of Asia, "yet if Catullus had not lived Horace might be counted the greatest lyricist in Latin" ("H," 225). Pound, too, in seeking his *nostos* detours to visit both the *clarae Europae urbes* and the dead of the classical past, which likewise informs our sense of his lyric greatness.

Though Pound in 1930 admired Horace's lyric ability less than Catullus', his discussion of Horace in relation to subsequent tradition and his

survey of various translators of the *Odes* foreshadows his own late desire
to translate him. After perusing four centuries of French and English
"approximations," Pound felt that Horace had remained untranslatable;
and "pleasing versions of individual poems do not dispose of the question"
("H," 218). The Elizabethans could not have translated Pound's Horace
because he "does not the least fit their period" and he lacks "the Elizabethan interest in magnificent and grandiloquent phrases" ("H," 218–19).
Pound found the eighteenth century, though "'founded on the *Ars
Poetica,*'" no more successful in rendering Horace's Latin, and their efforts
"unreadable" ("H," 218), which translates perhaps that neoclassical
imitation is irrelevant to understanding his own pursuit of *personae*. He
did concede that the period achieved at least the "superficial appearance of
unity by reason of its uniform metric";[10] no serious concession, however,
for the chief exponent of *verse libre* in his time. Pound attributed the
modern pleasure in Horace to his irony and to his complicated word order
("H," 219). (Think, here, of the *Cantos.*) In short, while admitting the
"tremendous fertility or stimulus that has resulted from failing to translate
him" ("H," 224), Pound condemned Horace three times in the same essay
for being "not good enough" and "not unified enough to absorb the translator or to cause a masterwork in the new language" comparable with
Douglas' *Aeneid*, Marlowe's *Elegies,* or Golding's *Metamorphoses* ("H,"
218, 224, 226). Seeing little chance of a real translation "unless someone
really were 'a Horace,'" Pound with increasing dramatic irony felt that,
while Douglas, Marlowe, and Golding were "full of untempered admiration for their originals, only such untempered admiration can produce the
energy necessary for surrender and fusion" ("H," 226). Given the obvious
sincerity of his own effort to translate Horace in 1964, Pound would seem
to have "circumvolved" from his remark here in 1930 that "It is difficult to
imagine anyone wanting to feel like Horace with sufficient force to produce the equivalent idiom" ("H," 226). Pound does indeed produce the
equivalent idiom, if only in three poems, which highlights how much he
has made his peace with Horace, if not therefore with himself.

While Pound rightly disparaged much of the great mass of Horatian
translation stored in the British Museum, he was trying hard with his selections to discredit both Horace and his English translators. Selecting from
Richard Moore (1621), John Smith (1649), and John Hanway (1730)
among others, Pound implied that Horace must be inferior because he has
inspired a host of inferior translations in English. Yet, without questioning
Pound's judgment of such translation, one could question his method and
implicit aims. Concluding his survey by calling the British Museum's
Horatian holdings of little interest to the public, Pound suggested that they
offered "small direct return" to the specialist and student of literature,

"either as light on Horace or as illustrative of the art of translating" ("H,"
226–27). While his own late translations, by contrast, delightfully demonstrate his superior skills as a translator and a poet, had Pound been less
biased against Horace and English poetry to begin with, he just as easily
and perhaps more helpfully could have stated a contrary thesis. Had he
selected translations of Horace by great English poets, Pound could have
convincingly shown not only Horace's genius for inspiring such translation, but also the development of English poetry in general. Pound's own
late translations of Horace suggest strongly how much this, in fact, was the
thesis that he himself eventually came to accept.

After his essay in *The Criterion,* Pound made one more, notably
caustic, comment about Horace. Apparently prompted by Pound's early
poetic treatment and by his essay that January, Louis Untermeyer sent him
in Rapallo some of his own Horatian parodies.[11] Untermeyer, in turn,
prompted Pound's parody of Horace's "Persicos odi":

> [I hate Persian pomp, boy,
> garlands bound with linden-bark displease me;
> cease chasing to where a late
>   rose may linger.
>
> I bid that you officious add nothing to
> simple myrtle: myrtle befits both
> you as a servant and me drinking
>   under the leafy vine.]
>   (*Odes,* 1.38)[12]
>
> The Persian buggahs, Joe,
> Strike me as a rotten show,
> Stinking of nard and musk
> Over the whole of their rind and husk;
> Wearing their soft-shell clothes
> Whichever way the wind blows,
> The Persian buggahs, Joe,
> Strike me as a rotten show.[13]

Pound here has transformed Horace's modest plea for simplicity over
ostentation into a philippic against "Persian" decadence that betrays the
speaker's own British-Horatian sense of superiority. With symmetry and a
slight note of ennui, Dobson at least preserved the thematic and tonal
balance of the original. But by dwelling on Horace's "Persicos apparatus"
(*Odes,* 1.38.1) in his "highbrow's" translation, Pound turns Horace into a
fin de siècle British imperialist. Especially with the diction off his refrain—
"buggahs" and "rotten show"—Pound captures the snobbery implicit in
such a figure. More important, however, by silhouetting his own animus
against all heretical assaults on his right to venerate myrtle *sub arta vite* of

his verse, Pound previews how he will eventually use Horace to justify himself.

Pound's imagist aversion for Horace's abstraction — "no method developed to meet the demands of such directness will serve to translate him" ("H," 225) — should give us pause. *Not* because Horace is not "abstract," but because Pound's examples of his abstraction, involving as they do an awareness of the importance to Pound of Botticelli's "Primavera" or Catullus' detour, are themselves, frankly, rather indirect, imprecise, and therefore "abstract" as in misleading. This intriguing, not to say shocking, revelation concerning Pound's imprecision points to another, which his commentators have been shamefully slow to appreciate, but which is apparent to anyone who has earnestly and repeatedly assaulted the *Cantos*: *rarely* in either Pound's poetry or his criticism does the "thing itself" mean what it appears to mean. Of course, meaning is ideogrammicly related to use or context, but context for Pound invariably entails far more than meets the eye. If all this seems "too suspicious," we should reply that Odyssean Pound himself has taught us to be wary. The man may be descended from Zeus (Longfellow), but he is also descended from Autolycus (horsethieves). For one final measurement, then, of Poundian parallax we might consider his treatment of Horace in both the short poetry and the *Cantos*. Pound's Horatian minimasks, so to speak, derive their significance, finally, less from who Pound is at the moment than from who he consistently aspires to be at the end. In fact, he wanted to be a great poet and the star he sighted by was Horace's boast about his own lyric greatness in *Odes* 3.30. Pound humbly began his career with this star in view, then distracted by the war (i.e., the world) and by an even brighter star (the *Aeneid*) he lost sight of the lesser one, but then more severely disoriented by a second war he rediscovered the lesser giant as if he were yet beholding its brighter companion. Now to prove the parable.

Pound amusingly alluded to several Horatian odes in "The Amphora" (*ALS*, 1908). In this early sonnet, Pound plays Horace by asking a servant to fetch him some wine from the storeroom; but instead of wine, Pound asks metaphorically for "some poet of the past" (*ALS*, 107). The dramatic situation derives from several odes. Horace once explained to Maecenas that he yearly celebrated his escape from a falling tree by drawing the cork from a "jar set to drink the smoke" (*Odes*, 3.8.11); Pound, too, requests his jar "from out the smoky room" (*ALS*, 107). Horace actually addressed a "faithful jar" (*Odes*, 3.21.4) that guarded the "gathered Massic" (*Odes*, 3.21.5); Pound himself asserts that he has drunk "Faller[n]ian and Massic of the Roman hoards" (*ALS*, 107). Horace honored the *Neptunalia* by bidding "Lyde" to "bring forth promptly the stored Caecuban" (*Odes*,

3.28.2–3); Pound, in turn, bids his "boy" to "search i' the gloom...well, and mark you that the draught be good" (*ALS*, 107). Besides deriving this mock *nekuia* or descent into the storeroom of the past from Horace, Pound also describes the kind of wine (poetry) he wants by alluding to Horace's *Odes* 3.30. Compare the monument of Horace's poetry,

> [which no greedy rain-cloud, no violent North-wind
> can destroy nor the countless
> toll of years and the flight of time...]
> (*Odes*, 3.30.3–5)

with Pound's first allusion to it:

> Yea, of such wine as all time's store affords
> From rich amphorae that nor years can blast
> With might of theirs and blows down-rainèd fast....
> (*ALS*, 107)

Since he revises (*reviso*) the past to discover himself, Pound modestly describes his own achievement in 1908 as receiving from his "boy" an "amphora" whose "clasp was Hood" (*ALS*, 107).[14] Nevertheless, as we see, young Pound knows clearly where he wants to go.

Pound's next, more mature treatments of Horace subtly show the gravitational force of both World War I and Virgil on his intended line (poetry) of sight (eyes: "I"'s). "Monumentum Aere, Etc." (*Blast*, 1914) constitutes a parodic proposition of Pound's Horatian ambition; "Dum Capitolium Scandet" (*Lustra*, 1917), an antithetical imitation of Horatian greatness; and Pound's private translation of *Odes* 4.10, with its suggestion of ambivalent anxiety, the perfect Propertian synthesis of a man about to embark upon an epic adventure (the *Cantos*) but quite unsure as to whether he will complete his quest for greatness. As implied by the title of the journal in which it appeared, "Monumentum Aere, Etc." proves rather audacious:

> You say that I take a good deal upon myself;
> That I strut in the robes of assumption.
>
> In a few years no one will remember the *buffo*,
> No one will remember the trivial parts of me,
> The comic detail will be absent.
> As for you, you will rot in the earth,
> And it is doubtful if even your manure will be rich enough
>
> To keep grass
> Over your grave.
> (*Per*, 146)

Having alluded to *Odes* 3.30 in "The Amphora" (*ALS,* 1908), Pound here in his title satirizes Horace's opening line, "I have completed a monument more lasting than bronze" (*Odes,* 3.30.1). Pound's "the trivial parts of me" reflects his preoccupation with the phrase "multaque pars mei" (*Odes,* 3.30.6; "a great part of me"), yet his negative rendering of it this time suggests he can only associate Horace's boast with himself through the guise of parody. The boast appeals to Pound's ego, but it does not yet apply to his work. Perhaps he even intends to humble Horace by imputing to him the strutting in "robes of assumption," and acting "the *buffo,*" that others see in himself. In short, Pound cleverly masks his strong desire to attain Horatian immortality both by lessening Horace and by projecting his own insecurity onto the "you" he attacks, who "will rot in the earth, etc."

In contrast to "Monumentum Aere, Etc," Pound's "Dum Capitolium Scandet" (*Lustra,* 1917) favorably imitates *Odes* 3.30. Pound's title refers to Horace's claim that he would be remembered "as long as the pontifex shall ascend the Capitol" (*Odes,* 3.30.8-9). Pound's poem depends on Horace's assertions that he "will not altogether die," that "a great part of [him] will escape the death-goddess," and that he "continuously in after-time will grow fresh with praise" (*Odes,* 3.30.6-8):

> How many will come after me
>   singing as well as I sing, none better;
> Telling the heart of their truth
>   as I have taught them to tell it;
> Fruit of my seed,
>   O my unnameable children.
> Know then that I loved you from afore-time,
> Clear speakers, naked in the sun, untrammelled.
>   (*Per,* 96)

This time Pound has hypostasized the idea of "multaque pars mei" into a "tribe of Pound," conspicuous for their Whitmanian "clear-speaking" and for being "untrammelled." In effect, he has fantasized the psychological situation of "Monumentum Aere" into the future, transforming his discontent for being among Horace's seed into his own seed's admiration for himself. Thus, here Pound honors Horace the better someday after his own poetic success to boast through him about his own work.

In July, 1917, Pound mailed his only early translation of Horace, of *Odes* 4.10, to James Joyce, lamenting their common mistreatment by public and publishers alike. He enclosed the translation to contrast his own and Joyce's neglect with that of Ligurinus, who the ode implies was beset by suitors:

[O cruel still and powerful with Venus' gifts,
when unhoped for† down will beset your pride,
and the locks, now wafting over your shoulders, have fallen,
and the hue, now outvying the red rose's blossom,
changed has turned Ligurinus into a bristly face,
you will say whenever you see yourself altered in the mirror,
"Alas, why was my intent today not the same for me as a boy,
or why to my present spirits do not my boyish cheeks return?"]
          (*Odes*, 4.10)

O cruel until now, mighty in Venus' gifts,
when unexpected falls thy feathery pride,
And all the locks, that hide
Thy shoulders now, be shent;
And colour that outdoes the Punic rose
Show but an ashen face, O Liguriné,
Thou shalt say,
To see thyself so altered in thy glass,
"Alas, the day!
"Why had I of these thoughts no trace
"In youth; or why, today,
These thoughts that have no face?"
          (*P/J*, 122–23)[15]

More revealingly, Horace's admonition to Ligurinus—you will live to regret either your pride or your bygone youth—becomes Pound's prophetically accurate warning to himself, on the verge of pursuing what Pisa proves to be a bittersweet success. Moreover, labeling his translation "mellifluous archaism" (*P/J*, 122) scarcely masks Pound's own Propertian anxiety, and we note the shift away from *Odes* 3.30 as a further indication of Pound's Virgilian (i.e., epic) concerns.

Curiously, even as he reversed Propertius' central transitionary poems (Propertius 2.34 and 3.1) in the *Homage* (1917), so Pound has intimated his epic ambition before manifesting how World War I prompted him to disparage Horace as an Augustan imperialist in both the *Homage* and *Mauberley* (1919). These parallel reversals demonstrate how Propertius' aesthetic crisis had indeed become a moral crisis for Pound, wherein events led him to revile the very poets he most wished to emulate. If this first war teaches Pound to ignore history, the second one would teach him to regret his neglect. With his *recusatio* poems Propertius himself has prompted us to wonder whether he morally, as well as aesthetically, rejected Augustan imperialism. Pound, however, has left little doubt about his own wartime discovery of Propertius' anti-imperialism. Soon to let this view of Propertius and his poetic envy of Virgil distort Propertius' respect for Virgil in section XII of the *Homage*, Pound also derides Horace for his

Augustanism in section II. As Pound's Apollo and Calliope inform Propertius, who is trying to write epic, that his genius is for love poetry, we sense Pound is talking to himself. After relating his dream about being on Helicon drinking "wherefrom father Ennius hath drunk" (*Per,* 210), Pound's Propertius begins his roll call of Roman martial events about which he was going to write: "I had rehearsed the Curian brothers, and made / remarks on the Horatian javelin / (Near Q. H. Flaccus' book-stall)" (*Per,* 210). Absent from the original, Pound's reference to Horace results instead from his association of Horace's oratory (as reflected in *Odes* 3.1-6) with the heroism of the Horatii that Propertius was "rehearsing." Thus, while underplaying his own epic hopes and fears, Pound through Propertius ridicules both Horace and Virgil for pandering Augustanism, which combined with his antipathy for the British establishment during the war clarifies why he eventually chose Ovid the impudent upstart for his epic mask in the *Cantos.*

Although Horace, like Virgil, did espouse Augustan imperialism, Pound's vituperation results strongly from his own complex reaction to World War I and the demise of British imperialism. This can be seen most clearly from Pound's bitterly ironic rejection of Horace's "humbug" in *Mauberley* (I.iv):

> Some quick to arm,
> some for adventure,
> some from fear of weakness,
> some from fear of censure,
> some for love of slaughter, in imagination,
> learning later...
> some in fear, learning love of slaughter;
>
> Died some, pro patria,
>   non "dulce" non "et decor"....
>   (*Per,* 190)

Pound's anaphora ("some...") intensifies his catalog of questionable motivations for going to war. But it also makes all the more emphatic his reversal, "Died some." The alliterating "d"'s of "Died some, pro patria / non 'dulce' non 'et decor'..." underscore Pound's denunciation of Horace's own patriotic sentiment, "To die for one's country is sweet and fitting" (*Odes,* 3.2.13).[16] Significantly, Pound had lost many acquaintances and friends, among them Gaudier-Brzeska, in the trenches ("walked eye-deep in hell"), and in rejecting Horace he repudiates what he saw as "old men's lies" and "deceits," politically motivated "infamy," and "usury age-old and age-thick." As with his opposite reading of Propertius, Pound's response to the war colors his reading of Horace; it also explains his mixed review in the *Criterion* 11 years later, and why it would take 29 years of epic endeavor and then another war before, suitably chastened, he returned to *Odes* 3.30.

Almost the obverse of his increasingly negative treatment in the short poetry, Pound's treatment of Horace in the *Cantos* from 1925 to 1948 confirms the antithetical moral and aesthetic impact on his career of both World Wars. For while the first war caused Pound to lose sight of *Odes* 3.30 and to adopt Ovid rather than Virgil as his epic mask, the second war chastened him to forego Ovid and return to *Odes* 3.30 as if he were responding to Virgil. Thus, from the nadir of *Mauberley* Pound gradually reaccepted Horace in the *Cantos* with his own increasing age. In fact, while half of his allusions occur at roughly equal intervals before 1948, half of them occur in 1948 alone. Moreover, Pound referred both to the *Epistles* and to the *Ars Poetica,* as well as to the *Odes,* which suggests if not an increasing, at least an enduring interest in Horace. Twice he alluded early and late in the *Cantos* to the same passage, each time with an impersonal and then a personal intent. In the thirties Pound treated Horace even-handedly in the *Cantos,* and then in 1948 he returned again to *Odes* 3.30, following his use of the poem in "The Amphora" (1908), "Monumentum Aere, Etc." (1914), and "Dum Capitolium Scandet" (1917), and preceding his final triumphant translation of it in 1964.

Pound's initial allusion to Horace in the *Cantos* seems the most difficult to fathom, until we recall his awareness of Horace's discordance as in *Odes* 3.15. Now the *Cantos* begins with Pound's homage first to Homer (Canto I), next to Ovid (Canto II), and then to Browning (Canto III). Thus, Canto IV becomes Pound's own beginning within the beginning of his epic poem, and for the poet who would rival Virgilian narration with Ovidian metamorphosis an apt first solo it is. Espying Ecbatan "in smoky light," with "Troy but a heap of smouldering boundary stones," the young ambitious poet would invoke the lords of his lyre, Aurunculeia as a substitute for Lesbia who is lost to time, and Cadmus for his own experience in founding polity, and proceeds to synthesize his own Botticellian "choros nympharum" beneath "the apple trees" (4/13). Pound realized, of course, that singing *eros* to the world of time, a matter as it were of "Muttering, muttering Ovid" (4/15) and of recognizing that "No wind is the king's wind" (4/16), would involve great peril for the poet. Hence the discordant note in his *reverdie* opening, which rhymes generally with his ambivalent attitude toward Horace recently caused by the war and his own epic ambitions, and rhymes specifically with Horace's celebration of spring's ability to banish care wherein Procne, while building her nest, is "tearfully lamenting Itys" (*Odes,* 4.12.5). Starting with "Ityn! / Et ter flebiliter, Ityn, Ityn!" (4/13), Pound in Canto IV anxiously feathers his nest with associations between the stories of Itys and Cabestan, as well as between Actaeon and Vidal. By playing on "ter" ("three"), the "ter" in Horace's "flebiliter" ("tearfully"), and also the English senses of a wind that rends (tears) and makes one weep (tears), Pound marks his own transitions from story to story. Just as Procne had changed into a swallow after serving Itys to Tereus for having raped her sister, so Marguerite of Chateau Roussillon jumped out a window after learning that her husband had served her Cabestan's heart in a dish. Pound's first transition, then, occurs with the swallows crying on the wind: "Ityn! / 'It is Cabestan's heart in the dish'" (4/13). Again, their cry signals Pound's second transition from Cabestan's to Actaeon's story: "'Tis. 'Tis. Ytis! / Actaeon..." (4/14). Just as Actaeon was torn apart by his own hounds for having ventured upon Diana bathing, so Vidal was almost killed by hounds after having grown mad over Loba de Perrautier. And "Itys" echoes even in Pound's third transition, which implies that Vidal has been the "old man seated / speaking in the low drone" (4/13) all along: "Then Actaeon: Vidal, / Vidal. It is old Vidal speaking..." (4/14). Doubtless Pound also had in mind the metamorphoses from the mythological figures Itys and Actaeon (sure destruction), to the troubadours Cabestan and Vidal (mixed results), to himself as a defender of the *ventus Veneris* in 1925 (an open question).[17]

Pound's second pair of allusions illustrates more clearly how the two world wars antithetically influenced his initially favorable attitude toward Horace. The first war aroused Pound into writing a Hellenic epic against his time, so prompting his close association of usury with Horace. In Canto XV (1925), Pound has described his Dantean hell, wherein appear:

> the beast with a hundred legs, USURA
> and the swill full of respecters,
> bowing to the lords of the place,
> explaining its advantages,
> and the laudatores temporis acti
> claiming that the sh-t used to be blacker and richer....
> (15/64)

Here Pound's Latin, "admirers of bygone time," in light of his own respect for the past, illustrates how he has repressed his youthful admiration for Horace, who had described the typical old man as an "admirer of bygone time when he was young" (*A.P.*, 173–74), by transforming it into an overt sense of betrayal. By contrast, after years of swimming against the current (how Swinburne could swim), only to end beached (bitched) at Pisa, Pound returns to Horace's portrait in Canto LXXX (1948), touchingly and knowingly having become what he earlier had scorned:

> "mi-hine eyes hev"
>   well yes they *have*
> seen a good deal of it
>   there is a good deal to be seen
> fairly tough and unblastable
>   and the hymn...
> well in contrast to the *god*-damned crooning
>   put me down for temporis acti....
>   (80/498–99)

Significantly, as Horace's "old man," Pound has witnessed less the Hebraic "glory of the coming of the Lord" than the Hellenic glory of his own youth, and of an ideal past, itself "fairly tough and unblastable" even by the present realities of modern warfare.

Pound's next two allusions to Horace, which refer to the Adamses, reflect this reacceptance of Horace in the *Cantos* of the thirties. At the end of Canto XXXIV (1934), Pound described John Quincy Adams, with obvious references to his own Hellenic endeavor, as "Constans proposito...Justum et Tenacem" (34/171). Pound has slightly modified the opening of Horace's *Odes* 3.3: "A man just and tenacious of purpose / not the passion of citizens bidding perversity / ... / shakes from his firm belief..." (*Odes,* 3.3.1–2, 4). The poem's first line, Adams himself had related, was inscribed on a cane made him as a gift.[18] Pound also has become more *constans* in appreciating Horace, for in Canto LXVII (1940) he again alludes approvingly to him, this time while admiring John Adams' assertions in the *Boston Gazette* just before the Revolution that English law did not apply to the American colonies: "I wish Massachusetts / knew what a democracy is, what a republic / Irritat mulcet et falsis terroribus implet..." (67/388). Horace's irritation with the playwright, who magically "annoys, appeases, and fills his heart with unwarranted fears" (*Ep.,* 2.1.212), has become not simply Adams' response to "Massachusettensis," the Loyalist Daniel Leonard, who would disguise the rule of men (empire) as the rule of law (a true republic),[19] but also Pound's to "Massachusetts" on the eve of World War II. So Pound's frustration with America, and surely he sensed how the war would jeopardize the *Cantos* at a time when his life's work was nearing completion, betrays gravely his own moral confusion or frustration with himself not just for getting caught upon the barb of time, but for being responsible, largely, for his own inability to achieve himself.

Thus, Pisa imposes time on the poet who would eschew time, allowing him to contemplate his mixed success. And as a final sign of his returning sympathy, Pound rediscovers his Horatian star in 1948 by alluding twice to *Odes* 3.30.[20] Moreover, in contrast to "Monumentum Aere, Etc." or even

"Dum Capitolium Scandet," where he self-consciously masked his admiration, here in the *Pisan Cantos* Pound movingly reflects his old man's (poet's) respect for "the old man's poet." In Canto LXXVII (1948), he returns to Horace's assertion that "As long as the pontifex will ascend the Capitol" (*Odes,* 3.30.8–9) he will be considered a great poet: "dum Capitolium scandet / the rest is explodable..." (77/467). Clearly with this homage Pound would now profess confidence in his own Hellenic achievement. And then in Canto LXXXIII (1948), Pound returns to Horace's opening line, "I have completed a monument more lasting than bronze" (*Odes,* 3.30.1), and to Yeats' punningly proud boast about his own poetic success in "The Peacock":

> ...I recalled the noise in the chimney
> as it were the wind in the chimney
>   but was in reality Uncle William
> downstairs composing
> that had made a great Peeeeacok
>   in the proide ov his oiye
>   had made a great peeeeeeecock in the...
> made a great peacock
>   in the proide of his oyyee
>
> proide ov his oy-ee
> as indeed he had, and perdurable
>
> a great peacock aere perennius....
>   (83/533–34)

Of course, Pound in retrospect is honoring the whole of Yeats' achievement, but his mimicry of Yeats' pronunciation ("oiye...oyyee...oy-ee") more importantly signifies the "new subtlety of eyes" (81/520) or masks that he has acquired while pondering his present poetic predicament. For comparing his achievement against what he had hoped to achieve compels Pound to dissemble yet again, even as he boasts about his own progress toward immortality ("I Ray perennius"). After all, he had contended to become not Horace but Virgil, and not Yeats but himself. In short, why insist on being a "great peacock," if indeed one has become a person, content at last with one's self?

While Word War I and a desire to write the *Cantos* prompted Pound to desert Horace, the struggle to complete his Hellenic epic and World War II (St. Elizabeths), by interrupting and then distorting his endeavors and thus precluding complete success, compelled his late return to translate from Horace's *Odes.* The man who said in 1930, "It is difficult to imagine anyone wanting to feel like Horace with sufficient force to produce the equivalent idiom" ("H," 226), would now provide three polished examples of criticism by translation to assess his own achievement. Having sought himself with *personae* throughout his career, yet foiled just short of epic success, Pound cannot make peace with Virgil because he has not, after all, found himself. Even Ovid, imitating Horace, was able to boast "Iamque opus exegi..." (*Meta.* 15.871ff), which suggests not only Pound's last mask but also that his own "opus non exactum est." Consequently, Pound does the only thing he can do, what he has done all along and what, by now, he does quite well: he adopts the mask of Horace to justify his final frustrated self as if his work were indeed "exactum." Through *Odes* 1.11 (1963),[21] Pound confesses his inability to achieve himself; through *Odes* 1.31 (1964) he rededicates himself to a Hellenic poetry that opposes the world; and through *Odes* 3.30 he proudly proclaims the immortality of his achievement. In short, Pound's reconciliation with Horace reflects an enforced reconciliation with himself, as a craftsman, a translator, and something more than a lyric poet. For though he twits the establishment by posing as Horace, we suspect he really wanted its admiration of himself as Virgil.

Besides affirming Horace's perennial ability to inspire translation, Pound's return illuminates his identification with Horace as the quintessential craftsman. Pound himself had always emphasized technique, leaving inspiration, as it were, to the gods. In Horace as a craftsman, Pound saw himself. What Pound has said of Horace, that he learned all he could without having the root and that he was a tessellation of bits, might finally be said of himself. Pound's Horace was an imitator; so is Pound. Horace lacked unity, was incongruous, exhibited kaleidoscopic association; so on occasion, is Pound. Himself an arranger of words, Pound has noted Horace's verbal arrangement; himself an ironist, he has mentioned Horace's irony; and himself a foe of rhetoric, he has pointed out Horace's absence of magnificent and grandiloquent phrases. Hence Pound's remark in 1930 that the real unity of an Horatian ode derives, in fact, from "the essential personal unity of Horace" ("H," 226), when coupled with his own final efforts at translating him, honors Horace the craftsman, or "joiner of bits," by implicitly acknowledging the same personal unity in his own work.

In *Odes* 1.11, Horace met young Leuconoe's superstitious belief with his usual Epicurean maxims. Pound, in turn, transforms the poem into an old man's advice to his young companion on how to face their end together:

> Tu ne quaesieris, scire nefas, quem mihi, quem tibi
> finem di dederint, Leuconoe, nec Babylonios

temptaris numeros. ut melius, quidquid erit, pati,
seu pluris hiemes seu tribuit Iuppiter ultimam,
quae nunc oppositis debilitat pumicibus mare
Tyrrhenum: sapias, vina liques, et spatio brevi
spem longam reseces. dum loquimur, fugerit invida
aetas: carpe diem, quam minimum credula postero.
　　　　　(Odes, 1.11)

[Seek not—to know is unordained—what end for me, for
you the gods have granted, Leuconoe, nor meddle with
Babylonian calculations. How much better to endure whatever comes
whether Jupiter has allotted us many winters, or this last,
which now breaks the Tuscan Sea upon the opposing
cliffs. Be wise, strain the wine, and with life short
cut back long hope. While we speak, envious time has
fled: seize the day, trusting as little as possible in tomorrow.]

Ask not ungainly askings of the end
Gods send us, me and thee, Leucothoe;
Nor juggle with the risks of Babylon,
　　　　Better to take whatever,
Several, or last, Jove sends us. Winter is winter,
Gnawing the Tyrrhene cliffs with the sea's tooth.

Take note of flavors, and clarities in the wine's manifest.
Cut loose long hope for a time.
We talk. Time runs in envy of us,
Holding our day more firm in unbelief.
　　　　　(CtC, 36)

Pound has absorbed Horace's wisdom better than Horace himself. Indeed, Horace published his poem at age forty-two; Pound first published his at age seventy-eight. The poet who for so long had sailed after knowledge of himself now counsels, "Ask not ungainly askings of the end," which for himself implies an acceptance of his inability to "gain" himself, and for the *jeune fille* that there is little future in their relationship. Yet Pound's "Leucothoe" (echoing Ovid's seagoddess and maid transformed into a frankincense bush) would share the poet's end, while Horace's "Leuconoe" was seeking her own end. "Babylonios...numeros" meant astrology to Horace; to Pound, intriguingly, perhaps either what it would take to spring him from the madhouse or his absolute magnitude among the stars. Horace's "hiemes" really suggests "years," though he obviously chose the word for its color; Pound's "Winter is winter" stoically emphasizes the fact of his final frustration, hinting that it need not have necessarily been so. While Horace meant what he said in "Be wise, strain the wine," Pound's own "Take note of flavors, and clarities in the wine's manifest," offers possibilities beyond wine itself, as in "The Amphora." And instead of moralizing like Horace about the brevity of life, Pound transmutes what he sadly has had to do once old ("Cut loose long hope") into what she happily should do yet young ("for a time"). Ever the phrase-maker, Horace closed with the conceit, "While we talk, time flies," and then the aphorism, "Seize the day." Pound, instead, sounding a bit like Lear to Cordelia if not Marvell in triumph, would, of course, defend himself against time with his talk, his secretary, and his Hellenic "unbelief."

The reactionary nature of Pound's unbelief congeals more clearly in his translation of *Odes* 1.31 (1964), where Horace's distinction between the crowd's pursuit of riches and the poet's simple life implies Pound's own lifelong Hellenic struggle against the Hebraic world.

> [What does the poet ask of enshrined
> Apollo? What does he beg pouring new
>   wine from the bowl? Not the rich
>   grain lands of fertile Sardinia,
>
> not the pleasing herds of hot
> Calabria, not Indian gold or ivory,
>   not fields that Liris' silent stream
>   cuts with its quiet water.
>
> Let those whom Fortune has permitted
> prune the vine with a Calenian sickle, and let the rich
>   merchant drain from golden cups
>   wine purchased with Syrian goods,
>
> he dear to the gods themselves, indeed three and four
> times a year revisiting the Atlantic sea
>   with impunity. My fare is olives,
>   mine chickory and light mallows.
>
> May you, Latona's son, both grant me healthy
> to enjoy those things provided but, I pray,
>   with a sound mind, and to live an old age neither
>   ugly nor lacking the lyre.]
>   (*Odes,* 1.31)
>
>
> By the flat cup and the splash of new vintage
> What, specifically, does the diviner ask of Apollo? Not
> Thick Sardinian corn-yield nor pleasant
> Ox-herds under the summer sun in Calabria, nor
> Ivory nor gold out of India, nor
> Land where Liris crumbles her bank in silence
> Though the water seems not to move.
>
> Let him to whom Fortune's book
> Gives vines in Oporto, ply pruning hook, to the

Profit of some seller that he, the seller,
May drain Syra from gold out-size basins, a
Drink even the Gods must pay for, since he found
It is merchandise, looking back three times,
Four times a year, unwrecked from Atlantic trade-routes.

Olives feed me, and endives and mallow roots.
Delight had I healthily in what lay handy provided.
Grant me now, Latoe:
                                    Full wit in my cleanly age,
Nor lyre lack me, to tune the page.
(*CtC,* 35)

Horace's poem commemorating the dedication of the Palatine Apollo elicits Pound's final demonstration of Hellenic poetry that ever resists the forces of materialism. With his "What, specifically, does the diviner ask of Apollo?", Pound transforms Horace's occasional opening into the rhetorical question of his own career, which generates his own triptych concerning the riches he never sought, a farewell outburst against the philistines of the world, and a brief prayer that circumscribes even his former poetic ambition. As a Horatian poet, Pound has pursued "not...cornyield nor... ox-herds...nor ivory nor gold...nor land." While Horace intended his portraits of vintner and merchant to complement his catalog of luxuries in order to increase the contrast with his own simple poet's life, Pound in his zeal against philistinism isolates, in order to vilify further, his own scapegoat for greed. Pound's alliteration of "ply pruning hook...profit," his repetition of "seller," and emphasis on "gold out-size basins" (vs. "flat cup" above) all heighten the original descriptions. Whereas Horace humorously suggested that the merchant must be dear to the gods since he could sail often and with impunity, Pound would have his merchant sell "Syra" even to the gods, "since he found it is merchandise." Here Pound's "three times, / four times a year, unwrecked" is sharpened by our awareness of the "shipwreck" of his own poetic career. Pound's version of the simple life contrasts all the more sharply with the preceding crescendo of materialism because he begins not in mid-stanza like Horace, but with a new third stanza. The syntax of Horace's last strophe, even for himself, is unusually convoluted, but Pound translates now with neat simplicity, employing both a rippling series of liquids and an emphatic end-rhyme to good effect. Moreover, while Horace was hoping to enjoy his vegetarian fare, Pound's "olives feed me, and...roots" suggests that he has more than his diet in mind. Indeed, "Delight had I healthily in what lay handy provided" indicates that he is not anticipating his old age, like Horace, but speaking in it. Thus, Pound's appeal to Apollo, the god of song, "grant me now," signals his chastened poet's wisdom to seek only for himself "full wit" and but a "lyre to tune the page."[22]

If Pound's rendering of 1.31 represents his envoi to Hellenic poetry, his translation of *Odes* 3.30 (1964) constitutes his final, proudly confident tribute, intended not for the profane, to his lasting fame as a poet. To those outside the shrine, Pound's poem may seem only the farewell flourish from a man often given to overstatement, and so, from a popular perspective, it is. More important, however, the poem gains from being a carefully considered, and therefore concealed, assessment of his own career by a poet who had early forsaken Horace in an ambitious quest to rival Virgil, but who eventually returns, mindful that he had "lost [his] center / fighting the world" (117/803), in a genuine effort to set his house in order before the end. Here valuations of lyric or epic greatness seem pointless, for Pound, boasting not through original poetry but through translation, and at that a translation of Horace, who had "acquired all that is acquirable, without having the root" (*LE*, 28), would offer us the subtle truth about himself as a Hellenic poet who rests his immortality (i.e., the survival of his personality) upon its ceaseless metamorphosis from the Eleusinian past. *Quies*, then, in the Hebraic sense of achieving psychic integrity or heaven-havens on earth, precisely because it has eluded Pound in life, has suddenly become unimportant to him in death.

> This monument will outlast metal and I made it
> More durable than the king's seat, higher than pyramids.
> Gnaw of wind and rain?
> > Impotent
> The flow of years to break it, however many.
>
> Bits of me, many bits, will dodge all funeral,
> O Libitina-Persephone and, after that,
> Sprout new praise. As long as
> Pontifex and the quiet girl pace the Capitol
> I shall be spoken where the wild flood Aufidus
> Lashes, and Daunus ruled the parched farmland:
>
> Power from lowliness: "First brought Aeolic song to
> > Italian fashion" —
> Wear pride, work's gain! O Muse Melpomene,
> By your will bind the laurel.
> > My hair, Delphic laurel.
> > (*Ctc*, 36–37)

Horace's proud song of triumph, asserting with increasing precision that he would not wholly die, that his fame would grow from age to age, and that he would be said the first to have composed Aeolic song in Italian verse, formed a fitting epilogue to the first three books of *Odes*. Similarly, Pound's lifelong interest in this particular poem from Horace, from Latin, and perhaps from any literature, reflects an equal if derivative pride in his own poetic achievement. Perhaps the key word of Horace's poem is "deduxisse," from "deduco," meaning "to lead down" as in time, or figuratively, "to spin out." In fact, Horace himself was asserting less the originality of his achievement than his capacity for having transformed Greek into Italian song.[23] In doing so, of course, he also set the matchless standard for lyric composition in Latin poetry. Thus, Pound's emulation, in the epilogue of his own career, of the poet he earlier had derided as "sometimes more, sometimes less than a translation" ("H," 217), conveys his Hellenic sense of himself as less an original than a traditional poet, whose originality lies in preserving poetic tradition by "making it new." Significantly, such Hellenism implies less that Pound lacks creative imagination, than that he has elevated translation to the craft of composition, as few, if any, have done before him, by using memory and association, paradoxically, to deduce himself from the past.

Pound's three divisions of Horace's undivided poem, then, reflect not only his reading of Horace, but also an estimation of his final poetic self. In his first section, Pound has essentially preserved Horace's own catalog of monuments, elements, and time, which his poetry will outlast, but he has done so with the transformative touches of a great American poet. Pound's "This monument" refers less, really, to the *Cantos* than to his overall achievement, and so he reverses Horace's verb in the opening line for emphasis: "...and I made it." Letting the words suggest their own meaning, he more precisely breaks Horace's "regalique situ pyramidum" ("royal site of the pyramids") into two equally appropriate images: "king's seat" and "pyramids." Pound's middle English diction of "Gnaw," "wind," and "rain" seems efficiently hard, clean, and forceful. And by making the line a question, having Horace's "impotens" ("violent") provide its opposite English derivative, and isolating the word between the question and the next line, he concisely allows "impotent" to do double duty: "Gnaw of wind and rain? / Impotent / The flow of years to break it, however many." Pound next manifests his conception of Horace as a craftsman and of himself as an executor of Eleusis in his especially Poundian metamorphosis of Horace's middle section dealing with his lasting fame as a poet. With both the third syllable of Horace's verb "vitabit" ("escape"), and the second syllable of his death-goddess, "Libitina," showing the way, Pound's final phrasing of "multaque pars mei" prefigures his own poetic renewal: "Bits of me, many bits, will dodge all funeral, / O Libitina-Persephone and, after that, / Sprout new praise."[24] Aside from his obvious gratitude that Maria has given him grandchildren, Pound's mention of Persephone (Koré: daughter) and his use of the Whitmanian verb, "sprout," further convey the vegetative vitality of his art. In addition, the erotic and aesthetic dimensions of Eleusis in Pound's art can be gleaned from Horace's allusion to the rites of the vestal virgins and the pontifices, by which he felt he was invoking the very perpetuity of Rome. For the Romans Vesta (Hestia) was the hearth-goddess, whose fire they associated with life itself, and whose *virgines* or daughters of the royal house were chosen by the *pontifex maximus* uttering the formula: *te, Amata, cupio*. Pound's "quiet girl" typifies his own ideal of feminine beauty that both insures the survival of humanity and inspires the poet's song, and his "pontifex" signifies the supreme diviner or seer or poet himself. Thus, Pound grafts Horace's allusion to the *vestalia* onto the clause glossing the river and first king of his Apulian homeland the better to appropriate Horace's index of immortality for himself. For while Horace linked his lasting fame to Rome the place, Pound having experienced firsthand the vanity of such a literal-minded approach, would now derive his glory from the Eleusinian or vegetative, erotic, and aesthetic principles of metamorphosis celebrated in his profoundly American (in the sense of rootless) art, the only "homeland" he knows. Finally, Pound isolates Horace's supreme assertion about the special originality of his composition in order to stress its unique importance for himself. In fact, Pound's conditional statement, colon, and stanzaic break all presage what his transformation of Horace's indirect statement into direct quotation propounds: "Power from lowliness: 'First brought Aeolic song to / Italian fashion.'" Himself born in Hailey, Idaho, perhaps Pound identifies with Horace's humble beginnings, but clearly here he no longer regards Horace as a "liar of no mean pomposity" ("H," 217) in order to promote his own success in having brought Latin and other linguistic song into English verse. Pound's "Wear pride, work's gain!" functions less ambiguously as self-address, whereas Horace's "sume superbiam" ("take pride") is cleverly addressed to the Muse responsible for his success. Curiously enough, though she ill suits Horace's lyric achievement, Melpomene as the Muse of tragedy ironically befits Pound. And so he closes his poem with the apostrophe to "O Muse Melpomene," revising Horace's "volens" ("graciously") into "by your will," as if to stress the legitimacy of her choice. On the other hand, laurel symbolizes triumph, or in Pound's case his capacity for having captured Daphne in song, and so he, unlike Horace, repeats the word in closing his poem. His final line, with its noun phrases as fragments of a more complete thought, and its restrictive adjective, "Delphic," allowing "laurel" to modulate fully the second time around, highlights Pound's own Horatian pride in his achievement: "O Muse Melpomene, / By your will bind the laurel. / My hair, the Delphic laurel."

Thus ends the last act of Pound's brilliant but bittersweet performance, a drama belied only by the tragedy of his being a man without a country. In his simpler time, Horace could appeal to Rome and Apuleia for his ultimate sense of self; Pound, by contrast, had neither Rome nor America in the end, and consequently became quite directionless: "M'amour, m'amour / what do I love and / where are you?" (117/802). His translation of *Odes* 3.30 reminds us of the opportunity to love (*agape*) that Pisa presented, which earlier had become a chance missed. Of course, Pound eventually honored Horace for the craftsmanship, translation, and lyricism for which we value his own verse, and yet in "settling" for Horace, Pound seems not only to have recognized the inherently Hebraic nature of his lifelong quest for selfhood, but also, therefore, to be denying the importance of ever sufficiently achieving such integrity in life. And he denies it less by further resisting the establishment, Virgilian, or Hebraic values of English poetry, than by claiming for himself a poetic immortality dependent upon the same Hellenic values he celebrated in his own verse. But simply to cease relating altogether to society and disappear into one's own creation, whether an ideal or a real republic (very much the risk of all Romantic and post-Romantic poetry, and one Pound had been preparing himself to take for a long time), is to conceive art *in vacuo,* without a practical or truly meaningful social and therefore natural dimension. Such escape signals a disavowal of responsibility, a refusal to "come home," and an unwillingness or inability to define one's self in relation to others, however frustrating the task may be. How can such impatience possibly be rooted? And, since rootless, how can it rightly lead to love, except of one's self and perhaps one's friends, and then but groundlessly? Certainly, civil disobedience, and the tradition of non-violence, has its place in democratic society, even as the majority must protect minority and individual rights, but Ezra Pound erred too far in his selfishness (*amor sui*). That much of the world wandered with him only proves the problem was larger than Pound, God bless him, whose work darkly reflects the moral vagrancy of our violent and often misspent time. So lest we disturb his dust too harshly, let us acknowledge how much he was one of us, and value how much he, though lost, may yet lead us to ourselves (*amor fratris*).

Conclusion

"Do not move / Let the wind speak /
that is paradise" (120/803)

The "Maiden Gathering Flowers" is a first century A.D. wall-painting from Stabiae, now housed in the National Museum of Naples. Along with Pompeii and Herculaneum, Stabiae was destroyed by the eruption of Mount Vesuvius in 79 A.D. In *The Story of Art* (Phaidon, 1950) E. H. Gombrich briefly admires this painting's "exquisite beauty and grace," seeing the maiden as "one of the Hours, picking a blossom as if in dance" (p. 77). Notwithstanding the Botticellian echoes of this identification, it is a beginning. The wall itself appears covered with an olive green wash, the color of nature, but also creating the customary effect in Roman art of a figure located in a perspectiveless background. The woman has been gathering flowers, as evidenced by the white and yellow bouquet in her basket. In fact, her clothes are of the same colors: a silk-white toga-like outer garment and a saffron full-length slip or gown. Moreover, she is presently plucking a white blossom with her right hand, precisely pinching her prey with all five fingers clearly articulated. Here we might draw the reasonable aetiological conclusion that she is demonstrating who she is: Flora the Roman goddess of flowers, or Chloris her Greek forebear. At any rate, she certainly is beautiful: taller than the tall plant, leisurely bare-footed, poised enough to pluck while walking, full-hipped, genteelly fingered, richly braceleted, and nobly dressed in fine linens, of cameo-white complexion, which we notice especially from the way her slip has slid alluringly off her right shoulder in the act of picking, and from the contrast between her bare neck and orange-red hair (itself a rarity), elegantly coiffed behind. This much we see, fondly imagining the power of her embrace from the obvious strength in her left arm and the length of her right, and yearning to know more about the formal beauty that lies yet veiled beneath her airy vestments, and to gaze upon the colored lights of her eyes forever hidden from our view.

Perhaps Gombrich is correct; perhaps she is one of the Hours, maybe Karpo (flowering) or Auxo (ripeness), who were associated with the seasons, and therefore the passing of time. And now we can appreciate the unknown artist's Keatsian ability to contemplate the problem of time in his work. Both maiden and plant *have grown*. She herself in her maidenhood emblematically rests (diastasis) between the gathered flowers held by her *sinister* arm and the bloom about to be pinched so *dextrously* between thumb and index finger. She is picking, reaching, turning, walking, and the wind is blowing as shown by the way her silks flutter out behind her lagging *left* foot. Time is implied, although the artist has frozen a moment of time, and therefore triumphed over time. And yet, clearly there is something forthright, or *moral* about this moment, as if with his depiction of her right hand, her right foot forward, and her glance to the right, the artist would have his *virgin* boldly, knowingly, and humanly *choose* to walk left into the past of death because doing so is *de rerum natura*. In other words, the innocent freedom of the maiden's choice to gather flowers announces the morality of the artist's decision to paint her. The tension of the painting, then, is less between time versus timelessness, than between the plant producing many flowers, the nubile maiden exquisitely balanced between innocence and experience, and the creative artist having produced his masterpiece versus mortality itself. That mortality mockingly leers at us even today through the serpentine crack running down the right third of the painting, breaking off her right arm, and through the underlying red clay of the wall (almost the color of her hair or of her bracelet), exposed on her left buttock and at the back of her left knee, which together threaten to separate her from nature, tumble her at the knees, and destroy her image altogether. In short, the painting represents less a static moment in time, finally, than a vortex of floral, human, and pictorial *semina* that proclaim their generic survivability through time, despite individual extinction. After all, an Hour is the hand-maiden of Venus, whose warm westerly wind (Zephyrus) during the recurrent miracle of Spring excites our reverence for those magic moments when the *genetrix* presides over life's earthly renewal, in spite of the existence of death.

So who is this woman, a veritable blossom of nature that inspires great art, imbued with life's mysterious capacity for perennial metamorphosis? Flora, Chloris, one of the Hours, Venus? Here we notice she is not looking our way. Visually, such coyness proves attractive because we can thus name her as we wish. If an Hour, why not a Nymph: someone mortal, young, fair, and female? She is obviously graceful, charming, and beautiful: why not one of the Charites (Gratiae), say Thaleia (the flowering)? Or perhaps Charis (Grace). Since she, too, was raped while garnering flowers, why not Persephone (Koré)? Why not for her love, beauty, and fertility, Aphrodite herself as Anchises saw her, or Lucretius' *alma Venus;* but not Plato's Urania, for assuredly this woman walks on the ground. And so perhaps we should speculate more mundanely about, say, the artist's daughter, wife, or mistress, who may have been named Lesbia, or Aurunculeia, or Cynthia, or Corinna, or.... Morally, of course, we do not have world enough or time to ignore her identity; we cannot afford to let her walk facelessly away. And so we must pursue her, determine her name, and come to know her. For we need her, because she is who we are. But who in the busy twentieth century cares about Stabiae's "Maiden Gathering Flowers," a faded wall-painting almost two-thousand years old of a mysterious subject herself receding rapidly into the mythological past? A pagan image so out of time and the right tradition, so poised between the end of one era and the beginning of another, that it could not possibly speak to us today? Ezra Pound cared, and he was passionately concerned all his life that we should care, too. And for this we honor him.

Let us now reverse the image, to contemplate not our pursuit of love *(eros),* but rather love's pursuit of us *(agape).* Anders Nygren, Bishop of Lund, has written a most interesting book entitled *Agape and Eros,* translated by Philip S. Watson (Westminster Press, 1953), in which he explores both the motif of *agape* as expressed in the New Testament and Paul's theology, and the motif of *eros* as expressed in Plato, Aristotle, and neo-platonism. Nygren then discusses Augustine's doctrine of *caritas* as a synthesis of *eros* and *agape* that endured throughout the Middle Ages until a renewal of *eros* in the Renaissance, which soon incited a renewal of *agape* in the Reformation. While Nygren has not gone unchallenged, and while his argument is theologically oriented, his book does fortuitously illuminate large areas of Pound's Hellenic-Hebraic thinking. We should remember that Plato's idealistic formulation of heavenly love in the *Symposium,* though exerting a tremendous influence on Christianity through Augustine, proves an exception to the ancient world's popular thinking about passion, beauty, and fertility as expressed in the worship of Aphrodite (Venus) and her son Eros (Cupid). In this pandemic sense Pound is probably more representative than Plato. But also, we recall Pound's refusal in "Axiomata" (1921) to speculate about the "intimate essence or *theos*" of the universe, which Whitmanian rule he adhered to throughout his career, much better than Whitman did. Similarly, our use of *agape* in reference to Pound has primarily concerned less God's love for man (or man's for God) than man's love for his fellow men. Employing Nygren as a foil, then, we see well, Confucius notwithstanding, that Pound's Hellenism coincides with vulgar (popular) *eros* of Graeco-Roman times, the erotic side of Nygren's *caritas*-synthesis during the Middle Ages, i.e., neoplatonism from

Plotinus through Erigena to Plethon, and less Ficino's than Botticelli's classicism during the Renaissance. Correspondingly, Hebraism, for Pound, coincides with Plato, who banished all imagists from his republic, with Judeo-Christian monotheism in general, and with Calvin's Protestant toleration of usury. No wonder, in his own time we find post-Protestant Pound on the reactionary, anti-Semitic side of the fascists.

How revealing it becomes to compare Pound's prodigal search for self through one *Latin* mask after another, a consciously selfish or erotic quest, with 1 Corinthians, chapter 13, Paul's great lyric on Christian love to the handful of believers at Corinth, a city known for its pagan decadence in 55 A.D. "Though I speak with the tongues of man and of angels..." (13:1), and "though I have the gift of prophecy, and understand all mysteries, and all knowledge...," without love "nihil sum" (13:2). Did Pound not employ many languages and even the gods in his verse? Did he not profess to be a seer, to revere the mysteries, and to sail after knowledge? Love "suffereth long, and is kind" and "envieth not" and "vaunteth not itself, is not puffed up" (13:4). Pound only grew more impatient, malignant, envious, and proud with age, in direct relation to his own frustration in achieving himself, the one important exception being Pisa where through suffering he learned patience. Love is not "ambitiosa" (13:5); Pound's ambition knew no limit, not even when thwarted by epic failure or faced with death. For Paul, love never fails; "but whether there be prophecies, they shall fail; whether there be tongues, they shall cease; whether there be knowledge, it shall vanish away" (13:8). Paul teaches that we know in part, and prophesy in part, "but when that which is perfect is come, evacuabitur quod ex parte est" (13:9-10). Sadly, Pound's became an increasingly desperate effort with higher and higher stakes to progress beyond "ex parte." And here we might associate Pound's almost sexual preoccupation with rootedness to the exiled artist's fear for his identity or manliness; "When I was a child, I spake as a child, I understood as a child, I thought as a child: but when I became a man, I put away childish things" (13:11). Paul insists that "now we see through a glass, darkly; but then face to face: now I know in part; but then I shall know even as also I am known" (13:12). What are Pound's masks, his eyes, "I" 's, if not mirrors in which he obscurely sought himself? What did he seek and indeed almost achieve at Pisa, if not distance on himself, or the perception of himself in his otherness? "And now," says Paul, "abideth faith, hope and charity [*agape*]; maior autem horum est charitas" (13:13), which Pound has "had sometimes," but "cannot make... flow thru" (116/797). By "flow thru" I submit he is not thinking *ad fontes* with the neoplatonics, but rather with Luther of his enemies whom he should have more tolerantly loved despite themselves, had not so much of himself been at risk.

Our point in rehearsing 1 Corinthians has not been to moralize about Pound, and even less to dwell upon the obvious; but rather to emphasize the deficiency in his Hellenic approach to reality. His word for what he lacked was "charity," and ours, "love" (*agape*); but perhaps a better word would be "patience." Patience (*pati:* to suffer) in Hebraic tradition used to be a virtue, as in the suffering of the Jews throughout history, that of the early Christians, and even of the Protestants during the Counter Reformation. Yet the tradition of *Puritanism* in America has been such that impatience or intolerance, practically speaking, became a virtue, until the eighteenth century and the Enlightenment when science began to compete with religion, the center of American government moved farther south from Boston to Philadelphia to Washington, and Calvinism deferred to Deism. Of course, Puritan intolerance betrays Puritan insecurity, even as the Founding Fathers after the Revolution began to feel more secure about their American experiment. *Impatience,* therefore, while not traditionally a particularly Jewish trait, has sometimes been a European Catholic and more recently an American Protestant or Puritan one. In America, Puritan impatience or intolerance replaces Hebraic patience, which in turn becomes a more statesmanlike or Hellenic virtue. One is tempted to relate Puritanism's psychological flip-flop to the broader history of Christian heresy: the Romans martyred the early Christians (a minority), who evolved into the Roman Catholic Church (a majority), which persecuted various dissenters, including the European Protestants (a minority), who as the Puritans (a majority) harassed many helpless non-conformists (women, Jews, Quakers, Indians, dancing-masters, etc.). Pound's dilemma as a post-Protestant, therefore, was one of where to go to join a majority, if only a moral majority. And his solution on leaving Wabash College in 1908 was to escape into Hellenic poetry, and to try and make that poetry prophetic by fleeing eventually to fascist Rome, where he became a member of an apparent majority and could then, predictably enough, proscribe all heretics (Roosevelt, Churchill, the Jews, etc.) from his New Jerusalem.

Besides identifying *impatience* with *Puritanism* and patience with our more secular leaders, because life for the Puritans was difficult, and for the Deists comparatively easy, we also in America have come to associate Hellenic patience with intellectual leisure and Hebraic impatience with physical labor. And since ours is a Puritan tradition, we frown on Hellenic consciousness as pleasure-seeking, frivolous, and evil but extol Hebraic conscience as work-oriented, industrious, and good. Those who can, do; those who cannot, teach, or even worse, write poetry! Quite obviously, Pound spent his impecunious career trying rationally to right the wrongs we have perpetrated against Hellenism in the name of righteousness, which in the industrialized West often seems to have earned its own material reward. Less obviously, however, as this task, which became his triune goal of lyric, dramatic, and epic self-fulfillment, grew increasingly difficult and finally impossible to achieve, Pound correspondingly lost his Hellenic patience (cool), and reverted irrationally to the good old sacred rage (intolerance) of Puritan New England. Hence, the chief *persona* of Pound's Latin masks, it would seem, was his *Hellenism* itself! Amazingly, Pound's Hellenism appears to be something of an American myth conceived by many of her writers to justify their alienation in this still incredibly anti-intellectual land. The self-exiled poet invents a Hellenic rootedness to conceal his own Puritan impatience, which once revealed, exposes him to the cure of Hebraic patience. Such is the route of the matter.

While we might forgive Pound his "stupid, suburban prejudices" (note his animosity even here), we must never forget he had them. Some would claim extenuating circumstances, that his passport was nullified (and so it was, figuratively speaking) and that he could not have left had he wanted to. What of his subsequent, quite voluntary, Rome Broadcasts? A more sophisticated version of this same argument might involve the implicitly Hebraic nature of his quest for self through time, asserting that had he been allowed to complete his epic identity "things would have been different." This, to me, seems disingenuous at best, as if anyone could not be charitable upon having his way first. But a better refutation of this view involves recognizing the explicitly Hellenic nature of Pound's aesthetics from the beginning of his career, which conscious predisposition, however long he was able to defer his date with destiny, inexorably led him into unconscious politico-economic excess. And here we are talking about memory and association, which eventually became for Pound a matter of the mind's "jumping without building" (110/780), as means of deducing one's self from the past. Metamorphosis leads one marvelously to the present, but what happens when one's present becomes unbearable as it often does due to the suffering inherent in life? Aesthetically, and therefore morally, we need to glimpse a bit of the future to bear our own present better. Without some sense of apocalypse, how can we achieve the necessary distance on ourselves to see ourselves not only as others see us, but also as we ourselves would like to be seen? The relevant word here is perspective, and without it one whores after strange gods. Perspective fosters communication, not confrontation; and implies peace, not war. It suggests not simply, as Pound said thinking of James during the first world war, "a recognition of differences, of the right of differences to exist, of interest in finding things different" (*LE,* 298); but also problem-solving or the reapplication of the differences learned to what was difficult to resolve in the first place, thereby preparing us for greater challenges in the future. Why should a man look upon the sun, if he does not then re-enter the cave to help others in their assent? Nor should he stare too long, else he will ruin his eyes.

In contrast to Pound himself, we might close by returning to Virgil in order to demonstrate conclusively his unspoken role as the father of a prodigal son who long yearned but never quite managed to come home. How profoundly Protestant, how anxiously American (an aftershock of the Revolution still with us) for an individual disliking himself simply to deny his immediate personal, societal, or historical past and to invent or discover another more suitable origin elsewhere. Because Pound was a modern *American* poet, whom he wanted to emulate says much about his initial sense of inferiority, and also his ultimate poetic ambition. That Pound trained his eye on Whitman who "broke the new wood" (*Per,* 80), on Milton who fathered the Puritan epic in English, on Dante whose Catholicism proved acceptable because unthreatening, on Virgil who conceived the foundation myth of Rome, and on Homer whose *nekuia* was "older than the rest" (*L,* 274) defines his own greatness of soul *(megalopsychia)*. Also, despite his professed preference for Homer (Odysseus), Pound necessarily over time sought to rival Virgil because, unlike Homer, Virgil was the first (and the last) to achieve epic selfhood by celebrating a paradisal millenium of sorts (the *pax et imperium Romanum*) in his verse. Surely aware that failing to achieve this great goal of Virgilian imitation would make him appear foolish, conceited, and vain, or worse, Pound aimed, nevertheless, to disprove by his own example T. S. Eliot's claim in 1944 before the Virgilian society ("What Is a Classic?") that the Mantuan was inimitable (i.e., a "classic"). We should remember how much Pound saw Eliot as his only serious competition for the crown of Virgil *redux;* in fact, it is hard not to interpret Pound's own interests in Ovid (Eleusis) and Confucius as his effort to outflank the chief poetic spokesman for Christendom in our time. At any rate, Pound sympathized with the cunning of an outcast Odysseus, who felt, as he tells Athena in book thirteen, virtually alone in his struggle to return home (*Ody.* V–XII). In turn, Pound enviously resented the piety of "snivelling" Aeneas, who was periodically reassured of his own destiny as the founder of Rome. Aeneas' *pietas* derives largely from his willing submission to fate: whether shouldering his father from Troy, or sacrificing all he could have had with Dido in Carthage, or accepting his responsibility as an agent of the gods in reaching Latium. Pound's impiety, therefore, results directly from his unwillingness to honor Virgil as his poetic father precisely because he would like to match (although Eliot said it could not be done) Virgil's poetic, political, paradisal achievement. In that he endeavored to realize heaven on earth, then, Pound was, as Terrell says in his *Companion to the*

Cantos, a religious poet. Unless, of course, Eliot was right and establishing such a haven of terrene delight cannot be done in time, which would make Pound pre-eminently Satanic for even trying, much less trying and failing for lack of love. In short, to paraphrase Propertius (4.8. 16), "Homer was his excuse, but really his reason was Virgil."

If Virgil was a proto-Christian for discerning the meaning of history, Pound was plainly post-Christian (and anti-Eliot) in refusing to accept Aeneas' submissive behavior the better to rival Virgil. It is tempting to praise Virgil for abiding by the historical past and to censure Pound for inventing his own syncretic, highly synchronic, and often mythical past, or for pretending to derive himself from such a past through the obvious self-justification of "translating" or "metamorphosing" from the dead. On the one hand, however, are we so sure that Virgil's past was *the* past? Are we even sure that Virgil, who once was Augustus' enemy, or who just as easily could have performed for Antony, or who sympathized so with luckless Dido and tragic Turnus, felt it so? Clearly, the prophecy of the *Aeneid,* its apocalyptic dimension, so to speak, concerns less the rich re-creation of Troy's last hours, or the prophecies like Helenus' that come true in the poem, or even the history-as-prophecy of Anchises' rehearsal in hell or that on Aeneas' shield, than it does the poem's plea, both to Augustus (*Aen.* VI. 851–53) and to posterity through its lines of ceaseless and impartial carnage (*Aen.* VII–XII), for peace and a sense of community between Trojan and Italian alike. Eliot's point about Rome as the mother of Christian Europe is well taken, although Virgil's world (even when distinguished from Augustus') seems more the wishful one of Anglican Eliot in 1944 or in 1951 ("Virgil and the Christian World"). On the other hand, however, despite the complex license Pound has taken with his predecessors, the distortion inherent in his method of deducing himself from the past, are we so sure that he *only* saw himself in his glass and then but darkly? Is there no grain of truth to Eleusis, to Pound's neopagan veneration of agricultural, sexual, and aesthetic renewal? Was there no such thing as Greek piety in the Archaic Age (pre-600 B.C.)? Or no millennial efficacy in the wisdom litera-ture of Hesiod (or Confucius)? Not even Virgil could have foreseen the European ramifications of Jupiter's promise to set neither spatial nor temporal limits on Rome's dominion without end (*Aen.* I 278–79). Con-versely, that Pound felt so permanently and profoundly drawn to that critical nexus between Hellenic and Hebraic tradition two thousand years ago (between the birth of Catullus and the death of Ovid) indicates not only the length of Virgil's shadow, but also the Herculean labor Pound would expend fleeing from his time into the pre-temporal or mythological past in order to redeem his time both for himself and for society, European and American, or the world at large. From a twentieth-century perspective

Virgil seems so young and innocent; Pound, so experienced and old. Yet as Eliot saw, Virgil was a mature poet writing about a mature society, in a mature language; Pound may have been as mature a poet, but he felt compelled to range world history (and pre-history) and to employ half-a-dozen tongues in order to enrich the meager soil of his own intrinsically American sense of place and speech. Such apparently, was the curse of Whitman's "barbaric yawp." We are reminded of Virgil's humility toward his own fortunate ripeness: "Then aloft search with your eyes and duly found pluck it with your hand; for of itself freely and easily it will follow, if you the fates call; otherwise not with any force will you be able to seize it nor to rend it with hard steel" (*Aen.* VI. 145–48). We are also reminded of Eliot's admonition in "Virgil and the Christian World" about the man who, having a deep conviction of his destiny but ceasing to act as an instrument, thinks of himself as the active source of what he does, whose pride is punished by disaster (*Poetry and Poets,* p. 144).

In retrospect Pound's problem of how to rival Virgil was far more difficult than Virgil's problem of how to rival Homer. But whereas Virgil securely acknowledged his predecessor, Pound anxiously (and perhaps wisely) disavowed any preoccupation with his. Virgil as Sibyl sets the pace with "facilis descensus Averno" (*Aen.* VI. 126): Remembering the past, any past, is not so hard. Yet he also cautions all pretenders with, "sed renovare gradum superasque evadere ad auras,/ hoc opus, hic labor est" (*Aen.* VI. 128–29): Imagining a future that includes both personal (poetic) and social (political) justice becomes the challenge. The Sibyl even warns Aeneas' uninitiated comrades ("profanum," not the "vulgus." He himself, after all, was of that vast American "vulgus," but was fatefully tempted by Virgil to seek polity even beyond poetry. Nor is there any indication that he ever read beyond the bough of book six, to Virgil's pointedly dispassionate judgment on his own imaginative endeavors to change the world through poetry, where Aeneas ascends to the upper world through the gate of false dreams ("falsa...insomnia"; *Aen.* VI. 896). The *Aeneid,* it may be, is less an incomplete poem because of its fifty-odd unfinished hexameters, or because of its few passages revised by Varius and Tucca, or because it lacks a marriage between Aeneas and Lavinia, or because it fails to celebrate Alba Longa and Rome as it does Latium in some sort of Divine Comedy, than because Virgil who as he lay dying insisted his poem be destroyed felt he had not sufficiently distanced himself from the autocratic designs of that "crapulous Presbyterian Caesar Augustus." Octavian interceded after Virgil's death to preserve the poet's elaborate justification of divine authority for himself as the august *imperator* who closed the Temple of Janus in 29 B.C., and so he gained the fiction he required. Virgil, it seems, perceiving the tears of things, and bored both by fanciful and genuine warfare, had few illusions about his own or his country's good fortune: "then everywhere emulous with frequent fires the broad plains shone brightly" (*Aen.* XI. 208–09). Nor did he presume with his epic to have ushered in the millennium of pagan Italy, much less the bimillennium of Christian Europe. And yet, *mirabile dictu,* he did just that! But after witnessing Pound's conscious efforts to imitate Virgil's unconscious achievement, we might well hope to be spared the experiments of all poets who are tempted beyond poetry by polity into seeking to save the world from itself. Perhaps, instead, we should simply beware of all false prophets. Perhaps, indeed, we should accept in theory the possibility of Pound's dream despite the haste and ominous impatience of Pound himself. If only Hellenism and Hebraism, *eros* and *agape,* memory and imagination could be melded together for world peace.... Postwar tensions between East and West again appear to be increasing so as to allow us yet another opportunity, maybe our last in this nuclear age, for a synthesis prior to annihilation that would surpass even Virgil's and prove Mr. Eliot wrong. Or has modern poetry ceded its moral authority to science as the new domain of human imagination ever seeking to transform the world?

As to the poet whose moral outrage masked his aesthetic crisis in 1917, and whose aesthetic outrage failed to mask his moral crisis in 1945, who retreated from his dearly cherished but largely secret dream of achieving Virgilian polity through poetry, claiming instead for his efforts an Eleusinian immortality through Horace, what shall be his epitaph? If Odysseus' return to Penelope can be read as an Hebraic (linear) quest for self through time, Aeneas' migration to Rome, in fact, represents an Hellenic (circular) return to Dardanus' homeland. Enough of models, and heroes destined to become something greater or other than themselves. Ezra Pound, by contrast, for all his desire "sa gret" was never quite able to conclude his adventures satisfactorily. Here Palinurus comes to mind, who as Aeneas' helmsman fell asleep and therefore overboard after much good service just before reaching Hesperia. So, too, does Misenas whom none surpassed in arousing men to war with bugle and song. Or posibly old Acoetes lamenting the lifeless body of his charge, cut down before his time. But beyond Virgil lingers that haunting *re-encounter* with Elpenor, whose careless dissipation atop "Circe's ingle" determined his unfortunate end:

> "But thou, O King, I bid remember me, unwept, unburied,
> "Heap up mine arms, be tomb by sea-board, and inscribed:
> "*A man of no fortune, and with a name to come.*
> "And set my oar up, that I swung mid fellows" (1/4).

Notes

Chapter 1

1. As Donald Davie, *Ezra Pound: Poet as Sculptor* (New York: Oxford Univ. Press, 1964), pp. 29-30, says, "Unless the *Divine Comedy* is to be called an epic, Pound has pronounced an anathema upon the whole epic tradition since Homer.... In the only modern poet who has essayed epic in the English-speaking world, this is noteworthy."

2. "OCiG," 147; Pound later added that "Virgil and Petrarch...probably pass, among the less exigeant, for colossi" (*LE,* 24). Perhaps Hugh Kenner, *The Poetry of Ezra Pound* (New York: New Directions, 1951), p. 30, best appreciates Pound's point: "He places Virgil and Petrarch as 'dubious cases' with an eye on Homer and the troubadours."

3. *GB,* 113; in 1934 Pound recounted W. B. Yeats' story of the "plain sailor" who when asked about "Aeneas as hero" could only reply, "Ach, a hero, him a hero? Bi gob, I t'ought he was a priest" (*ABC,* 44).

4. Ezra Pound, "Virgil," *Il Mare,* V.xxvi (Rapallo, Feb. 4, 1933), 3.

5. All references to Virgil's text are from *P. Vergili Maronis Opera,* ed. by Frederic A. Hirtzel (Oxford: Clarendon Press, 1966); throughout the book, I have bracketed my prose translations from the Latin.

6. All references to Douglas' text are from *Virgil's Aeneid, Translated into Scottish Verse by Gavin Douglas, Bishop of Dunkeld,* ed. with notes and glossary by David F. C. Coldwell, 4 vols. (Edinburgh and London: Wm. Blackwood & Sons, LTD., 1951-56).

7. In 1917, after a short selection from Aeneas' descent into hell, Pound had said, "[Douglas] gets more poetry out of Virgil than any other translator. At least he gives some clue to Dante's respect from the Mantuan" (*LE,* 245), thereby implying that Douglas made hell come alive for him as Virgil did for Dante.

8. Ll. 116–19 from Pound's initial selection of the Sibyl describing the bough (Douglas, VI.ii.112–42 [*Aeneid,* VI.131–48]).

9. Although Pound never mentions it, Coldwell shows that Douglas often supplemented his own knowledge of classical mythology with commentaries on Virgil.

10. Surrey, II.1–13 (*Aeneid.* II.1–9); again, we note Pound's youthful interest in exile.

11. As C. S. Lewis, *English Literature in the Sixteenth Century Excluding Drama* (Oxford: Clarendon Press, 1954), p. 234, has said, Surrey is guilty of "putting Virgil in corsets."

12. See *A Preface to Paradise Lost* (Oxford: Oxford Univ. Press, 1942), pp. 12–50.

13. *GB*, 83; in 1918 Pound implored, "consider the definiteness of Dante's presentation, as compared with Milton's rhetoric" (*PD*, 7).

14. Herbert N. Schneidou, *Ezra Pound: The Image and The Real* (Baton Rouge: Louisiana State Univ. Press, 1969), pp. 56–73.

15. For Pound's poetic statement of this view, see 39/195; for his defiant restatement, see 74/435, 91/610, and 106/754. Leon Surette, *A Light from Eleusis: A Study of Ezra Pound's Cantos* (New York: Oxford Univ. Press, 1979), passim but especially pp. 40–56, syncretizes even further when he conflates Eleusis with the *nekuia,* Circe, and Aphrodite; for a more chastened estimation of Eleusis, which *remains* mysterious, see George E. Mylonas, *Eleusis and the Eleusinian Mysteries* (Princeton: Princeton Univ. Press, 1961), as well as any one of Martin P. Nilsson's numerous books on the subject.

16. For an excellent survey of Pound's religious position that relates his polytheism to his belief in neo-Platonism, Confucianism, and certain elements of Catholic thinking, see Clark Emery, *Ideas into Action* (Coral Gables: Univ. of Miami Press, 1958), pp. 1–22.

17. George Bornstein, *The Postromantic Consciousness of Ezra Pound* (Univ. of Victoria: English Literary Studies, 1977), pp. 19–34.

18. "The French Poets," *The Little Review* (Feb. 1918), rpt. *Make It New: Essays By Ezra Pound* (New Haven: Yale Univ. Press, 1935), p. 214.

Chapter 2

1. Donald Hall, "Ezra Pound: An Interview," *Ezra Pound,* ed. by Grace Schulman (New York: McGraw-Hill Book Co., 1974), p. 30.

2. Pound shared Landor's preference for Catullus over Horace, and especially like Catullus 31, 51, and 61, which were also Landor's three favorites; see *The Longer Prose Works of W. S. Landor,* ed. w. notes and index by C. G. Crump, 2 (London: J. M. Dent and Co., 1893), pp. 197–242.

3. All references to Catullus' text are from *C. Valerii Catulli: Carmina,* ed. by R. A. B. Mynors (Oxford: Clarendon Press, 1958).

4. John Espey, "Toward Propertius," *Paideuma,* 1.1 (1972), 68.

5. See E. T. Merrill's *Catullus* (Cambridge: Harvard Univ. Press, 1893), p. 72.

6. *PD* (1938 ed.), 60; in 1934 Pound claimed that Catullus alone was able to master Sappho's meter, that he was "better than Sappho for economy of words," or at least not "inferior" to her (*ABC*, 48).

7. Pound elaborated in 1934: "Our work [in 1916] was the work of outlaws.... The upper strata of society was rotten...the whole mind of the exploiting class was trivial, idiotic, and...the best conversation was found in *quadriviis et angiportis*" (*GB,* postscript).

8. "Ezra Pound and Catullus," *Ezra Pound: Perspectives,* ed. w. intro. by Noel Stock (Chicago: Henry Regnery Co., 1965), pp. 61–62.

9. See D. O. Ross' discussion of the "*amicitia* metaphor" in *Style and Tradition in Catullus* (Cambridge: Harvard Univ. Press 1969), pp. 80–95. "Amicitia" means roughly, "political alliance," and the metaphor suggests that Catullus used his affair with Lesbia to imply a larger, more chaotic world view.

10. Pound embedded his diptych in a section of wider Catullan allusion within the canto, including references to Cat. 2 and 3, as well as to Cat. 72 and 70; see Ronald Bush, *The Genesis of Ezra Pound's Cantos* (Princeton: Princeton Univ. Press, 1976), pp. 119-20, for a short gloss of this section. Pound's patchwork technique, here, foreshadows his more overtly dramatic effort in the *Homage* (begun in 1917, published in 1919) to build a "living personality" out of his own interpretation of Propertius' elegies.

11. "There is no useful English version of Catullus" (*LE,* 38), "It would be worth ten years of a man's life to translate Catullus" ("H," 226), and "No one has succeeded in translating Catullus into English" (*SP,* 294).

12. A shorter version of Catullus 26 appeared in *Papillon: Quattuor Epigrammata* (Milano: Vani Scheiwiller, 30 Ottobre, 1956), and the poem has often been reprinted, with minor variations; late in his career, Pound also translated Catullus 85 (*CtC,* 33).

13. Discerning such rhythm in "songs actually sung by the people at out-of-door festivities" (*SR,* 39), Pound noted that Catullus 34 "follows the classic dance of worship" (*SR,* 40). In fact, children could responsively sing the poem (see Merrill, *Catullus,* p. 60).

14. Espey, *Paideuma,* 1.1, p. 65, notes that Catullus' poem has inspired a long line of parodic efforts; see also, Hugh Witemeyer, *The Poetry of Ezra Pound: Forms and Renewal, 1908-1920* (Berkeley and Los Angeles: Univ. of Cal. Press, 1969), p. 114.

15. Witemeyer, *The Poetry of Ezra Pound,* pp. 139-41, explains that Pound intended with his poem to undercut Hermann Hagedorn's idealistic portrait of a cabaret dancer.

16. Pound the imagist also liked lyric Catullus 46 and invective Catullus 39: "Catullus' 'Iam ver egelidos refert tepores' would go straight into the best sort of chinese ideograph, the eleven lines are full of direct and definite statement, and the poem is very emotional" ("H," 225), and "In Rimbaud the image stands clear, unemcumbered by non-functioning words; to get anything like this directness of presentation one must go back to Catullus, perhaps to the poem which contains *dentes habet*" (*LE,* 33).

17. As Whigham (Stock, *Perspectives,* pp. 73-74) has noted, Catullus 61 exudes a marked Greek flavor, especially with its invocation to Hymen and its closing true epithalamium (see Merrill, *Catullus,* p. 96).

18. *SR,* 96; Catullus did anticipate "higher love" with his concern not only for Lesbia, but also for Roman society, as implied by the *amicitia* metaphor. Pound has alluded, here, to the distich in Catullus 72 (see n.10, above) whose diction—"ut gnatos diligit et generos"—Ross (p. 89) cites to support the *amicitia* metaphor.

19. For an account of Pound's own auspicious encounter during the summer of 1907 with the little maid of nine who alone of all Burgos had dared to tell the king's ban to the Cid, see Charles Norman, *Ezra Pound* (New York: The MacMillan Company, 1960), pp. 17-18.

20. See Wendy Flory, *Ezra Pound and the Cantos: A Record of Struggle* (New Haven: Yale Univ. Press, 1980), pp. 113-14.

21. Hugh Kenner, *The Pound Era* (Berkeley and Los Angeles: Univ. of Cal. Press, 1971), pp. 112-13.

22. "The grand bogies for young men who really want to learn strophe writing are Catullus and Villon. I personally have been reduced to setting them to music as I cannot translate them" (*ABC,* 104-105); and, "Having done Villon and Cavalcanti..., there remained 'Collis O Heliconii' (half-done, and no small technical problem)" (*GtK,* 368). Both

Donald Gallup (May 4, 1976) and R. Murray Schaefer (May 11, 1976) have written me that Pound's apparently unfinished score for Catullus 61 has yet to be found.

23. Ezra Pound, "M. Antonius Flamininus [sic] and John Keats: A Kinship in Genius," *The Book News Monthly,* 26.6 (Feb. 1908), 446; *Lusus* I, *Hieronymi Fracastorii et Marci Antonii Flaminii Carmina* (Veronae: ex typographica Petri Antonii Berni, MDCCXL), pp. 191–92, begins:

> [O you who inhabit the charming shores
> of Sirmio, fair Muse of Catullus, and
> who teach the blessed forest of citrus
> to resound pretty Lesbia. . . .]

24. Noel Stock, *The Life of Ezra Pound* (New York: Random House, 1970), p. 184.

25. [Sirmio, little eye of pensulas and islands,
> whatever in clear lakes and the vast sea
> each Neptune bears, how willingly and how happy
> I return to you, myself hardly believing
> that I have left Thynia and the Bithynian
> plains and that I see you in safety. O what
> is more blessed than the resolution of cares,
> when the mind puts aside its burden, and
> weary with foreign toil we have come to our
> hearth and repose on our longed for couch?
> This alone is worth labors so great. Hail,
> O charming Sirmio, and delight in your master's
> delight; and you, O waves of the Lydian lake,
> laugh, whatever there is of laughter at home.] (31)

26. For a more complete discussion of " 'Blandula, Tenella, Vagula' " as Pound's homage to a traditiion of lyric inspiration, see Ron Thomas, "Catullus, Flaminius, and Pound in ' "Blandula, Tenella, Vagula," ' " *Paideuma,* 5.3 (1976), 407–12; for Pound's use of "tenella" in the poem's title, see Espey, *Paideuma,* 1.1, p. 64; and for Hadrian's influence on the poem, see Witemeyer, p. 99n.

27. For a more complete discussion of Pound's elegiac return to Sirmio in the *Pisan Cantos,* see Ron Thomas, "The Catullan Landscape in Pound's Poetry," *Contemporary Poetry,* 4.1 (Spring 1981), 66–78.

Chapter 3

1. Pound's few Propertian allusions in the *Cantos* follow the Catullan pattern by dividing into early (lyrical) and late (elegiac) categories: see 5/17 and 20/89 (Propertius 2.20.28), as well as 74/443 (*Homage* IX.2), 110/780–81 (Propertius, 2.13.26), and 113/790 (Propertius 2.13.29–30).

2. Pound first associated Propertius with Provence when speaking of a medieval school that "set to explaining the nature of love and its effects... 'Ingenium nobis ipsa puella f[a]cit,' as Propertius puts it" (*LE,* 103; see also *LE,* 145–46 and 343–44); eventually, he associated him with Hellas: "There is a line in Propertius about *ingenium nobis f[a]cit.* But the subject is not greatly developed. I mean that Propertius remains mostly inside the classic world and classic aesthetic. Plastic to coitus. Plastic plus immediate satisfaction" (*LE,* 151).

3. All references to Propertius' text are from *Sexti Properti Carmina,* ed. by E. A. Barber (Oxford: Clarendon Press, 1960); Pound himself used *Catulli Tibulli Propertii Carmina,* ed. by Lucianus Mueller (Leipsig: B. G. Teubner, 1892), which occasionally made a difference in his reading.

4. For Dowson's poem, see *The Poetry of Ernest Dowson,* ed. with intro. by Desmond Flower (Rutherford, Madison, Teaneck: Fairleigh Dickenson Univ. Press, 1967), pp. 84–85; see also K. K. Ruthven's *A Guide to Ezra Pound's Personae (1926)* (Berkeley and Los Angeles: Univ. of Cal. Press, 1969), pp. 211–12, for a discussion of its influence on Pound's "Satiemus."

5. Besides Dowson and Propertius 2.15, Pound's "the fair dead" echoes his version of Propertius 2.28C with its catalog of beautiful women; also "bright glad days" echoes the "candida...soles" of Catullus 8.3 and 8, and the urgency of Catullus 5.1 and 5–6.

6. After *Canzoni,* Pound often praised Propertius' metrical ability (*LE,* 101; *L,* 87, 91, and 160; and *ABC,* 49), which admiration he may have derived from the classicist, J. W. Mackail (see *Latin Literature* [1894; rpt. New York: Frederick Ungar Publishing Co., 1966], p. 124). While several critics have suggested that Pound reproduced Propertius' meter in the *Homage,* J. P. Sullivan, in *Ezra Pound and Sextus Propertius* (Austin: Univ. of Texas Press, 1964), pp. 82–85, relates the elegiac couplet's closure to Pound's frequent reproduction of the sense (rather than rhythm) of a given couplet.

7. Reflecting his early late-romanticism, Pound in 1911 admired Propertius' virtù by quoting

   'Quoscumque smaragdos
   Quosve dedit flavo lumine chrysolithos' (2.16.43–44)

   —'the honey-coloured light' " (*SP,* 29). By contrast in Canto VII (1925) he recalled his former aestheticism by again using the expression "Smaragdos, chrysolithos" (7/25).

8. The "Ride to Lanuvium" itself occurs in Propertius' last book, when the affair with Cynthia, whether real or imagined, was over, and when he was trying least to write love-elegy and most to write on more public, Roman themes. Nor did Pound use the poem in writing the *Homage.*

9. Vincent E. Miller, in "The Serious Wit of Pound's *Homage to Sextus Propertius,"* *Contemporary Literature,* 16.4 (Aug. 1975), 452–62, suggests that Remy de Gourmont had a similar influence on Pound in his poem, helping him to modernize his language and to find his public voice; see also, Bush, *Genesis,* pp. 173–75.

10. In July, 1916, Pound told Iris Barry that if she could not find any "decent translations" of Propertius he would "have to rig up something" (*L,* 91). His jest to Joyce two years later displays his difficulty in publishing what he had indeed "rigged up": "I have as much trouble as you do in getting printed...the publishers-reading public seem to be horripiled by the most unforseeable turns of language" (*PJ,* 144). Four months later he remarked to Joyce, "I hope my Propertian ravings will amuse you *IF* I ever find anyone to print 'em" (*PJ,* 145). In December, 1918, he told Marianne Moore: "My last and best work, (*Propertius,,* has just dodged two publishers, one of whom [Mathews] wants to print half the book [*QPA*], leaving out the best of it" (*L,* 143). Pound again complained to Moore in February, 1919, about his struggles to get Harriet Monroe to print deserving authors: "I have nothing but my name on the cover [of *Poetry*]. And the prospects of a very mutilated piece of my Propertius appearing in her paper, because it would be criminal for me to refuse 10/10; and because it don't matter...in the least

what appears or does not appear. . . . The elect will see, ultimately, the English publication of the series" (*L*, 148). Pound's poem was "mutilated" in that only part of it appeared in *Poetry* in March, and then part in *The New Age* from June through August of that year. The poem made its first complete appearance that October in *Quia Pauper Amavi,* and only after appearing in *Poems: 1918-21* (1921), *Personae* (1926), and *Selected Poems* (1928) was it printed separately in 1934 — a measure of how long publishers and public took to accept the work on its own merits.

11. *PJ,* 247; though Pound's title partially repeats Ovid's line from the *Ars Amatoria* (2.165) — "I am the poet of the poor *because as a poor man I have loved*" — he obviously chose it to represent his view of Propertius (a pun on "paupertas" meaning "poverty" in Latin) resisting Maecenas' demands, and of himself fighting for artistic freedom during his London years.

12. Gardner Hale, *Poetry,* 14 (April 1919), 52; for similar negative reactions, see Robert Nichols, *The Observer,* Jan. 11, 1920, p. 6; W. R. Childe, *The New Age,* 26.11 (Jan. 15, 1920), 179; Harriet Monroe, *The English Journal,* 20 (Jan. 1931), 86-87; Martin Gilkes, *English,* 2 (1938), 77; Robert Graves, *The Crowning Privilege* (London: Cassell and Co., Ltd., 1944), pp. 212-13; and Gilbert Highet, *Horizon,* 33 (Jan. 1961), 116.

13. Pound's disdain for classical philology dated from his college days; see his early but revealing "Raphaelite Latin," *The Book News Monthly,* 25.1 (Sept. 1906), 31, and "M. Antonius Flamininus [*sic*] and John Keats: A Kinship in Genius," *The Book News Monthly,* 26.6 (Feb. 1908), 445. For the most recent discussions of Pound's mistranslation, see Gordon M. Messing, "Pound's Propertius: The Homage and the Damage," in *Poetry and Poetics from Ancient Greece to the Renaissance: Studies in Honor of James Hutton,* ed. by G. M. Kirkwood (Ithaca: Cornell Univ. Press, 1975), pp. 116-26, and Mark Turner, "Propertius Through the Looking Glass: A Fragmentary Glance at the Construction of Pound's *Homage,*" *Paideuma,* 5 (1976), 262.

14. Although Ruthven, *Guide,* p. 117, feels that Pound here was referring to Kandinsky — "Form alone, even if quite abstract and geometrical, has its inner timbre, and is a spiritual entity" — in 1916 he did honor Epstein's appreciation of form by saying, " 'Cynthia prima fuit?' What does it matter? Epstein is a slow worker perhaps" (*GB*, 99).

15. The first separate edition of the *Homage* in 1934 prompted R. P. Blackmur, with "The Masks of Ezra Pound," *Hound and Horn,* 7 (Jan.-March, 1934), 177-212, to initiate a stream of enlightened reviews; see especially John Speirs, "Mr. Pound's Propertius," *Scrutiny,* 3.4 (March 1935), 409-18; James Laughlin, "Ezra Pound's Propertius," *Sewanee Review,* 46 (Oct.-Dec. 1938), 480-91; Lawrence Richardson, "Ezra Pound's *Homage to Sextus Propertius,*" *Yale Poetry Review,* 6 (1947), 21-29; and "The Poet as Translator," *TLS,* Sept. 18, 1953, p. 596.

16. Only in "How to Read" (1928) did Pound define his neologism: "[*Logopoeia* is] 'the dance of the intellect among words,' that is to say, it employs words not only for their direct meaning, but it takes count in a special way of habits of usage, of the context we expect to find with the word, its usual concomitants, of its known acceptances, and of ironical play. It holds the aesthetic context which is peculiarly the domain of verbal manifestation" (*LE,* 25); in 1934 he added that with *logopoeia,* "you take the greater risk of using the word in some special relation to 'usage,' that is, to the kind of context in which the reader expects, or is accustomed, to find it. This is the last means to develop, it can only be used by the sophisticated" (*ABC,* 37-38).

17. Just as Davie (*Sculptor,* p. 88) legitimately labels the "logopoeic" relationship between Propertius and Laforgue "unconvincing, and irrelevant to the *Homage,*" so Kenner (*Ezra Pound,* p. 163) rightly recognizes the *Homage's* ironic techniques as "central to Pound's mature poetic practice."

18. *The New Age,* 26.5 (Dec. 4, 1919), 82; Adrian Collins (*The New Age,* 26.4 [Nov. 27, 1919], 62) first suggested that "Pound has developed the small germ of humor in Propertius—so small that no one else has noticed it—till it overruns his whole work."

19. Mueller, 4.1.39–42; Barber reads "detinuisse" (3.2.3; "detained"), but the idea of charming is still the same.

20. Responding to Hale, Pound admitted making only one error: his mistranslation of Propertius' reference to the Marcian aquaduct—"Marcius liquor"—as "Marcian vintage" (*L,* 149–50); the discovery of which, he explained in 1931, Hale himself "got not from his own intelligence or from a knowledge of Latin but from using an annotated edtn" (*L,* 230). Here Pound also chastised Harriet Monroe for putting "poetic quality below pedantry or even below scholastic distinction" (*L,* 230).

21. As for his mythological inaccuracies, Pound flippantly responded to Collins by asking why, if horses can fly, they cannot sing (*The New Age,* 26.5 [Dec. 4, 1919], 82). James Laughlin ((*Sewanee Review,* 46 [Oct.–Dec. 1938], 488) suggests that Pound transmutes his distaste for Christianity into Propertius' affected scorn for mythological personages, wherein the Roman divinities become stock characters in the Sunday comics. A more likely answer involves (a) Pound's ignorance of Propertius' Alexandrianism, (b) his projection of Ovid's often satiric treatment of myth onto Propertius, and (c) his unwillingness to render Propertius' *exempla* in scholarly, i.e., pedantic, fashion.

22. Though 11.2.34.83–84 in Mueller's edition differ slightly from Barber's, their gist is the same: "Nor less with these themes of love or, if less, in diction has the melodious 'swan' yielded to the unskilled song of the goose" (2.32.83–84).

23. While the evolution from Cynthia to Roman historical themes is clear enough in Propertius' work, Pound has raised the consciousness of some classicists concerning the significance of that evolution: To what degree is Propertius' aesthetic refusal to write epic, as epitomized by his frequent use of the *recusatio,* also a moral refusal to espouse Augustan imperialism? Besides Sullivan (including his *Propertius, A Critical Introduction* [Cambridge: Cambridge Univ. Press, 1976], passim), see *The Elegies of Propertius,* ed. with intro. and com. by H. E. Butler and E. A. Barber (1934; rpt. Oxford: Clarendon Press, 1964), p. lxv; Hugh E. Pillinger, "Some Callimachean Influences on Propertius, Book 4," *HSCP,* 73 (1969), 171–99; W. R. Johnson, "The Emotions of Patriotism: Propertius 4.6," *CSCA,* 6 (1973), 151–80; Margaret Hubbard, *Propertius* (London: Duckworth Press, 1974), esp. pp. 97–115, 134–36, and 160; and Steele Commager, *A Prolegomenon to Propertius* (Cincinnati: Univ. of Cincinnati Press, 1974), pp. 1 and 37–77.

24. For Propertius' more complicated arrangement, see Otto Skutsch, "The Structure of Propertius' *Monobiblos,*" *CP,* 58 (1963), 238–39.

Chapter 4

1. Pound had studied Ovid in the spring of 1903 during his sophomore year at the University of Pennsylvania.

2. Pound clarified his appreciation of *Ovid: Metamorphoses* 8.197–200, merely translated in passing here (*SR,* 15), when he said, "I am much more grateful for the five minutes during which a certain lecturer emphasized young Icarus begorming himself with Daedalus' wax than for all the dead hours he spent in trying to make me a scholar" (*LE,* 241).

3. That it was printed in Holland (if, in fact, it really was), Pound attributed to the "Puritan pest already beginning" (*ABC,* 135).

4. This line was apparently censored in 1917.

5. All references to Marlowe's text are from *Ovid's Elegies Translated by Christopher Marlowe,* ed. by Frederick Etchells and Hugh Macdonald (London: Spottiswoodie, Ballantyne and Co., 1925).

6. In 1934 Pound discussed this passage, including its reference to "pedants," as if he was defending the *Homage:* "The men who tried to fit English to rules they found in Latin grammarians have been largely forgotten, but the men who filled their minds with the feel of the Latin have left us the deathless criteria" (*ABC,* 135); in 1964 he again selected the passage (*CtC,* 37–38).

7. All references to Ovid's text are from *Ovid: Metamorphoses* 2 vol., ed. with an English translation by Frank Justus Miller (New York: G. P. Putnam's Sons, 1933).

8. All references to Golding's text are from *Shakespeare's Ovid Being Arthur Golding's Translation of the Metamorphoses,* ed. by W. H. D. Rouse (1906; rpt. Carbondale: Southern Illinois Univ. Press, 1961).

9. Cf. "...Scythiam septemque triones / horrifier invasit Boreas..." (*Meta.* 1.64–65) and "...the blasts of blustring *Boreas* raigne / In Scythia and in other landes set under *Charles* his waine" (Golding, 1.73–74). On the English asterism, see the *Oxford English Dictionary.*

10. Catullus closed his poem by claiming that the gods, with religion not yet scorned, had been wont to visit mortal company, but now that men had begun to sin, they no longer visited nor suffered themselves to be touched by daylight (64.384–408). Pound's allusion registers his interest in Sirmio and the gods, following " 'Blandula, Tenella, Vagula' " (*Canzoni,* 1911), but preceding the initial version of Canto I (*Poetry,* 1917).

11. Michael Alexander, *The Poetric Achievement of Ezra Pound* (Univ. of Cal. Press: Berkeley and Los Angeles, 1979), p. 21.

12. "Beauty in art reminds one what is worth while...even this pother about the gods reminds one that something is worth while. It draws one to consider time wasted.... The cult of beauty and the delineation of ugliness are not in mutual opposition" (*LE,* 45).

13. W. B. Yeats, in *A Packet for Ezra Pound* (Dublin: The Cuala Press, 1929), pp. 2–3, has famously restated Pound's explanation of his poem's structure: The *Cantos* "will [when finished] display a structure like that of a Bach Fugue. There will be no plot, no chronicle of events, no logic of discourse, but two themes, the descent into Hades from Homer, a metamorphosis from Ovid, and mixed with these medieval or modern historical characters." While underscoring the programmatic importance to Pound's epic of Ovid and therefore canto II, Yeats' statement and Pound's own later one (see Mary de Rachewiltz, *Discretions* [Boston: Little, Brown and Co., 1971], p. 159) might lead one to expect an emphasis on Ovidian physical metamorphosis; instead Pound has

chosen to emphasize the "magic moments" of the gods returning to himself and his audience.

14. Massimo Bacigalupo, *The Formed Trace: The Later Poetry of Ezra Pound* (Columbia Univ. Press: New York, 1980), p. 35.

15. For a discussion of myth and the *Cantos* from a Homeric rather than Ovidian point of view, see Lillian Feder, *Ancient Myth in Modern Poetry* (Princeton: Princeton Univ. Press, 1971), pp. 90–120, 200–18, and 293–306; for a discussion of metamorphosis, but not Ovid or myth, in the *Cantos,* see Sister M. Bernetta Quinn, *The Metamorphic Tradition in Modern Poetry* (New Brunswick, N.J.: Rutgers Univ. Press, 1955), pp. 14–48; see also, George Dekker, *Sailing After Knowledge* (London: Routledge & Kegan Paul), pp. 62–84.

16. Daniel Pearlman, *The Barb of Time* (New York: Oxford Univ. Press, 1969), p. 48, suggests that much of the scholarship devoted to this canto (see E. M. Glenn, *The Analyst,* No. 18) has slighted its relationship to the *Cantos* as a whole; in this formal sense Eugene Nassar, *The Cantos of Ezra Pound* (Baltimore and London: John Hopkins Univ. Press, 1975), p. 20, calls the poem a "dominant vortex piece"; and Bush (*Genesis,* p. 265) labels its central episode a "parable."

17. With his picture of Bacchus' justice dwarfed by his cruelty, Ovid seems to be condemning those abusing power in imperial Rome; see Brooks Otis, *Ovid As Epic Poet* (Cambridge: Cambridge Univ. Press, 1966), pp. 122–45. In this respect, Pound's piety ironically coincides better with Virgil and Horace's Augustanism.

18. For the tale of Acoetes, Pound relied on *Meta.* 3.597–691, as comparison with the Homeric Hymn to Dionysus (VII) — the other principal source for the story — quickly shows.

19. For this suggestion, see Flory, *Pound and the Cantos,* pp. 131–32.

20. Michael Bernstein, *The Tale of the Tribe: Ezra Pound and the Modern Verse Epic* (Princeton: Princeton Univ. Press, 1980), p. 166.

21. T. S. Eliot, *After Strange Gods,* (New York: Harcourt, Brace and Company, 1934), see especially pp. 33–53.

22. Jean Seznec, *The Survival of the Pagan Gods,* trs. from French by Barbara F. Sessions (New York: Pantheon, 1953).

23. M. L. Rosenthal, *Sailing into the Unknown Yeats, Pound, and Eliot* (New York: Oxford Univ. Press, 1978), p. 23.

24. See Bion, *Lament for Adonis,* Theocritus, *Id.* 15, and Ovid, *Meta.* 10.503–59 and 708–739; see also, *The Oxford Classical Dictionary,* p. 8.

25. In her reading of canto XLVII, Flory, *Pound and the Cantos* (pp. 142–45), stresses that "sexual love" brings "the gift of healing"; for similar emphases on sexual illumination, see Christine Brooke-Rose, *A ZBC of Ezra Pound* (Berkeley and Los Angeles: Univ. of Cal. Press, 1971), p. 135, and Pearlman (pp. 187–88). One might better accept Rosenthal's characterization of Pound's Odyssean imagination as "the ultimate embodiment of the male creative principle...penetrating the female principle of responsive, maleable reality" (p. 17), so long as we distinguish Pound's powers of memory and association from romantic visionary transcendence.

26. Bornstein, *Postromantic Consciousness* (pp. 21–22, and n. 6), first notes the obscurity of this passage, which underscores Pound's mysteriousness about Eleusis in general.

27. R. L. Stevenson, *Essays by Robert Louis Stevenson,* w. intro. by William Lyon Phelps (New York: Charles Scribner's Sons, 1892), pp. 54–56.

28. Lowell, *History* (New York: Farrar, Straus and Giroux, 1973), p. 140.

29. See Bernstein, *Tale of the Tribe* (esp. pp. 48–58), for a helpful discussion of the importance of Confucian historiography to Pound's *Cantos.*

30. Ezra Pound, *Jefferson and/or Mussolini* (1935; rpt. New York: Liveright, 1970), p. 113; I am indebted to Bacigalupo, *Formed Trace* (p. 185), for this point.

31. "Tintern Abbey" (11. 88–93), *The Poetical Works of Wordsworth, Cambridge Edition,* rev. w. new intro. by Paul D. Sheats (Boston: Houghton Mifflin Company, 1982), p. 92.

32. Upon this premise, Bernstein, *Tale of the Tribe* (pp. 3–25), predicates his illuminating theoretical discussion of Pound and the modern verse epic.

33. Cf. Mary de Rachewiltz, *Discretions* (p. 22), recalling her parents' house in Venice before the war: "And on the studio bookcase the great Ovid bound in wooden boards...."

34. "Modern Beauty" (1. 18), in *Poetry of the Victorian Period,* 3rd edition, ed. with notes by Jerome Hamilton Buckley and George Benjamin Woods (Glenview, Illinois: Scott, Foresman and Company, 1965), p. 887.

35. "To Althea, from Prison" (11. 5–8), "The Triumph of Charis" (11. 11–12), and "Song, Go, Lovely Rose" (11. 13–15) in *The Norton Anthology of Poetry,* revised, ed. Alexander W. Allison et al. (New York: W. W. Norton & Company, Inc., 1975), pp. 362, 260, and 305.

36. While perceiving a paucity of "mental action" in Pound's poetry as a whole, George Bornstein, *Postromantic Consciousness* (p. 70), acutely describes canto LXXXI and this passage in particular as "the closest mimesis of triumphant mental action in *The Cantos.*"

37. For a biographical interpretation of these lines, see Flory, *Pound and the Cantos,* p. 217.

38. W. S. Blunt's double sonnet, "With Esther," appears in M. E. Spear's *The Pocket Book of Verse* (New York: Pocket Books, Inc., 1940), p. 276:

> ...When I set
> The world before me and survey...
> —Its mean ambitions, its scant fantasies,
> ....
> ...and when I keep
> Calmly the count of my own life and see
>   On what poor stuff my manhood's dreams were fed
> Till I too learn'd what dole of vanity
>   Will serve a human soul for daily bread,
> —Then I remember that I once was young
> And lived with Esther the world's gods among.
>   (11.8–10, 22–28)

39. L1. 7–8, in *The Collected Poems of W. B. Yeats* (1933; rpt. New York: Macmillan Publishing Co., Inc., 1956), p. 20.

40. *Pur.* 26.143, in *Dante Alighieri: The Divine Comedy, Purgatorio,* Italian text and translation, by Charles S. Singleton (Princeton: Princeton Univ. Press, 1973), p. 289.

41. George Kearns, *Guide to Ezra Pound's Selected Cantos* (New Brunswick, New Jersey: Rutgers Univ. Press, 1980), pp. 177–78; it should be pointed out that Kearns is glossing only the first half of the canto.

42. W. B. Yeats, "The Peacock," ll. 1–3, *Collected Poems,* p. 119.

43. Once known as Cadmus' daughter Ino, but now a sea-goddess, Leucothea pities Odysseus and bids him to desert his raft and swim to Phaeacia with the aid of her veil; there he releases the veil, which floats back out to Ino (*Ody.* V.333–53, and 458–62); see also, Brooke-Rose (pp. 3–4, 15–16, and 150–56) and Hugh Kenner, "Leucothea's Bikini: Mimetic Homage" (Stock, *Perspectives,* pp. 25–40).

44. Pound quotes, "Est deus in nobis" (the first half of *Fas.* 6.3), from:

> [I will sing the truth, but some will say I have lied
> and will think that no deities have been seen by mortal.
> There is a god in us; with him stirring we grow warm:
> His impulse holds the seeds of inspiration.
> It is especially right for me to have seen the gods' faces,
> whether because I am a seer, or because I sing of sacred things.]
>   (Fas. 6.3–8)

[He also associated Ovid's "est Deus in nobis, agitante calescemus illo" (*Fas.* 6.3) with Richard of St. Victor's remark, "Ignis quidquid in nobis est," which he translated, "There is a certain fire within us" (*SP,* 74).

Chapter 5

1. J. P. Sullivan, in "Ezra Pound and the Classics," in *New Approaches to Ezra Pound,* ed. by Eva Hesse (London: Faber and Faber, 1969), p. 222, says, "On Horace, Pound is more puzzling and ambivalent. He sides of course with Propertius as against Horace's 'public' Augustanism, but he includes him among the four Latin poets who matter"; referring to Pound's translations of Horace (*CtC,* 35–37), Sullivan (*Approaches,* p. 223) adds that "Horace has long been regarded — for his attitudes rather than his verse — as the old man's poet *par excellence*. It may be that only in Pound's later years did the Horatian 'experience' strike a resonance in him."

2. Pound studied Horace's *Odes* in the spring of 1902 during his freshman year at the University of Pennsylvania, as well as his *Satires* and *Epistles* in the following spring during his sophomore year there.

3. *SR,* 88; in his next sentence, Pound described Daniel as the craftsman "whom Dante found 'best verse-wright in the fostering tongue,' the *lingua materna,* Provençal Langue d'Oc" (*SR,* 88); again, in 1934 Pound praised the birds' music in "L'Aura Amara" by alluding to Horace's 3.30.1: "That is why the monument outlasts the bronze casting" (*ABC,* 54). T. S. Eliot's dedication of *The Wasteland* (1922) to Pound as *il miglior fabbro* ("the better craftsman") foreshadows Pound's eventual association of his own and Horace's "craftsmanship."

4. In referring to Anatole France's commentary on *Odes* 1.11 (*SR*, 96), Pound anticipated his own allusion to the poem in "Surgit Fama" (*Lustra*, 1917) and his translation of it in 1963 (see also, *CtC*, 36).

5. Ezra Pound, "Orazio," *Il Mare* 11.25.1241 (Rapallo, Dec. 24, 1932), p. 4.

6. "H," 217; on "simple," Landor (*Works*, vol. 10, ed. by Charles G. Crump [London: J. M. Dent and Co., 1893], p. 101), had questioned both Horace's "choice of words" and his "*transpositions* of them," praising instead the "simple" syntax of Catullus and Ovid; for Landor's other Horatian criticism, see *Works* II.86 and 100–105, IV. 25, and X.45.

7. "H," 218; Pound later commented that Horace could "start in the tone 'O wife of indigent Ibycus / Why *will* you play about with flappers' and introduce his *stellis nebulam spargere* ["cast a cloud over the stars"] without creating an incongruity" ("H," 226). Horace's conceit of comparing hag and maids to cloud and stars (*Od. 3.15.5–6*) illustrates how often he achieved a kind of "discordia concors" in his work.

8. "H," 217; Pound later added that Horace had "the knack of interpolating [the] Greek treasure trove in pseudo Greek meters" ("H," 226); in 1934 he cautioned Mary Barnard: "Try writing Sapphics. And *not* persistently using a spondee, like that Blighter Horace, for the second foot" (*L*, 252). But Horace's innovation of fixing both the length of the fourth syllable and the caesura after the fifth reflected his desire to resolve the conflict between the word accent (Greek had no word accent, or stress) and the verse ictus of the line. As D. O. Ross points out, in *Backgrounds to Augustan Poetry: Gallus, Elegy, and Rome* (Cambridge: Cambridge Univ. Press, 1975), p. 135, "Horace's use of *modos* (freely translatable as 'meter') may thus indicate his 'Latinizing' of Aeolic meters, his discovery of how he could use most effectively the resources of his native language."

9. See *Odes* 1.25, 3.15, and 4.13.

10. "H," 226; Pound earlier had said that Pope really was a poet of "the Elizabethan satiric style, more or less born out of Horace, and a little improved or at least regularized" (*LE*, 287).

11. See Louis Untermeyer's *Collected Parodies* (New York: Harcourt, Brace and Co., 1926), pp. 81–210.

12. All references to Horace's text are from *Q. Horati Flacci: Opera*, ed. by H. W. Garrod (Oxford: Clarendon Press, 1967).

13. *Readies for Bob Brown's Machine*, ed. by Bob Brown (Cagnes-sur-Mer: Roving Eye Press, 1931), p. 114; Landor himself alluded amusingly to *Odes* 1.38 in his *Works*, II.103; and, quite probably, Pound was influenced by H. A. Dobson's shorter version of the poem, which Crump has appended to Landor's allusion:
   Davus, I detest
   Persian decoration;
   Roses and the rest,
   Davus, I detest.
   Simple myrtle best
   Suits our modest station;
   Davus, I detest
   Persian decoration. (*Works*, XII.103, n. 4)

14. Pound has alluded indirectly to Horace in "Song in the Manner of Housman" (*Ca*, 38; see A. E. Housman's translation of *Od.* 4.11), "Surgit Fama" (*Per*, 90; see *Odes* 1.11), and "The Patterns" (*Per*, 103; see *Odes* 1.22 and 2.5, as well as *Cantos*, 50/249).

15. Pound's rendering of Horace's "pluma superbiae" (*Od.* 4.10.2) as "feathery pride" perhaps results from remembering Yeats' "The Peacock" (1914), which concludes, "His ghost will be gay / Adding feather to feather / For the pride of his eye" (*Collected Poems*, 119). Horace's use of "pluma" ("down"), if it is "pluma," for the youth's first "beard" is unique; Pound's "Liguriné" seems derived from the variant, "Ligurine."

16. Though Pound substituted the noun, "decor," for Horace's adjective, "decorum," treating this line satirically was popular among the poets reacting to World War I; see, for example, Wilfred Owen's, "Dulce et Decorum Est."

17. In canto LXXVIII (1948), Pound again alluded to *Odes* 4.12.5, as well as to the Roman tradition of closing the temple of Janus to signify peace, this time personally appreciating how "no wind is the king's": "ter flebiliter: Ityn / to close the temple of Janus bifronte / the two-faced bastard..." (*Cantos*, 477.).

18. See *The Diary of John Quincy Adams: 1794-1845,* ed. by Allan Nevins (New York: Longmans, Green, and Co., 1928), p. 568.

19. See *The Works of John Adams,* ed. with bibliography and notes by Charles Francis Adams (Boston: Little and Brown, 1850-1856), vol. 4, p. 57.

20. For Pound's implicit comparison of Horace's "shipwreck" under Pyrrha's spell and his own under "Circe" 's, see *Odes* 1.5.4-5 and canto LXXX (*Cantos*, 495).

21. Pound's "ne quaesaris" (91/612 and 98/684), a present passive subjunctive of the variant "quaeso" (?), echoes Horace's "ne quaesieris" (*Odes* 1.11.1), which suggests that he began to meditate this first translation as early as 1955, at age seventy, a sign given the importance of these translations in justifying his failure, that he felt the vanity of writing anything after Pisa that could salvage epic success.

22. At the end of his version of *Odes* 1.31, Pound alluded with *"phrenes empedoi"* (*CtC*, 35) to Circe's command that Odysseus visit soothsaying Tiresias in Hades, whose "mind [abides] steadfast" while others flit about as shades (*Ody.* X.490-95); in canto LXXX (1948) Pound earlier had implied that he, too, like blind old Tiresias in hell, "still hath his mind entire" (80/494).

23. Because "deduxisse" probably echoes the "deductum carmen" of Virgil's own statement of Alexandrian poetics (*Ec.* 6.3-5), Horace in lines 13-14 was, more precisely, claiming for himself the double heritage of Greece and Alexandria; for a full discussion of what Horace meant by "Aeolium carmen ad Italos deduxisse modos" (*Odes* 3.30.13-14), see Ross, *Augustan Poetry,* pp. 134-36.

24. In "many bits," Kenner (*Era*, p. 548) perceives Pound's remembering "his many years' cunning attention to details."

Appendix

Pound's Formal Training in Latin

According to his academic transcripts and the appropriate course descriptions from the University of Pennsylvania (he took no Latin at Hamilton College during his junior and senior years, 1903-04 and 1904-05), Pound compiled the following record in Latin:

a) He was admitted to the freshman class in 1901, in part, on the basis of his Latin preliminary exams.

b) His coursework and grades (e.g., "distinguished," "good," "pass," "no pass") during his freshman and sophomore years (for a total of 21 credits) are as follows:

	Fall	*Spring*
1901–02 (6 hrs. total)	Lat. 1, 2 hrs., pass (Livy: sel. from Bks. I, XXI, and XXII)	Lat. 1, 2 hrs., pass (same)
	Lat. 2, 1 hr., good (Horace: *Odes*)	Lat. 2, 1 hr., good (same)
1902–03 (15 hrs. total)	Lat. 432, 3 hrs., pass (Cicero: *De Senectute* or *De Amicitia; Letters*)	Lat. 434, 3 hrs., good (Horace: *Satires* and *Epistles*)
	Lat. 439, 3 hrs., pass (Catullus and Tibullus)	Lat. 441, 3 hrs., pass (Propertius and Ovid)
		Lat. 443, 3 hrs., good (Virgil and Lucretius)

c) In 1905–06 Pound took a Latin Pro-Seminary (Catullus, Martial, and Tacitus) for three credits; and on April 30, 1906, he passed his Pro-Seminary exam for a minor in Latin as part of his M.A. degree in "Romanics," i.e., Romance Languages, itself conferred on June 13, 1906.

This information was obtained from the University of Pennsylvania Archives, North Arcade, Franklin Field E6, Philadelphia, Pennsylvania, 19174.

Select Bibliography

Works by Pound

Pound, Ezra. *A Lume Spento.* 1908; rpt. New York: New Directions, 1965.
——. *ABC of Reading.* 1934; rpt. Norwalk: New Directions, 1951.
——. "A Brief Note." *The Little Review,* 5 (Aug. 1918), 6–9.
——. *The Cantos.* 1970; rpt. New York: New Directions, 1973.
——. *Canzoni.* London: Elkin Mathews, 1911.
——. "Catullus," in *Papillon: Quattuor Epigrammata.* Milano: Vani Scheiwiller, 30 Ottobre, 1956.
——. "Catullus and Martial." *Edge,* 5 (May 1957), 34.
——. "The Draughty House." *The European,* 12.5 (London, Jan. 1959), 284.
——. "The Draughty House." *Furioso,* 1.2 (New Year's Issue), 5.
——. "Eighth Canto." *The Dial,* 72.5 (May 1922), 505–509.
——. *Ezra Pound to Louis Untermeyer: Nine Letters Written to Louis Untermeyer by Ezra Pound.* Ed. J. A. Robbins. Bloomington: Indiana Univ. Press, 1963.
——. "The Flagellants." *The New Age,* 26 (Jan. 22, 1920), 195.
——. *Gaudier-Brzeska: A Memoir.* 1916; rpt. London: The Marvell Press, 1960.
——. *Guide to Kulchur.* 1938; rpt. London: Peter Owen, Ltd., 1952.
——. "Horace." *The Criterion,* 9.35 (Jan. 1930), 217–27.
——. *Impact.* Ed. with intro. by Noel Stock. Chicago: Henry Regnery Co., 1960.
——. *Instigations: Together with an Essay on the Chinese Written Character by Ernest Fenellosa.* New York: Boni and Liverwright, 1920.
——. *Jefferson and/or Mussolini.* 1935; rpt. New York: Liveright, 1970.
——. *Literary Essays.* Ed. with intro. by T. S. Eliot. 1954; rpt. New York: New Directions, 1968.
——. "*The Little Review* Calendar." *The Little Review,* VIII. 2 (Spring 1922), 2 and 40.
——. *Lustra.* New York: Alfred Knopf, 1971.
——. "M. Antonius Flamininus [sic] and John Keats: A Kinship in Genius." *The Book News Monthly,* 26.6 (Feb. 1908), 445–47.
——. *Make It New: Essays By Ezra Pound.* New Haven: Yale Univ. Press, 1935.
——. "On Criticism in General." *The Criterion,* 1.2 (Jan. 1923), 143–56.
——. "Orazio." *Il Mare,* 11.25.1241 (Rapallo, Dec. 24, 1932), 4.

————. *Patria Mia.* (1913); 1950; rpt. London: Peter Owen, 1962.

————. *Pavannes and Divagations.* New York: New Directions, 1958.

————. *Pavannes and Divisions.* New York: Alfred Knopf, 1918.

————. *Personae.* London: Elkin Mathews, 1909.

————. *Personae.* 1926; rpt. New York: New Directions, 1971.

————. *Poems: 1918–1921.* New York: Boni and Liverwright, 1921.

————. "Poems from the Propertius Series." *Poetry,* 13.6 (Mar. 1919), 291–99.

————. *Polite Essays,* 1937; rpt. Freeport, New York: Books for Libraries Press, Inc., 1967.

————. *Pound/Joyce: The Letters of Ezra Pound to James Joyce, with Pound's Essays on Joyce.* Ed. with com. by Forrest Read. 1965; rpt. New York: New Directions, 1967.

————. "Propertius and Mr. Pound." *The Observer,* 25 (Jan. 1920), 5.

————. "Raphaelite Latin." *The Book News Monthly,* 25.1 (Sept. 1906), 31–34.

————. *Selected Letters: 1907–1941.* Ed. Donald Paige. 1950; rpt. New York: New Directions, 1971.

————. *Selected Poems.* Ed. with intro. by T. S. Eliot. London: Faber and Faber, 1928.

————. *Selected Prose: 1909–1965.* Ed. with intro. by William Cookson. London: Faber and Faber, 1973.

————. "Small Magazines." *The English Journal,* 19 (Nov. 1930), 689–704.

————. *The Spirit of Romance.* 1910; rpt. New York: New Directions, 1968.

————. "Three Cantos, I." *Poetry,* 10.3 (June 1917), 113–21.

————. "Three Cantos, II." *Poetry,* 10.4 (July 1917), 180–88.

————. "Three Cantos, III." *Poetry,* 10.5 (Aug. 1917), 248–54.

————. "To the Editor." *The English Journal,* 24 (Jan. 1931), 230–31.

————. Transcripts of the Shortwave Broadcasts from Rome, Dec. 7, 1941–July 25, 1943. U.S. Federal Communications Commission: Library of Congress, 1952. (Microfilm.)

————. *The Translations of Ezra Pound.* Ed. Hugh Kenner. London: Faber and Faber, 1970.

————. Untitled [Pound's Reply to Collins' Review of *QPA*]. *The New Age,* 26.5 (Dec. 4, 1919), 82–83.

————. "Virgilio." *Il Mare,* 5.26.1247 (Rapallo, Feb. 4, 1933), 3.

Works about Pound

Alexander, Michael. *The Poetic Achievement of Ezra Pound.* Berkeley and Los Angeles: Univ. of Cal. Press, 1979.

Alvarez, A. "Ezra Pound: the Qualities and Limitations of Translation-Poetry." *EIC,* 6 (Apr. 1956), 171–89.

Annotated Index to the Cantos of Ezra Pound. Ed. John H. Edwards and William W. Vasse. Berkeley and Los Angeles: Univ. of Cal. Press, 1957.

Anon. "The Poet as Translator." *Times Literary Supplement* (Sept. 18, 1953), p. 596.

Bacigalupo, Massimo. *The Forméd Trace: The Later Poetry of Ezra Pound.* New York: Columbia Univ. Press, 1980.

Bernstein, Michael André. *The Tale of the Tribe: Ezra Pound and the Modern Verse Epic.* Princeton: Princeton Univ. Press, 1980.

Blackmur, R. P. "The Masks of Ezra Pound." *Hound and Horn,* 7 (Jan.–March, 1934), 177–212.

Bornstein, George. *The Postromantic Consciousness of Ezra Pound.* Univ. of Victoria: English Literary Studies, 1977.

Bottrall, Ronald. "XXX Cantos of Ezra Pound." *Scrutiny,* 9 (1933), 112–22.

Brooke-Rose, Christine. *The ZBC of Ezra Pound.* Berkeley and Los Angeles: Univ. of Cal. Press, 1971.

Bush, Ronald. *The Genesis of Ezra Pound's Cantos.* Princeton: Princeton Univ. Press, 1976.

Childe, W. R. "Catholicism." *The New Age,* 26.11 (Jan. 15, 1920), 179.

Collins, Adrian. "Quia Pauper Amavi." *The New Age,* 26.4 (Nov. 27, 1919), 62.

Cookson, William. "Ezra Pound and Myth: A Reader's Guide to Canto II." *Agenda,* 15. ii–iii (1977), 87–92.

Davie, Donald. *Ezra Pound: Poet as Sculptor.* New York: Oxford Univ. Press, 1964.

Dekker, George. *Sailing After Knowledge.* London: Routledge & Kegan Paul, 1963.

Emery, Clark. *Ideas into Action.* Coral Gables: Univ. of Miami Press, 1958.

end to torment: A Memoir of Ezra Pound by H.D. Ed. by Norman Holmes Pearson and Michael King. New York: New Directions, 1979.

Espey, John J. "Addenda." *Analyst* (Northwestern Univ.), No. III (1953), 10–11.

———. "Toward Propertius." *Paideuma,* 1.1 (Spring-Summer, 1972), 63–74.

Flory, Wendy. *Ezra Pound and the Cantos: A Record of Struggle.* New Haven: Yale Univ. Press, 1980.

Gallup, Donald C. *A Bibliography of Ezra Pound.* 2nd ed., 1963; rpt. London: Hart-Davis, 1969.

———. Letter from Donald C. Gallup to Ronald E. Thomas. Unpublished (May 4, 1976).

Gilkes, Martin. "The Discovery of Ezra Pound." *English,* 2 (1938), 74–83.

Glenn, E. M. "A Guide to Ezra Pound's *Cantos* (I–IV)." *Analyst,* No. 1 (1953), 1–7.

Hale, W. G. "Pegasus Impounded." *Poetry,* 14 (Apr. 1919), 52–55.

Hall, Donald. "Ezra Pound: An Interview," in *Ezra Pound.* Ed. Grace Schulman. New York: McGraw-Hill Book Co., 1974, pp. 29–30.

Highet, Gilbert. "Beer-Bottle on the Pediment." *Horizon,* 3.3 (Jan. 1961), 116–18.

Hutchinson, Patricia. "Ezra Pound and Thomas Hardy." *Southern Review,* 4 (Jan. 1968), 90–104.

Kearns, George. *Guide to Ezra Pound's Selected Cantos.* New Brunswick, New Jersey: Rutgers Univ. Press, 1980.

Kenner, Hugh. *The Poetry of Ezra Pound.* Norwalk: New Directions, 1968.

———. *The Pound Era.* Berkeley and Los Angeles: Univ. of Cal. Press, 1971.

Klinck, Dennis R. "Pound's 'Gods': The Many and the One." *Southern Review: Literary and Interdisciplinary Essays,* 11 (1978), 296–315.

Laughlin, James. "Ezra Pound's Propertius." *Sewanee Review,* 46 (Oct.–Dec. 1938), 480–91.

Laurie, Peter Hamilton. "The Poet and the Mysteries: Pound's Eleusis." *DAI,* 37 (1976), 309A (Brown Univ.).

Lewis, Wyndham. "Mr. Ezra Pound." *The Observer,* 25 (Jan. 18, 1920), 5.

McDougal, Stuart Y. "The Presence of Pater in ' "Blandula, Tenella, Vagula." ' " *Paideuma,* 4.2–3 (Fall-Winter, 1975), 317–21.

Messing, Gordon M. "Pound's Propertius: The Homage and the Damage," in *Poetry and Poetics from Ancient Greece to the Renaissance: Studies in Honor of James Hutton.* Ed. by G. M. Kirkwood. Ithaca: Cornell Univ. Press, 1975.

Miller, Vincent E. "The Serious Wit of Pound's Homage to Sextus Propertius." *Contemporary Literature,* 16.4 (Autumn 1975), 452–62.

Miyake, Akiko. "The Greek-Egyptian Mysteries in Pound's '*The Little Review* Calendar' and in Cantos 1–7." *Paideuma,* 7 (1978), 73–111.

Monk, Donald. "How to Misread: Pound's Use of Translation," in *Ezra Pound: The London Years: 1908–1920.* Ed. by Philip Grover. New York: *AMS,* 1976, pp. 61–88.

Monroe, Harriet. "To the Editor." *The English Journal,* 20 (Jan. 1931), 86–87.

Nassar, Eugene. *The Cantos of Ezra Pound.* Baltimore and London: Johns Hopkins Univ. Press, 1975.

Nichols, Robert. "Poetry and Mr. Pound." *The Observer,* 24 (Jan. 11, 1920), 6.

Norman, Charles. *Ezra Pound*. New York: The MacMillan Company, 1960.

Peacock, Alan J. "Pound, Horace and Canto IV." *English Language Notes,* 17 (June 1980), 288-292.

Pearlman, Daniel. *The Barb of Time*. New York: Oxford Univ. Press, 1969.

Peck, John. "Pound's Idylls." Unpublished dissertation (Stanford, 1973).

Pound, Ezra. College Transcrips. Unpublished (Hamilton College: 1903-1904; 1904-1905).

———. College Transcripts. Unpublished (The University of Pennsylvania: 1901-1902; 1902-1903; 1905-1906).

Rachewiltz, Mary de. *Discretions*. Boston: Little, Brown, and Co., 1971.

Read, Forrest. *'76: One World and The Cantos of Ezra Pound*. Chapel Hill: Univ. of North Carolina Press, 1981.

Reck, Michael. "A Confrontation Between Ezra Pound and Allen Ginsberg." *The Evergreen Review,* 55 (June 1968), 26-29 and 84.

Richardson, Lawrence. "Ezra Pound's *Homage to Sextus Propertius*." *Yale Poetry Review,* 6 (1947), 21-29.

Rosenthal, M. L. *Sailing into the Unknown: Yeats, Pound, and Eliot*. New York: Oxford Univ. Press, 1978.

Ruthven, K. K. *A Guide to Ezra Pound's Personae (1926)*. Berkeley and Los Angeles: Univ. of Cal. Press, 1969.

Sanders, Frederick K. *John Adams Speaking: Pound's Sources for the Adams Cantos,* Orono, Maine: Univ. of Maine Press, n.d.

Schaefer, R. Murray. Letter from R. Murray Schaefer to Ronald E. Thomas. Unpublished (May 11, 1976).

Schneidou, Herbert N. *Ezra Pound: The Image and the Real*. Baton Rouge: Louisiana State Univ. Press, 1969.

Speirs, John. "Mr. Pound's Propertius." *Scrutiny,* 3.4 (Mar. 1935), 409-418.

Stock, Noel. *The Life of Ezra Pound*. New York: Random House, 1970.

Sullivan, J. P. "Ezra Pound and the Classics," in *New Approaches to Ezra Pound*. Ed. Eva Hesse. London: Faber and Faber, 1969.

———. *Ezra Pound and Sextus Propertius*. Austin: Univ. of Texas Press, 1964.

Surette, Leon. *A Light from Eleusis: A Study of Ezra Pound's Cantos*. New York: Oxford Univ. Press, 1979.

Terrell, Carroll F. *A Companion to the Cantos of Ezra Pound*. Berkeley, Los Angeles, London: Univ. of Cal. Press, 1980.

Thomas, Ronald E. "The Catullan Landscape in Pound's Poetry." *Contemporary Poetry,* 4.1 (Spring 1981), 66-78.

———. "Catullus, Flaminius, and Pound in ' "Blandula, Tenella, Vagula." ' " *Paideuma,* 5.3 (Winter 1976), 407-412.

Turner, Mark. "Propertius Through the Looking Glass: A Fragmentary Glance at the Construction of Pound's *Homage*." *Paideuma,* 5 (1976), 241-65.

Whigham, Peter. "Ezra Pound and Catullus," in *Ezra Pound: Perspectives*. Ed. with intro. by Noel Stock. Chicago: Henry Regnery Co., 1965.

Witemeyer, Hugh. *The Poetry of Ezra Pound: Forms and Renewal, 1908-1920*. Berkeley: Univ. of Cal. Press, 1969.

Yeats, W. B. *A Packet for Ezra Pound*. Dublin: Cuala Press, 1929.

Other Works

Abrams, Meyer Howard. *Natural Supernaturalism: Tradition and Revolution in Romantic*

Literature. New York: Norton, 1971.

Active Anthology. Ed. Ezra Pound. London: Faber and Faber, 1933.

The Aeneid of Virgil. Trans. by Allen Mandelbaum. 1961; rpt. Toronto, New York, London, and Sydney: Bantam Books, 1981.

The American Heritage Dictionary of the English Language. Ed. by William Morris. Boston: Houghton Mifflin Company, 1978.

Arnold, Matthew. *Culture and Anarchy.* Ed. w. intro. and notes by Ian Gregory. Indianapolis and New York: Bobbs-Merrill Company, Inc., 1971.

Biblia Vulgata. Ed. by Alberto Colunga and Laurentio Turrado. 4th ed. Matriti: Biblioteca de Autores Cristianos, 1965.

Bloom, Harold. *The Anxiety of Influence: A Theory of Poetry.* London; New York: Oxford Univ. Press, 1975.

C. Valerii Catulli Carmina. Ed. by R. A. B. Mynors. Oxford: Clarendon Press, 1958.

Catulli Tibulli Propertii Carmina. Ed. by Lucianus Mueller. Leipsig: B. G. Teubner, 1892.

Catullus. Ed. E. T. Merrill. Cambridge: Harvard Univ. Press, 1893.

Catullus, Tibullus, and Pervilgilium Veneris. Trans. by F. W. Cornish, J. P. Postgate, and J. W. Mackail. 1913; rev. 1950; rpt. Cambridge: Harvard Univ. Press; London: William Heinmann Ltd., 1968.

The Chinese Written Character as a Medium for Poetry. Ed. Ezra Pound. (1917); London: Villiers Publishing, Ltd., 1936.

The Collected Dialogues of Plato. Ed. with intro and notes by Edith Hamilton and Huntington Cairns. Trans. by Lane Cooper, et al. 1961; rpt. Princeton: Princeton Univ. Press, 1969.

The Collected Poems of Wilfred Owen. Ed. with intro. and notes by C. Day Lewis and with mem. by Edmund Blunden. London: Chatto and Windus, 1964.

Commager, Steele. *A Prolegomenon to Propertius.* Cincinnati: Univ. of Cincinnati Press, 1974.

The Compact Edition of the Oxford English Dictionary. 2 vols. Ed. James A. H. Murray, et al. 1933; rpt. New York: Oxford Univ. Press, 1971.

The Complete Poems of A. E. Housman. Ed. with intro. by Basil Davenport and his. of the text by T. B. Haber. New York: Henry Holt and Co., 1959.

The Complete Poetical Works of Austin Dobson. Ed. Alban Dobson. London: Oxford Univ. Press, 1923.

The Complete Works of W. S. Landor. 10 vols. Ed. Charles G. Crump. London: J. M. Dent and Co., 1893.

Confucius to Cummings: An Anthology of Poetry. Ed. Ezra Pound and Marcella Spann. New York: New Directions, 1964.

Dante Alighieri: The Divine Comedy, Purgatorio. Trans. by Charles S. Singleton. Princeton: Princeton Univ. Press, 1973.

The Diary of John Quincy Adams: 1794-1845. Ed. Allan Nevins. New York: Longmans, Green, and Co., 1928.

The Elegies of Propertius. Ed. with intro. and com. by H. E. Butler and E. A. Barber. 1934; rpt. Oxford: Clarendon Press, 1964.

Eliot, T. S. *After Strange Gods.* New York: Harcourt, Brace and Company, 1934.

———. *On Poetry and Poets.* New York: Farrar, Straus and Cudahy, 1957.

———. *Selected Essays.* New York: Harcourt Brace and Co., 1950.

Essays by Robert Louis Stevenson. Intro. by William Lyon Phelps. New York: Charles Scribner's Sons, 1892.

Feder, Lillian. *Ancient Myth in Modern Poetry.* Princeton: Princeton Univ. Press, 1971.

Galinsky, G. Karl. *Ovid's Metamorphoses: An Introduction to the Basic Aspects.* Berkeley and Los Angeles: Univ. of Cal. Press, 1975.

Gombrich, E. H. *The Story of Art.* 1950; rev. 1966; rpt. London: Phaidon Press Ltd., 1967.

Gordon, A. E. "Cults at Aricia." *Univ. of Cal. Pub. in Classical Archaeology,* II. i. (1934), 1–20.

Graves, Robert. *The Crowning Privilege.* London: Cassell and Co., 1955.

The Greek Bucolic Poets. Trans. by J. M. Edmonds. 1912; rev. 1928; rpt. Cambridge: Harvard Univ. Press; London: William Heinemann LTD, 1950.

The Greek New Testament. Ed. by Kurt Aland, Matthew Black, Bruce M. Metzger, and Allen Wikgren. London: United Bible Societies, 1966.

Henry Howard, Earl of Surrey: Poems. Ed. with intro., notes, and glossary by Emrys Jones. Oxford: Clarendon Press, 1970.

Hesiod, The Homeric Hymns, and Homerica. Trans. by Hugh G. Evelyn-White. 1914; rev. 1936; rpt. Cambridge: Harvard Univ. Press; London: William Heinemann LTD, 1950.

Hesiod: Works and Days. Ed. with Prolegomena and com. by M. L. West. Oxford: Clarendon Press, 1978.

Hieronymi Fracastorii et Marci Antonii Flaminii Carmina. [n.ed.]. Veronae: ex typographica Petri Antonii Berni, MDCCXL.

Homer: the Odyssey. 2 vols. Ed. with English trans. by A. T. Murray. Cambridge: Harvard Univ. Press; London: William Heinemann, Ltd., 1953.

Horace: The Odes and Epodes. Trans. by C. E. Bennett. London: William Heinemann; New York: G. P. Putnam's Sons, 1929.

Hubbard, Margaret. *Propertius.* London: Duckworth Press, 1974.

Johnson, W. R. "The Emotions of Patriotism: Propertius 4.6." *CSCA,* 6 (1973), 151–80.

Latin Poetry in Verse Translation. Ed. L. R. Lind. Boston: Houghton Mifflin, 1957.

Lewis, C. S. *A Preface to Paradise Lost.* Oxford: Oxford Univ. Press, 1942.

———. *English Literature in the Sixteenth Century Excluding Drama.* Oxford: Clarendon Press, 1954.

Lewis, Charlton T. and Charles Short. *A Latin Dictionary Founded on Andrews' Edition of Freund's Latin Dictionary.* Oxford: Clarendon Press, 1955.

Liddell, Henry George and Robert Scott. *A Greek-English Lexicon.* Rev. ed. Oxford: Clarendon Press 1925–40.

Lowell, Robert. *History.* New York: Farrar, Straus and Giroux, 1973.

Mackail, J. W. *Latin Literature.* 1895; rpt. New York: Frederick Ungar Publishing Co., 1966.

The Metamorphoses. Trans. w. intro by Horace Gregory. New York: Viking Press, 1958.

Mylonas, George E. *Eleusis and the Eleusinian Mysteries.* Princeton: Princeton Univ. Press, 1961.

The New Golden Bough. Abridged Edn. Ed. w. notes and foreword by Theodor H. Gaster. New York: S. G. Phillips, Inc., 1959.

Nilsson, Martin P. *Greek Popular Religion.* New York: Columbia Univ. Press, 1940.

The Norton Anthology of Poetry. Rev. and ed. by Alexander W. Allison et al. New York: W. W. Norton & Company, Inc., 1975.

Nygren, Anders. *Agape and Eros.* Trans. by Philip S. Watson. Philadelphia: Westminster Press, 1953.

The Odyssey. Trans. by Robert Fitzgerald, w. drawings by Hans Erni. New York: Doubleday & Company, Inc. 1961.

The Open Bible. King James Version. Ed. by Manford G. Gutzke, et al. Nashville, Camden, New York: Thomas Nelson Publishers, 1975.

Otis, Brooks. *Ovid as Epic Poet.* Cambridge: Cambridge Univ. Press, 1966.

Ovid: Fasti. Ed. with English trans. by Sir James George Frazer. New York: G. P. Putnam's

Sons; London: William Heinemann, Ltd., 1931.

Ovid: Metamorphoses. 2 vols. Ed. with English trans. by Frank Justus Miller. New York: G. P. Putnam's Sons; London: William Heinemann, Ltd., 1933.

Ovid's Elegies Translated by Christopher Marlowe. Ed. Frederick Etchells and Hugh MacDonald. London: Spottiswoodie, Ballantyne, and Co., 1925.

The Oxford Book of Greek Verse. Ed. Gilbert Murray, et. al. 1930; rpt. Oxford: Clarendon Press, 1938.

The Oxford Classical Dictionary. Ed. by N. G. L. Hammond and H. H. Scullard. 2nd ed. 1970; rpt. Oxford: Clarendon Press, 1977.

P. Vergili Maronis Opera. Ed. Frederick A. Hirtzel. Oxford: Clarendon Press, 1966.

The Pastoral Elegy: An Anthology. Trans. and ed. w. intro, com, and notes by Harry Joshua Leon. Austin: Univ. of Texas Press, 1939.

Pillinger, Hugh E. "Some Callimachean Influences on Propertius, Book 4." *HSCP,* 73 (1969), 171-99.

The Pocket Book of Verse. Ed. M. E. Speare. New York: Pocket Books, Inc., 1940.

The Poetical Works of Wordsworth, Cambridge Edition. Rev. w. new into. by Paul D. Sheats. Boston: Houghton Mifflin Company, 1982.

The Poetry of Ernest Dowson. Ed. with intro. by Desmond Flower. 1967; rpt. Rutherford, Madison, Teaneck: Fairleigh Dickenson Univ. Press, 1970.

Poetry of the Victorian Period. 3rd ed. Ed. w. notes by Jerome Hamilton Buckley and George Benjamin Woods. Glenview, Illinois: Scott, Foresman and Company, 1965.

Preece, Warren E. Editor. *The New Encyclopaedia Britannica.* 30 vols; 15th ed. 1974; rpt. Chicago, etc.: Encyclopaedia Britannica, Inc., 1982.

Propertius. Trans. by H. E. Butler. 1912; rpt. Cambridge: Harvard Univ. Press; London: William Heinemann LTD, 1939.

Q. Horati Flacci Opera. Ed. H. W. Garrod. Oxford: Clarendon Press, 1967.

Quinn, Sister M. Bernetta. *The Metamorphic Tradition in Modern Poetry.* New Brunswick: Rutgers Univ. Press, 1955.

Readies for Bob Brown's Machine. Ed. Bob Brown. Cagnessur-Mer: Roving Eye Press, 1931.

Richard of St. Victor: Benjamin Minor. Trans. into English by S. V. Yankowski. Ansbach, West Germany: Wiedfeld and Mehl, 1960.

Richardo Da S. Vittore: Pensieri Sull' Amore. Ed. Ezra Pound. Milano: Vanni Scheiwiller, 1956.

Ross, D. O. *Backgrounds to Augustan Poetry: Gallus, Elegy, and Rome.* Cambridge: Cambridge Univ. Press, 1975.

————. *Style and Tradition in Catullus.* Cambridge: Harvard Univ. Press, 1969.

The Scriptores Historiae Augustae. Ed. David Magie. Cambridge: Harvard Univ. Press; London: William Heinemann Ltd., 1953-1954.

Selected Poems of Thomas Hood. Ed. John Clubbe. Cambridge: Harvard Univ. Press, 1970.

Sex. Propertii Elegiae. Ed. Lucianus Mueller. Leipsig: B. G. Teubner, 1894.

Sexti Properti Carmina. Ed. E. A. Barber. Oxford: Clarendon Press, 1960.

Seznec, Jean. *The Survival of the Pagan Gods.* Trans. from French by Barbara Sessions. New York: Pantheon, 1953.

Shakespeare's Ovid Being Arthur Golding's Translation of the Metamorphoses. Ed. W. H. D. Rouse. 1906; rpt. Carbondale: Southern Illinois Univ. Press, 1961.

Skutsch, Otto. "The Structure of Propertius' *Monobiblos.*" *CP,* 58 (1963), 238-39.

Stead, C. K. *The New Poetic.* London: Hutchinson Univ. Library, 1964.

Sullivan, J. P. *Propertius: A Critical Introduction.* Cambridge: Cambridge Univ. Press, 1976.

Terrell, Carroll F. [Rpt. from Thomas Taylor's *Eleusinian and Bacchic Mysteries.*]

Paideuma, 7 (1978), 155–74.

Untermeyer, Lewis. *Collected Parodies.* New York: Harcourt, Brace, and Co., 1926.

Virgil. 2 vols. Trans. by H. Rushton Fairclough. Rev. ed. Cambridge: Harvard Univ. Press; London: William Heinemann Ltd., 1978.

Virgil's Aeneid Translated into Scottish Verse by Gavin Douglas, Bishop of Dunkeld. 4 vols. Ed. with notes and glossary by David F. C. Coldwell. Edinburgh and London: William Blackwood and Sons, Ltd., 1951–56.

Wind, Edgar. *Pagan Mysteries in the Renaissance.* New Haven: Yale Univ. Press, 1958.

The Works of Geoffrey Chaucer. Ed. F. N. Robinson. 2nd ed., 1933; rpt. Boston: Houghton Mifflin, 1961.

The Works of John Adams. 10 vols. Ed. w. biog. and n. by Charles Francis Adams. Boston: Little and Brown, 1850–1856.

Yeats, W. B. *The Collected Poems of W. B. Yeats.* 1933; rpt. London: Macmillan Publishing Co., Inc., 1956.

Index

Adams, Charles Francis, 72, 89
Adams, John, 72, 88, 102, 130
Adonis, 86
Agape (Christian love): 2, 143-45, 150; Pound's
    movement toward at Pisa, 89, 92, 101,
    105-7, 112, 139
Alexander, Michael, 70, 82, 84, 90, 92
Amicitia, 152n.9, 153n.18
Anacreon, 111
Anti-Semitism: Eliot's, 82; Pound's, 2, 3, 68, 81-
    82, 88, 96, 144, 145
Aphrodite, 18, 26, 36, 78, 98, 109, 143; in the
    Cantos, 23, 57, 61, 75, 81, 89, 101, 103,
    106. *See also* Cythera, Venus
Apollo, 135
Apuleius, 60
Artemis, 67, 78. *See also* Delia, Diana
Athena, 75, 99
Aubade, 61, 98, 111
Augurellus, Aurelius, 118
Augustine, Saint, 143
Aurunculeia, 30-31, 36, 128, 143

Bacigalupo, Massimo, 71, 113
Barber, E.A., 41
Bard, Joseph, 102
Barry, Iris, 119
Baudelaire, Charles, 99
Beardsley, Aubrey, 100
Bernstein, Michael, 78, 111-12, 160n.29
Blake, William, 19
Bloom, Harold, 4
Blunt, W.S., 107, 160n.38
Bodenheim, Max, 50
Borgia, Caesare, 79
Bornstein, George, 19, 160n.26, 160n.36
Boston Gazette, 130
Botticelli, Sandro, 101, 119, 128, 144
    Birth of Venus, 75, 79, 97
    Calumnia, 83
    Primavera, 98, 119, 123

Browning, Robert, 33, 36, 39, 49, 78, 82, 128
Bunting, Basil, 102
Bush, Ronald, 34
Byron, Lord George Gordon, 19

Candor, Pound's Hellenic, 91-92, 97, 105
Caritas: canto XXX, 77; the *Homage,* 58; Pisa,
    88, 91, 97, 105. *See also Agape*
Catullus, Gaius Valerius, 3, 4, 5, 6, 9, 17, 20, 55,
    57, 86, 98, 104, 109, 123, 148
    Carmina, 5
    Catullus 4, 28
    Catullus 11, 24
    Catullus 26, 26-27
    Catullus 29, 22
    Catullus 31, 31-35
    Catullus 34, 27, 29, 31, 40
    Catullus 39, 120
    Catullus 43, 22-23
    Catullus 46, 120
    Catullus, 51, 22-25, 26, 31
    Catullus, 58, 24-26, 45, 69
    Catullus 61, 27, 29-31, 40
    Catullus 64, 35, 68, 81, 112, 158
    Catullus 68, 29
    Catullus 86, 29
    Pound's allusions to, 27-37
    Pound's translations of, 22-27
Cavalcanti, Guido, 23, 30, 45, 76, 82, 92
Ceres, 100. *See also* Demeter
Chaucer, Geoffrey, 13, 19, 64, 78, 102, 106
    Romaunt of the Rose, 60
Chloris (Flora), 81, 119, 141, 142. *See also*
    frontispiece
Circe, 26, 36, 79, 80, 81, 88, 99
Clowes, William, 109
Coetus (coitus), 81, 83, 87, 88, 97, 103, 105
Coleridge, Samuel Taylor, 19
Collins, Adrian, 50, 157n.18
Confucius (Kung Chiu), 88, 89, 91, 92, 99, 106,
    108, 143, 147

historiography of, 3, 5, 112, 160n.29
Pound's translations of, 90-91
Cummings, E.E., 81, 90
Curie, Pierre, 76
Cynthia, 27, 40, 41, 47, 143
Cythera (Cytheria), 98, 100. *See also*
  Aphrodite, Venus

Daniel, 23, 34, 108, 161n.3
Dante, Alighieri, 10, 16, 23, 80, 82, 96, 98, 129,
  147
Davie, Donald, 151n.1, 157n.17
Deduco: in Alexandrian poetics, 6, 137,
  163n.23
De Gourmont, Remy, 18, 81
Delia, 98. *See also* Artemis, Diana
De Mailla, Père de Meyriac, 72, 89, 90
Demeter, 18, 99. *See also* Ceres
De Vega, Lope, 99
Diana, 27, 75. *See also* Artemis, Delia
Dionysus, 71, 86. *See also* Zagreus
Dobson, H.A., 122
Dolmetsch, Arnold, 68-69, 102
Douglas, C.H., 58
Douglas, Gavin
  translation of *Aeneid* by, 10-15, 62, 121
Dowson, Ernest, 43-44
Duccio, Agostino di, 83, 107
Duce, il, 5, 59, 96. *See also* Mussolini

Ecclesiastes, 101
Eleusis, 2, 18, 27, 40, 67, 69, 147, 152n.15,
  160n.26; *Pisan Cantos* and, 90, 93-94,
  101-102, 105, 109; post-Pisan cantos and,
  113, 114, 116; Pound's poetic
  immortality and, 57, 113, 136, 137-38,
  150; pre-Pisan cantos and, 72, 77, 80, 81,
  82, 83-85, 86, 87. *See also* Demeter,
  Persephone
Eliot, T.S., 4, 19, 46-47, 50, 51, 84, 87, 90, 102,
  114, 147-49, 150, 161n.3
  After Strange Gods, 82
  On Poetry and Poets, 149
  Prufrock and Other Conversations, 44, 46
  "Virgil and the Christian World," 148
  "What is a Classic?", 147
Elizabeth I (Queen Bess), 64, 114
Elizondo, Padre José, 100, 101
Elpenor, 58, 79, 150
Erigena, Scottus, 92, 107
Eros (pagan love), 2; aborted by usury, 83; in
  canto XXXIX, 79; Cynthia and, 57;
  Eleusis and, 18, 81; Helen and, 63; Inès
  and, 78; Lesbia and, 23; at Pisa, 90, 91,
  92, 97, 99, 101, 106, 111; in society, 118,
  128; woman and, 84; versus *agape,* 72,
  143, 144, 150
Espey, John, 22

Fenollosa, Ernest, 16, 21, 90
Flaminius, M.A., 32, 61, 154
Flory, Wendy, 113
Ford, Ford Madox, 16, 21, 90, 94
Frazer, Sir James G., 13, 18, 79, 81, 100
Frost, Robert, 90

Gaudier-Brzeska, Henry, 47, 127
Gemistho (Georgious Gemisthuo, sometimes
  called Plethon), 107
Gods, the: Pound's belief in, 66, 70, 75, 97, 115,
  116; significance of their return, 35, 36,
  59, 71, 72, 81, 97, 99, 112. *See also*
  individual deities; Ovid: *Metamorphoses*
Golden bough, 13-14
Golding, Arthur
  translation of *Metamorphoses* by, 62-65, 121
Gombrich, E.H.: *Story of Art,* 141, 142
Gonzaga, Francesco, 78, 83
Grosseteste, Robert de, 92, 107

Hale, William Gardner, 49, 50, 51, 58
Hardy, Thomas, 48, 89
Hebraism, 19, 28, 69, 86, 94, 110, 117, 134, 150;
  Pound's quest for selfhood and, 1, 2, 139;
  Hellenic myth and, 58, 59, 63, 71, 112;
  Pound's thinking and, 143-46; Odysseus
  and, 150
Hellenism, 19, 28, 36, 77, 78, 85, 86, 94, 109, 110,
  117, 129, 134, 135, 136, 150; components
  of for Pound, 2-3, 106; fascism and, 43,
  69, 72, 81-82; Hebraic history and, 58, 59,
  63, 71, 112; achieved through memory
  and association, 137; Pound's thinking
  and, 143-46; Aeneas and, 150
Hemingway, Ernest, 90
Heresy, 82, 145
Hermes, 75, 85
Hesiod, 88, 148
  Works and Days, 85, 86
History, 72, 88-89, 94, 112, 126
Homer, 2, 4, 10, 15, 20, 35, 81, 84, 90, 128
  Iliad, 54
  Odyssey, 9, 79-80, 88, 94, 104, 112, 147
Horace (Quintus Horatius Flaccus), 3, 4, 6, 21,
  24, 28, 55, 104, 113, 150
  Ars Poetica, 128
  Epistles, 128, 130
  Odes 1.4, 119
  Odes 1.11, 117, 132-33
  Odes 1.31, 117, 132, 134-36
  Odes 1.38, 122
  Odes 3.1, 118
  Odes 3.1-6, 120, 127
  Odes 3.2, 127
  Odes 3.3, 130
  Odes 3.8, 123
  Odes 3.15, 119, 128

Odes 3.21, 123
Odes 3.28, 123-24
Odes 3.30, 6, 110, 116, 117, 118, 123, 124, 125, 126, 128, 130, 131, 132, 136-39
Odes 4.10, 124, 125
Pound's ambivalence toward, 118-19, 128, 161n.1
Pound's boasting through, 110, 117, 138
Pound's *Cantos* and, 128-31
Pound's criticism and, 117-23
Pound's early poetry and, 122-28
Pound's late translations of, 131-39
Pound's reconciliation with, 131-32

James, Henry, 146
Janus, 7
John, Saint, 100
Jonson, Ben, 85, 98
Jowett, Benjamin, 109
Joyce, James, 82, 89, 125

Kearns, George, 109
Keats, John, 19, 142
Kenner, Hugh, 21, 35, 48, 68, 157n.17
Knowing, classical: associative memory, 2, 78, 86, 89-90, 137, 146, 150, 159n.25; metamorphosis, 2, 20, 53-54, 79, 86, 128, 142, 146, 158n.13; Ειδω , 84, 103
Knowing, romantic: apocalypse, 2, 78, 87, 146, 148; imaginative vision, 2, 78, 86, 137, 150, 159n.25; romantic poetry, risk of, 139; romanticism, Pound's misrepresentation of, 19
Koré, 76, 80, 93, 98, 100, 109, 142. *See also* Persephone

Laforgue, Jules, 46, 50, 51
Landor, Walter Savage, 21, 24, 98, 119, 152n.2
Lawrence, D.H., 82
Legge, James, 72, 89
Lesbia: her creeking sandal, 29-30; Pound's Catullan contrast and, 5, 21, 24-25, 26, 36; Pound's nostalgia for, 2, 29, 34, 143
Leuconoe, 132, 133
Leucothea (Homer's Ino), 75, 113-14, 161n.43
Leucothoe: for Leuconoe, 133; Ovid's Ino, 72, 75, 113-14; Ovid's other goddess, 113-14; Propertius' Ino, 54
Lewis, C.S., 15
Lewis, Wyndham, 50, 90, 114
Logopoeia, 50-58; defined, 156n.16
Lombardos, Pietro and Tullio, 108
Longfellow, Henry Wadsworth, 123
Lorimer, G.H., 102
Lovelace, Richard, 102
Lowell, Robert, 88
Lucretius (Titus Lucretius Carus), 71, 143

"Maiden Gathering Flowers" (wall-painting, Stabiae, 1st century A.D.), frontispiece, 141-43
McDaniel, W., 21
Mackail, J.W., on Propertius, 44-46, 51
Malatesta, Sigismunde, 75-76, 98-99, 102, 107
Marlowe, Christopher, 100, 121
translation of Ovid's *Amores* by, 60-62
Masks, Pound's Latin (defined), 3-7
Mathews, R.H., 72, 89
Megalopsychia (magnanimity), Pound's, 25-26, 117-18, 147
Mencken, H.L., 102
Metastasio, Pietro, 35, 36, 115
Micah, 98
Migne, Jacques-Paul, 107
Milton, John, 5, 6, 9, 19, 58, 64, 147; identified with Virgil, 15-16; his latinism, 17-18; his Puritanism, 18; his rhetoric, 16
"Miltonism" (defined), 15
Monroe, Harriet, 25, 47, 71, 118, 155n.10
Mueller, Lucianus, 41, 43
Mussolini, Benito, 88, 95-96, 101. *See also* Duce, il
Mylonas, George, 84, 152n.15
Mysteries. *See* Eleusis
Myth, 59-60, 67-69, 112. *See also* the Gods

Nassar, Eugene, 81
Nature, 89, 92-95
Nekuia, 2, 10, 75, 147, 152n.15; in "The Amphora," 124; in canto LXXXII, 90, 93, 94; in Douglas' *Aeneid,* 13; in the *Homage,* 40
Neo-Platonism, 4, 98, 106, 143-44. *See also* Erigena, Gemistho, Grosseteste, Plotinus
Nilsson, Martin P., 85, 86, 152n.15
Nygren, Anders: *Agape and Eros,* 143

Orage, A.R., 50, 58
Ovid (Publius Ovidius Naso), 2, 3, 4, 5, 19, 20, 21, 32, 36, 55, 104, 120, 127, 128, 132, 147
Amores, 61-62, 101
Ars Amatoria, 60
Fasti, 114, 115, 119
Golding's translation of, 62-65
Marlowe's translation of, 60-62
Metamorphoses, 2, 5, 71, 132
Acoetes, 73-75
Acteon, 64, 65, 69-70, 129
Apollo and Daphne, 66
Arachne, 96
Atalanta, 62-63, 65
Bacchus, 62, 63, 72-74
Cadmus, 64, 65, 75, 76, 128
Cupid and Psyche, 60
Cyclops, 64
Daedalus and Icarus, 60, 64

Glaucus, 65, 66-67, 80
Leucothoe, 113-14
Meleager, 64
Midas, 64, 65
Minyas' daughters, 64
Pan and Syrinx, 68
Pentheus, 72-75
Persephone, 62, 64, 65, 67
Philemon and Baucis, 65, 41
Procne, 65
Pound on translations of, 59-65
Pound's *Pisan Cantos* and, 88-113
Pound's poetry before *Cantos* and, 65-71
Pound's post-Pisan cantos and, 113-16
Pound's pre-Pisan cantos and, 71-88

Pater, Walter, 30, 44, 45
Pearlman, Daniel, 111
Persephone (Proserpina), 18, 40, 62, 64, 65, 77, 80, 84, 94, 137, 142. *See also* Koré
Pindar, 30
Plato, 69, 106, 113, 143, 144
Plotinus, 104, 144
Polity, Pound's pursuit of, 2, 10, 19, 36, 59, 71, 72, 75, 85, 88, 106, 109, 150
Pontifex, Pound as, 116, 138
Pound, Dorothy (wife), 31
Pound, Ezra
    attitude toward publishers of, 47, 155n.10
    attitude toward war of, 47-48, 126-27
    eyes ("I"'s) of, 42, 43, 57, 81, 104, 110, 111, 131, 144, 147
    knowledge of Latin by, 3, 4, 48, 165
    political convictions of, 1, 3, 26-27, 95-96, 112-13
    Rome broadcasts by, 88, 89, 91, 146
    school studies of, 2, 3
Pound, *Cantos* of, 3, 4, 10, 11, 12, 13, 15, 21, 26, 29, 30, 33, 39, 43, 50, 53, 54, 55, 57, 58, 59, 60, 62, 63, 65, 67, 68, 69, 70, 71, 123, 124
    Canto I, 10, 41, 58, 75, 80, 84, 93, 128, 150
    Canto II, 24, 58, 63, 65, 71, 72-75, 76, 84, 99, 104, 112, 128, 159n.16
    Canto III, 30, 35, 78, 101, 128
    Canto IV, 30-31, 76, 85, 128-29
    Canto V, 30, 31, 35
    Canto VIII, 58
    Canto X, 102
    Canto XI, 76
    Canto XII, 75
    Canto XIII, 90
    Canto XIV, 75, 81
    Canto XV, 75, 129
    Canto XVI, 75, 76
    Canto XVII, 72, 75-76, 109
    Canto XIX, 76
    Canto XX, 31, 101

Canto XXVII, 72, 76-77
Canto XXVIII, 31
Canto XXX, 27, 72, 79, 82
Canto XXXIV, 130
Canto XXXIX, 27, 72, 79-81, 99, 104
Canto XLV, 72, 82-84
Canto LVII, 72, 82, 84-85, 86, 88, 93
Canto LXV, 72
Canto LXVII, 130
Canto LXXIV, 26, 89, 90, 91, 92, 96, 98
Canto LXXVI, 90, 91, 96, 98, 99, 100
Canto LXXVII, 92, 96, 99, 131
Canto LXXVIII, 96, 99
Canto LXXIX, 6, 57, 72, 89, 92, 99-100
Canto LXXX, 89, 90, 96, 100, 129-30
Canto LXXXI, 6, 72, 81, 84, 87, 89, 90, 97, 100, 101-7, 110, 111, 131
Canto LXXXII, 90, 93, 94
Canto LXXXIII, 6, 72, 89, 90, 93, 104, 107-11, 131
Canto LXXXIV, 96
Canto LXXXV, 94, 114
Canto XC, 72, 113
Canto XCI, 114-15
Canto XCIII, 115
Canto XCV, 114
Canto XCVII, 115
Canto XCVIII, 114
Canto CII, 114
Canto CIII, 115
Canto CIV, 115
Canto CV, 115
Canto CVI, 72, 113, 115
Canto CX, 85, 113, 115
Canto CXIII, 115
Canto CXVI, 88, 105, 113
Canto CXVII, 72, 115, 139
Canto CXX, 101
Cantos LII-LXXI, 89, 91
A Draft of The Cantos 17-27, 75, 76
A Draft of XXX Cantos, 77
Drafts and Fragments, 6
The Fifth Decad of Cantos XLII-LI, 81
Pisan Cantos, 5, 19, 36, 59, 61, 72, 88-113, 131
Rock-Drill, 113
Thrones, 113
Ur-canto I, 32, 33, 34, 35, 36, 78, 115-16
Ur-canto II, 22, 23, 24, 25, 26, 30, 34, 45, 78
Ur-canto III, 40
Pound, *Homage to Sextus Propertius* of, 5, 17, 18, 27, 28, 37, 61, 62, 70, 126; as Pound's rejection of aestheticism, 39-44; as Pound's reaction to pressures and critics, 39, 44-50; as a reflection of Pound's poetic crisis, 39, 47-48, 50-58
Pound, prose of:
    The ABC of Reading, 10, 12, 14, 61, 64
    "Arnold Dolmetsch," 68-69

"Axiomata," 71, 143
"Calendar of the New Era," 71
"Cavalcanti," 9
Gaudier-Brzeska: A Memoir, 1
"Genesis," 71
"Horace," 119-22, 131-32
"How To Read," 9, 60
Instigations, 65
Make It New, 92
"Notes on Elizabethan Classicists," 10, 15, 60
Pavannes and Divisions, 65
"Religio: Or a Child's Guide to Knowledge," 70
The Spirit of Romance, 32, 39, 60, 68, 118
"Terra Italica," 18
Pound, short poetry (excluding the *Homage*) of:
"The Amphora," 123-24, 125, 128, 133
"'Blandula, Tenella, Vagula,'" 32-33, 34
Canzoni, 39-43, 44, 58
Cathay, 90
"The Coming of War: Actaeon," 69-70
Confucius to Cummings, 61, 64
"Dum Capitolium Scandet," 125, 128, 131
"The Flame," 32
"Guillaume de Lorris Belated: A Vision of Italy," 32
"An Idyl for Glaucus," 66-67
"Lesbia Illa," 24, 25
A Lume Spento, 65, 84
Lustra, 25, 34, 47, 65, 70, 109
"Masks," 65-66
Mauberley, 5, 28, 37, 39, 43, 44, 50, 53, 58, 70, 102, 105, 126, 127, 128
Moeurs Contemporaines, 47
"Monumentum Aere, Etc.," 124, 125, 128, 130
Personae, 40, 50, 65, 66
"Phasellus Ille," 28
Pisan Cantos, 5, 19, 36, 59, 61, 72, 88-113, 131
Quia Pauper Amavi, 47, 49, 50
"The Return," 67-68, 69
Ripostes, 65, 67
"Satiemus," 40, 43-44
"The Study in Aesthetics," 36
"To A Friend Writing on the Cabaret Dancers," 29
"The Tree," 66, 67, 68, 70, 75, 86, 109
Pound, translations by:
Catullus 26 ("The Draughty House"), 26-27
Catullus 43 ("To Formianus' Young Lady Friend..."), 22
Catullus 51 (in ur-canto II), 22-24, 25, 26
Catullus 58 (in ur-canto II), 24-26
Confucius' *Ta Hsüeh* (*The Great Learning*), 90
Confucius' *Chung Yung* (*The Unwobbling Pivot*), 90
du Bellay's (Vitalli's) "Rome," 40, 43
Flaminius' *Lusus* I, 32
Horace's *Odes* 1.11, 132-34
Horace's *Odes* 1.31, 134-36
Horace's *Odes* 3.30, 136-39
Horace's *Odes* 4.10, 124, 125
Propertius 2.28C ("Prayer for His Lady's Life" and *Homage* IX.2,3), 40-43, 51
Pound, Maria (daughter), 108, 111, 137
Propertius, Sextus, 3, 4, 5, 6, 18, 20, 21, 27, 31, 36, 61, 104, 120, 126
aesthetic crisis of, 47-48, 49, 56-58, 126
anti-imperialism of, 5, 44, 49, 57, 120, 126-27
Elegiae, 5, 39-58
Monobiblos, 2, 5, 41
Pound's *Canzoni* and, 39-43
Pound's *Homage* and, 44-58
"Ride to Lanuvium," 44-45, 155n.8

Quies (rest), Pound's failure to achieve, 111, 117, 136

Recusatio, 56, 126, 157n.23
Rex nemorensis, Pound as, 27, 100
Roethke, Theodore, 86
Roots, 86, 119, 135, 136, 139
Rosenthal, M.L., 84
Ross, David O., Jr., 152n.9, 153n.18, 162n.8
Rossetti, Dante Gabriel, 44, 45
Rudge, Olga, 88, 98

St. Elizabeths, 36, 60, 113, 115, 131
Santayana, George, 26, 102
Sappho, 18, 21, 23, 31
Schneidou, Herbert N., 16, 152n.14
Seznec, Jean, 82
Shakespear, Olivia and Dorothy, 40
Shakespeare, William, 64, 103
Shelley, Percy Bysshe, 19
Sirmio, 6, 20, 21, 28, 31-37, 154n.25
Socrates, 109, 113
Soncinus, Hieronymous, 49
Spenser, Edmund, 19
Spire, André, 102
Stead, C.K., 46
Steffens, Lincoln, 76
Stevenson, Robert Louis, 87
Sullivan, J.P., 50, 161n.1
Surrette, Leon, 81, 93, 152n.15
Surrey, Henry Howard, Earl of
"Certain Bokes of Virgiles Aeneais," 15
Swinburne, Algernon Charles, 28, 90, 94, 95, 129
Symons, Arthur, 100

Tennyson, Lord Alfred, 45
Terrell, Carroll, 113, 147

Time: Hebraic, historical, calendar, 2, 36, 80, 110, 130; Hellenic, mythical, natural, 2, 70, 82, 97, 98, 105; problem of its redemption, 77, 84-86, 97, 142, 148
Tovarisch, 77, 83
Translation, 2, 60, 132
Twain, Mark (Samuel L. Clemens), 80

Untermeyer, Louis, 122
Usura (usury), 18, 53, 82, 96, 129

Vates (seer), Pound as, 71-72, 81, 88, 100, 114, 161n.44
Venice, 75, 109
Venus, 11, 12, 57, 78, 97, 142, 143. *See also* Aphrodite, Cythera
Vesta, 138
Vidal, Peire, 23, 129
Virgil (Publius Vergilius Maro), 3, 6, 18, 19, 20, 88, 97, 106, 112, 113, 116, 126, 127, 128, 132, 136, 139
  Aeneid, 4, 6, 9-15, 94, 123
  Bimillenium of his birth, 58, 79
  Douglas' translation of, 10-15
  Eclogues, 6, 55
  as Pound's poetic father, 147-50

Pound's rejection of, 4, 9-10
Propertius' admiration for, 54-56
Voce tinnula, 30, 31, 101

Wabash College, 2, 145
Waller, Edmund, 102
Whigham, Peter, 26
Witemeyer, Hugh, 71, 118
Whitman, Walt, 86, 90, 93, 95, 98, 125, 137, 143, 147, 149
  "Lilacs," 88
  "Out of the Cradle," 94
Wilhelm, James, 113
Williams, William Carlos, 40, 90
Woolman, John, 88
Wordsworth, William, 17, 19, 49, 58, 93

Yeats, William Butler, 4, 19, 47, 49, 50, 79, 82, 90, 94, 100, 104, 107, 114
  "Down By the Sally Gardens," 108
  A Packet for Ezra Pound, 78, 158n.13
  "The Peacock," 110, 131
  Responsibilities, 44, 46

Zagreus, 71, 75, 99. *See also* Dionysus